DEDICATION

*This is dedicated to everyone
experiencing rejection in one form or another.*

PERMISSIONS

REJECTED
for a
PURPOSE:

**How God Uses Rejection to
Help You Find + Fulfill Your Destiny**

**By
O. J. TOKS**

Rejected for a Purpose: How God Uses Rejection to Help You Find and Fulfill Your Destiny

Published by
The Elevator Group Faith,
an imprint of The Elevator Group
Paoli, Pennsylvania

Copyright © 2010 by O. J. Toks

Library of Congress Control Number: 2010927182

Trade Paperback: ISBN 10: 0-9820384-3-7
ISBN 13: 978-0-9820384-3-7

Published in the United States by The Elevator Group.

Jacket and interior design by Stephanie Vance-Patience

This book was printed in the United States.

To order additional copies of this book, contact:
The Elevator Group
PO Box 207
Paoli, PA 19301
610-296-4966 (p)
610-644-4436 (f)
www.TheElevatorGroup.com
www.TEGFaith.com
info@TheElevatorGroup.com

ACKNOWLEDGEMENTS

Thank you, Father, for granting me the privilege and grace to write this work. I'm humbled and honored to be used in this capacity. Thank you for giving hope, closure, revelation, and inspiration to all those for whom You've written this book. Thanks for helping them realize that You were right there with them when they were crying, depressed, distraught, down-and-out, feeling worthless, feeling left out, and feeling like failures. Thank you for using this book to help them see the value of their experiences, and to understand that through those experiences, You were leading them to find unprecedented success and fulfill their destinies.

To my family: Captain J.N. & Mrs. E. O. Adeoye, Damilola, Junior and Rotimi, thank you for all your prayers, support, and encouragement. Thank you for challenging, inspiring, and believing in me to fulfill my dreams.

To Pastors Joel & Victoria Osteen: thank you for giving me hope and inspiration.

To Pastor Steve Parson and Pastors Calvin and Barbara Duncan: I'm grateful for the times I spent under your tutelage.

To Pastor Craig Johnson, Pastor Steve Austin, John Bowman, Violet Hernandez, and Russell and Carol Myers Wyatt: thank you for believing in me, supporting me, and your invaluable counsel regarding this book.

To Pastor Todd Hull and my *C30 The Journey* and *Latitude* Compass Class Family, Tunji Abifarin, Titus and Nora Benny, Chris and Monique Gamez, Jarod Cooper, Candace Thomas, Rigel Garcia, Rudy Morales, Craig and Naisha Ford Jr., Yolanda Medina, Leslie Romero, Kim Loving, Felipe and Jessica Casarez, Kwaku Nornoo, Jarusha Harris, Bonny Olvera, Rachael Manraj, Delsena Draper, Marie King, Christine Laredo, Sonia Gonzalez, and Shirley Phlegm: thanks for all your support, prayers, and encouragement.

To Sheilah Vance and The Elevator Group: thank you for embracing me and taking me under your wing. Thank you for your professionalism and expertise in making this work the exquisite book that it is. I appreciate your efforts in presenting this book to the masses.

And to you, dear reader: I commend you for picking up this book. I pray that by the time you reach the last page, your need for reading it would have been adequately met.

TABLE OF CONTENTS

INTRODUCTION

J ennifer conducted herself like the poster child for outstanding single women. "The man who marries you will be a very lucky guy" was a common compliment for her. Jennifer was simply adorable. She had a successful career as a CPA in a thriving accounting firm. She was also involved with her church, and she served in a community program for unwed teenage mothers, where she was an inspiration to them.

Despite her glamorous looks she carried herself with meekness. She was affable, hospitable and approachable. She was a virtuous woman; she feared God and prayed often.

Like an angel from the sky, Dan emerged as the lucky man everyone had been telling her about for the past few years. When she and Dan first met, so many sparks flew between them that it was surprising that they did not cause a power outage. Their chemistry went way beyond the scope of the average college science major's class. The overwhelming endorsements Jennifer received about Dan from her friends, parents, and pastor, in addition to her love for him, assured her that he was *the one*.

After dating for a few months, Dan popped *the question* on a breezy, bright, sunny afternoon amid a sea of tourists and unsuspecting onlookers on the 86th floor of the Empire State Building. Jennifer said yes before Dan dropped on one knee and popped out a two carat diamond ring. The wedding date was set and elaborate plans were made for a first-class wedding.

A week before their wedding, while Jennifer was going over last minute details with her wedding coordinator, Dan called her on her cell. Dan's conversation with Jennifer went something like this:

"Hello honey...uuuh...I...I don't know how to say this...but...it's not you...uuuh...it's me...uuuh...you're beautiful, you...you're an angel...you did nothing wrong...you'll find someone else...I'm sorry...I can't marry you...it's not you...it's me...I don't deserve you...I'm sorry...please...tell everyone...I'm sorry...please mail the ring back to my address..." Click!

* * *

Tommy felt like the outcast of his family. He was always the brunt of their jokes. He wasn't as cool as his older brother, Richard, the entrepreneur. He wasn't smart like his older sister, Mary-Ann, who plied her trade in the state attorney's office. And, he was not athletic, nor did he possess a commanding presence like his father who was a college football All-American. Worse still, he failed to meet his father's expectations as he didn't make the cut to play varsity football. And when his mom reprimanded him, he resented hearing her berate him for not being more like his brother and sister. Life in his high school was no better than home. His classmates always made fun of him. He was teased for being shy and chubby. His instructor scolded him for not paying attention in class and said that he would never amount to anything. Given these circumstances, is it any wonder that Tommy contemplated suicide?

* * *

George had dedicated a decade of his life working for one of the biggest banks in the country. His tenure at the financial behemoth earned him a senior manager's title and a high-end, five-figure income which helped him take care of his *six-figure* mortgage, stay-at-home wife ,and three kids, two of which were in college. George had endured and survived several changes at his workplace. He had been through a few mergers, splits, outsourcings, downsizings, and "uprisings."

During those corporate shakeups, George had often been

charged with the heart-wrenching task of firing workers. Over the years, in following orders passed down to him from his superiors, George had learned to layoff employees, some of whom where friends, without letting their termination overwhelm him. George had just finished informing some individuals that the company no longer needed them when he walked into his office to find, on his desk, his own marching orders.

George battled a severe attack of depression after his unceremonious and abrupt dismissal from the company he had spent ten years working for. The price he paid all those years he worked for the company was not just limited to his mental and physical efforts; he also paid the price of not spending enough time with his family, especially his wife. Not long after he broke the news to his wife about his sudden unemployment, he had to pay another price proposed by his wife—she asked for a divorce.

* * *

Paul and his wife pastored a local church in the city in which they lived. Twenty-one months prior, the church's board hired them after their predecessor resigned out of frustration from leading the house of worship. After seeking God's counsel about their plans to lead the church, Paul and his wife were inspired to take their new church in a new direction. Full of faith and trust in God, Paul and his wife took up the challenge and, slowly but surely, they began to turn things around.

Attendance went up, church membership doubled, more teenagers came to service, more couples stayed married, and more people dedicated their lives to God. The progress of their church was attributed to the way Paul and Sarah followed God's lead by effectively ministering to the needs of their congregants. Paul and his wife's "unconventional" style of ministry even attracted individuals and families from demographics different than most of the original members of the church.

That, however, did not sit well with the church board. Some of the original members of the church felt the same way and expressed their disapproval by *leaving* the church. The remainder of the original members, backed by the influence of most of the board, began to make the new members feel unwelcome. The few board members who supported their pastor's approach were forced out. Paul and his wife took a much needed two-week vacation to rejuvenate themselves and rekindle their marriage. Shortly after they got back from their sabbatical, they went to church early on a Sunday morning to prepare for the morning service. Imagine their surprise when they saw another person's name on the pastor's parking spot. Their surprise was complete when they saw a memo thanking Paul and his wife for their service, but also informing them that Paul was no longer the pastor.

* * *

I stood behind a wooden lectern on a platform ready to deliver my speech. I was at a relationship conference co-hosted by *VISION*, a student organization at Virginia Commonwealth University, my alma mater. At that time, I was the organization's coordinator, and we were able to secure a 500-seat auditorium at the Student Commons for the event.

In preparation for the seminar, I wore different hats. I was the host, organizer, advertiser, praise dancer, prayer warrior, usher, deacon, and one of the speakers. Despite my sincere efforts to ensure the success of the event, I was reprimanded by another organizer for delegating tasks to the wrong people. The speaker for day one of the two-day event cancelled because of an emergency. I was forced to find a suitable replacement 24 hours before the event. For that, I also got a friendly rebuke.

Thanks to my uncoordinated organizational efforts, most of the 500 seats were empty for both days of the event. Even more were empty on the second day—the day that *I* spoke. There were about 25 people who showed up for the first day. About 30 percent of them were the group that led praise and worship, 25 percent accounted for the praise dancers, other singers, and sound technicians. The remaining forty-five percent were the seminar attendees. On the second day, the day on which I spoke, about twelve people showed up for the event; half of which were the singers, dancers, sound technicians and yours truly.

On the night of the second day of the seminar, I stood before that lectern and looked at the handful of individuals in the audience. I mulled over the things I went through to organize the event. I felt that the sea of empty chairs before me symbolized the theme of my discussion. For the first time, I decided to talk about a subject that had been seeded in my heart about three-and-a-half years before.

I had developed feelings for a particular lady whom I had been checking out for a few months. After much fantasizing, self-induced hallucinations, soul-searching, counseling and prayer, I eventually mustered the courage to share my heart with this woman. But, "fortunately" for me, her feelings were not congruent with mine. She declined my affections, and I was disappointed. Nevertheless, I used my disappointment as my appointment to write my first book, *While You Are Single*.... Although the lady *turned me down*, she inadvertently *turned me on* to a path to my destiny.

Two-and-a-half years later, another lady caught my attention. Fortunately, again, my attempts at getting to know her met the same fate. I was rebuffed again. In fact, I felt like this lady indirectly blew me off. I was ticked off! I shouldn't have been upset, though, because prior to approaching the lady about my interest in her, I had asked God to ensure that the relationship would not even start if it would not work out for us. That was the same request I made to God regarding my first crush, too. In both cases, the results were the same. I was rejected. After the second refusal, while dealing with my disappointment, I discovered something about being rejected. It was that discovery which gave rise to my message at the conference.

I was hardly in the meat of the message when I heard a lady sitting in the front row begin to sob. After the seminar, she approached me and thanked me for the message. She disclosed to me that her fiancé had called off their engagement. That left her distraught and initially dissuaded her from coming to the seminar. Reluctantly, she still came to the event, and she was glad that she did.

According to her, what I revealed about rejection encouraged and enlightened her as to why her fiancé broke up with her. The relief and understanding expressed by most of the other conference attendees confirmed my belief that I had given them information which God wanted me to present to them. It also confirmed that other people needed to hear this information. Here it is.

Even if you cannot relate to the rejection that the characters in this chapter and I experienced, let me assure you that this book is for you. If you've been mistreated or told that you're not good enough, smart enough, and that you would not amount to anything, this book is for you. This is for you if you've ever been described as "different" and this label was not meant to be a compliment. This is for the woman who is still searching for *Mr. Right* because the men who she thought fit that profile treated her like *Ms. Wrong*. This is for the bachelor who is still single because the women who could have changed his marital status thought that he was "too nice."

If you've ever been given a vote of no confidence, treated like an outcast, called incompetent, had your employment terminated, been backstabbed by your family, friends, co-workers, clergy or significant other, this writing will help you understand that the people who neglected, refused or dismissed you might have done you the biggest favor of your life. By the time you've read through these pages, you'll have a better understanding of why you've been rejected, why God uses rejection, the merits of rejection, and how God utilizes your experiences to help you find and fulfill your destiny. This book will help you discover that you've been rejected for a purpose.

Chapter 1

Why Does It Happen to Us?

Afters church one Sunday, I spotted the familiar face of a beautiful, well-dressed lady. Although she was attractive, the look on her face was not. In fact, her expression was in sharp contrast to the one I saw just weeks before.

Weeks before, I saw her joy and admiration for the man she was about to marry. She glowed in her fiancé's presence, and he seemed excited, too. I don't know why the first thought that crossed my mind when I saw her now was that her trip to the altar was cancelled.

She was about a dozen people away from me, and I was not in any particular mood to exchange pleasantries, nor was I trying to push through people to reach her. I just let her be and hoped that all was well with her. A few moments later, I was at the mouth of the parking garage, and about two arms' length away from the lady in question. She still had the same sad look on her face. As she walked ahead of me toward her vehicle, I called out to her. She slowed down, looked back over her right shoulder, and acknowledged my greeting.

I asked how her Thanksgiving had been, and she responded by saying that it had been fine—with the same blank expression. I asked her how she was doing, and she unconvincingly told me that she was doing okay. I asked her again how she was doing, and then she spilled the beans. She told me that the engagement was off, and that she experienced the rejection on the week of Thanksgiving. Going through that kind of experience might force anyone to ask: "What is there to be thankful for?"

I was saddened by what she told me. I didn't even know what to say, especially since I had been happy for them and encouraged them about their pending marriage weeks before. In not so many words, I did my best to encourage her. She managed to force a faint smile, thanked me, and then we parted to our respective cars.

Rejection is in the air. It has always been and, as long as we exist, it will continue to be—for better—or for worse. How we *respond* to it determines which side of its effect we end up in. And when rejection is in the air, love, usually, is not. It's been a few years since I've discovered how universal rejection is. Yet, I've also realized that it is an *effective* tool that God uses to help us find and fulfill our destinies.

The revelation of the relevance of rejection to help us align ourselves with God's plan has invaluably transformed my life for the *better*. It can for you, too. And it is with this in mind that I attempt to address the subject in a manner that is balanced, real, informative, applicable, and helpful to you.

Perhaps you want to know why that guy or lady broke up with you. Maybe you want to know why you didn't get that job or why you got divorced. You might be wondering why some people don't like you, why others do not acknowledge you, why some dismiss you, why some look down on you, or why no one has ever asked you out. You might also want to know why your text message, phone call, voice mail or email was never returned; or why you lost out on the bid, failed to make the cut, had your idea rebuffed or never got a response to your application or proposal.

Whatever the case, rejection is something that we all face in life. We experience it at various times and in various forms— abuse, adversity, demotion, eviction, exclusion, failure, neglect, and prejudice. Rejection happens at various places—school, social events, work, home, and, sometimes, even at church. It hurts to be treated like you are not important. It's demoralizing to be treated as worthless. Nevertheless, despite the sourness of the experience, being rejected might be the best thing that ever happened *for* you.

I once heard a story about a duck that was trying to find itself. The duck saw a squirrel climb up a tree and decided that it would do the same. It was barely a few inches from the ground, on the trunk of the tree, when it flopped on its back. The duck was disappointed and dejected at its failure to mimic the squirrel. The duck then saw a bird swoop over it and decided that it would fly. The duck flapped its wings incessantly and made some progress a few feet up in the air, but it got tired and dropped faster than it went up. This time around, the duck was even more depressed and felt that it was good for nothing.

When the duck dropped from the air it landed on a pond. Swoosh! The duck glided on the water. Excited, exhilarated, and with a sense of accomplishment, the duck displayed its true colors as it coasted on the water. Eureka! The duck found itself. The inability of the duck to duplicate what the squirrel and bird did helped it find its niche. The duck felt restricted. It felt hindered. But, its experience helped it find its strength.

Like the duck, we often encounter setbacks in life. In our attempts to find fulfillment, some of us try to be like others who seem to be successful at who they are and what they do. Sometimes we look to them to validate us and give us our identities. And when we are unable to be like them or duplicate their successes, we feel like we've failed. At times, not only are they unable to validate us, some of them also invalidate or demean, hinder, and wrongly classify us. This leaves us frustrated and unfulfilled as we are yet to discover ourselves. The people we trusted to help us in our quest either couldn't help us with our identities, or made us feel like we were useless. Little do we know that our *setbacks* in life could turn out to be *setups* for life. When people and circumstances set us on our backs, where else can we go but *up*?

There are numerous synonyms for rejection. Some of them include: prevent, hinder, frustrate, throw out, cast off, repel, repudiate, brush-off, exclude, turndown, constrain, restrain, inhibit, "ejection," etc. If you've been put-down, passed over, held back, divorced or fired from your job, you've been rejected. But why do some people reject us? Why do some individuals turn us down? Why do some people dismiss us? The reasons vary; nevertheless, I believe that there are three main causes of rejection.

1. People reject us when we do not meet their expectations.

In this case we get rejected for *being* wrong or *doing* wrong. By being wrong, I mean that we are wrong for something or someone. We are turned down, refused or overlooked because we are not what they are looking for. We're not the right candidate for what they want us to do, or be. We're rebuffed because we do not have the qualifications or credentials.

This is where you get rejected because you don't fit the profile. You don't have the looks. You don't get the job because you don't have the required education and or experience. This is where you get rejected because you're not from a certain ethnicity, denomination, or religion. This is where you're not accepted because you're not an alumnus of a certain school, a member of a certain fraternity, organization, or club.

This is where a guy rejects a lady because she's not blonde or blue-eyed, brunette or green-eyed, red-headed or brown-eyed and attractive to him. Another rejects a lady because she's not light-skinned, tall, and physically endowed. A lady rejects a guy because he is not dark-skinned, bald-headed, and rolling in the dough. This is where you're passed over because your weight is not within a particular range. This is where someone is rejected because she is not a homemaker like Martha Stewart, does not cook like Rachael Ray, and does not live in a mansion with a yacht to match. This is where you are shunned because you're not spiritual, intellectual, sophisticated, or cool.

In all those cases, the individuals were rejected because they were wrong for what was expected of them. They were refused because they did not meet the requirements of those whom they wanted to be affiliated with.

By *doing* wrong, I mean getting rejected for doing the wrong thing. For example, a guy loses his job because he put his supervisor in a head lock. A student gets expelled from school because the student assaulted an instructor. A lady is rejected by her boyfriend, not only because she badmouthed him, but also because she did it in public.

If a wife annuls her marriage because her husband was unfaithful, a guy's job is terminated because he came late to work, a lady is dismissed by her friends because she slandered them behind their back, and a minister is asked to leave his church because he was insubordinate and incited the church members against their leadership, the individuals were dismissed because they *did* wrong.

When we don't meet people's expectations either by being wrong for their requirements, or doing wrong in the form of mishandling what they wanted us to do, we experience their disapproval. The expectations of those who turn us down might be reasonable or ridiculous; regardless, they reject us when we do not meet their expectations.

However, herein lies a problem. We can understand being passed over for not fitting the required profile. Even though we feel terrible, at least we can understand why we've been rejected. If we choose to, we can redeem ourselves by trying to meet the expectations of those who rebuffed us. A lady can work on sculpting herself to the specifications of the man she is trying to please. A guy can change his habit to ensure that he gets to work on time. A husband can ask his wife for forgiveness, spare no expense in winning her back, and faithfully attend counseling.

You see, friend, if you don't land a job or get a promotion because you lack the required education and experience, you can get the education and experience. If you get rejected because your hair is not a certain color, you can always bleach it accordingly. If you get dismissed because you don't have green eyes, you can get a pair of green contact lenses. If you are ignored because of your weight, you can hit the gym. Some women feel that if they are turned down because their body is not curvaceous, they can go under the knife. Some feel that if they are passed over because they are not physically endowed, they can buy Wonderbra® bras or silicon. Other women feel that, if they are refused because they do not look young enough, they can inject Botox®.

Even so, how do you explain it when a lady still gets rejected despite the fact that she is a bombshell, intelligent, and full of self confidence? How do you explain when a guy does not land a job that he obviously has the credentials for? How do you explain when you still get rejected when you are *stellar* for the position? How do you explain when you are still looked down upon and put at arms length when you do what is expected of you? How do you explain why you get rejected even when you are spiritual, intelligent, philosophical and cool, but still unaccepted by those who wanted you to possess the aforementioned traits?

A major challenge with this reality is that you can understand if you were rebuffed because you did not fit a profile or possess certain traits. You can understand when you are cast off because of something you did wrong. And if you choose to, you can make amends by educating yourself, going for counseling, or turning a new leaf.

However, if you're dismissed despite your work ethic, aspirations, and credibility, then what exactly can you work on since you're already doing the things that society in general says that you are supposed to be doing?

When you are the poster child for what people want and they still do not accept you, how do you handle this? How can you redeem yourself? You don't even know why they turned you down. If you knew the reason, you would make the necessary adjustments. But since you don't know why you were rejected, you don't know what to do to combat the situation. You don't know where you are lacking. So you are forced to ask yourself these gnawing questions: "What is wrong with me? Why don't people want me? Why is this happening to me? What is the problem exactly?"

Well, if those cases apply to you, then it's likely that you've been asking the wrong questions. You should not be asking yourself, "What's wrong with me?" You should be asking yourself, "What's right with me?" This brings me to the second reason why we get rejected, which is not because we did not meet expectations. It's because we exceeded them.

2. People reject us when we exceed their expectations.

Sometimes people reject us when we exceed their expectations. This is where we get rejected for being right or doing right. By *being* right, I mean that we are the right candidate—or too good of a candidate for what was expected of us. For example, a lady rejects a guy because he's "too nice" and too much of a gentleman. A lady is denied a position at a church because the church leadership felt that her credentials went beyond what *they classified* as a woman's role within their fellowship.

This is where a well-mannered, well-dressed and beautiful lady is rejected by other women because they assume that she is conceited and because unlike them, she usually draws the attention of a lot of gentlemen who fall over themselves to win her affection. This is where a guy is rejected by other guys because he went to an Ivy League school while they went to schools full of poison ivy. This is where you hear a recruiter say something like, "We can't afford to pay you...you're overqualified for the job," so, you are not hired. This is where you hear people say things like, "You think you are all that? You think that you are better than us? Who do you think you are?"

This is also where a lady is rejected by a guy because her pay grade is higher than his. She has her own house, but he lives in an apartment—with his mother. Please don't misunderstand me. If the lady rejects him based on their material possessions, she would be rejecting him because he did not meet her expectations. However, this is not the point I'm making here. She has no problem with where he is now. She's aware of his financial struggles, but she still loves and cares about him. She accepts him as he is. She believes in him and sees his potential, but he, out of his insecurity, has a problem with her accomplishments. He's got a problem with her having more things than him, so he feels intimidated by her accomplishments and pushes her away.

If you are rejected for *doing* right, it's because you did the right thing while others wanted to do the wrong thing and wanted you to do the same. For example, a lady is dismissed by a guy because she does not want to be physically intimate with him before their wedding day. A board member of a church is asked to resign and leave the fellowship because he cautioned the board about misusing church funds. A pastor loses half of his members because his vision for the fellowship goes beyond *just* his parishioner's needs. A lady does not get an overdue promotion and is mysteriously fired because she turned down her boss's romantic advances toward her. In these cases, the individuals were rejected because they exceeded the expectations of those who turned them down.

When you are refused because you exceeded expectations, sometimes it is because people are intimidated by your accomplishments, your standards, your dreams, visions, or aspirations. You've raised the bar, and they feel like you are making them look bad or incompetent. As a result, they "hate" on you. Being ignored and dismissed because you do the right things, treat people well, and have the experience, education, or expertise that qualifies you, signifies that you were rejected for exceeding expectations.

The third reason why people reject us is somewhat a combination of the first two. It's because we did right and wrong at the same time. By this I mean that we might have done the right things, but at the wrong time.

3. People reject us when we try to accomplish things with them at the wrong time.

We also experience rejection when we do things at the wrong time. The things we did might have been right, but it wasn't the proper time to carry them out. For example, a wife gets the cold shoulder from her husband when she confronts him about an issue while he is with his friends, watching the Super Bowl, and his mouth is stuffed full of Kentucky Fried Chicken. A guy is rebuffed by a lady, not because she didn't care for him, but because she was still healing from a recent breakup. A youth pastor's request for additional funding for more programs for young people is struck down because his church was managing some financial constraints. A lady's proposal to enhance her firm ends up in the trash pile because, at the time she proposed her project, her company did not have the necessary resources to execute her idea. In all these cases, the individuals were rejected because of the timing of their requests.

You might have graduated cum laude with an MBA from Harvard, but you likely wouldn't have landed a job at Bear Stearns around the time the investment bank collapsed amid the mortgage crisis. Experiencing rejection as a result of bad timing is not so much because of who you are, or what you do, but because of *when* you do.

With this in mind, it's imperative for us to be cognizant of the fact that timing is a very important factor in what we do. Because of this importance and the need to adequately explain the relevance of timing as a reason why we get rejected, I'll be talking more about timing in chapter 4.

IT'S A CHAUFFEUR THAT DRIVES YOU TO YOUR DESTINY

Once again, people reject us when we don't meet their expectations, when we exceed their expectations, and when we try to accomplish things with them at the wrong time. While it is important for us to find out why people reject us, I believe that it's even more important for us to find out why God allows us to experience rejection. Whether you've been dismissed because you did wrong, did right, or did both simultaneously, it's beneficial for you to know that God allows you to be rejected so that you can *meet* His expectations.

God's expectations are for you to fulfill your call. God uses rejection as a chauffeur to drive you to your destiny. Whether it's to do something, go somewhere, or be with someone, God employs rejection as a vehicle to transport you to your purpose.

At this juncture, it will be pertinent for us to reference a scripture that revolutionized this book:

The stone which the builders rejected has become the chief cornerstone. (Psalm 118:22 NKJV)

According to the apostle Peter, the stone was Jesus and the builders were the scribes and chief priests of His day (Acts 4:7-11). Jesus became who he claimed to be. He was the Messiah, the Christ, the anointed One. Similarly, just like Christ was "re-ejected" into His purpose, you are also pushed to your destiny. So, why don't you personalize that scripture? Look at that passage afresh with the perspective that you are that stone.

The passage said that the stone which was rejected had become the chief cornerstone. If you noticed, the passage refers to the stone which the builders rejected; it did not say that the stone was rejected by destroyers. It said that the stone was rejected by *builders*. This is significant. It's one thing to be turned down by someone you're not familiar with, but it's another thing when you are refused by a "builder." I want you to think of a builder as someone who is supposed to build you up.

A builder, like a building, is someone who is supposed to support you. It's one thing for you to be rejected by someone you don't really know, but it's another thing when you get the cold shoulder from someone who's close to you. It's more agonizing when someone who you look up to rejects you. It's devastating when someone who's supposed to build you up tears you down.

That builder could be a leader; it could be your parent, spouse, significant other, pastor, mentor, boss, or friend. It's more hurtful to be betrayed by someone whom you respected, admired and desired to build you up, rather than someone who did not mean much to you.

Furthermore, notice that the stone was just a stone before it got rejected, but after it was cast off it became the "chief cornerstone." What comes to your mind when you think of a stone? Usually, I think of something you step on, kick around, throw around, and play with. It's something that's useless by itself. I think of something unstable—a piece of stone that is here today, there tomorrow, gone tomorrow, due to people kicking it around and playing with it.

The stone was just a stone before it got rejected, but it became the chief cornerstone after it was rebuffed. God does not want you to be a stone. God does not want people to step on you, play with you, kick you around, "throw you for a loop," or throw you around. He wants you to be a chief cornerstone. He wants you to become who He created you to be. Unfortunately, people do treat us like stones. They step on us. They step on our dreams and on our self esteem. They play us for a fool. They play with our minds and emotions. They use and exploit us. As with a stone, they dismiss us as defective, useless, and good for nothing.

Notwithstanding, God uses their thrust to propel us to our destiny. The stone was *transformed* after being tossed. The rejection served as a catalyst to change the stone into a cornerstone. A cornerstone is a foundation stone. It's a stone used in construction to hold walls together. It's basically the foundation of a building. By binding structures together, the stone was fulfilling its purpose. The spiritual significance as it pertains to Christ is that Jesus is the foundation of the church and every other thing He has for His children. Christ, the stone, who was rejected by the scribes and religious leaders, the builders, became a chief cornerstone. He turned out to be the foundation and pillar of the church.

The rejection He experienced, ultimately on the cross, enabled Him to fulfill His destiny of not only becoming the foundation of the church, but also *paving* the way for everyone to be reconciled to God. This stone, which was discarded as useless, became useful *through* rejection. This stone which was discarded as nothing, through rejection, became something. This stone found and fulfilled His purpose; and this was facilitated by the rejection He underwent.

Likewise, you are the foundation of the purpose God has for you. The aforementioned scripture revealed that the stone became a chief. "Chief" is a title. If you have a title, this means that you have a function. If you have a function, this means that you have a purpose. More so, the stone became a chief cornerstone. In order for you to fulfill your purpose, you need to be *positioned* to do so. Hence, the chief *cornerstone*.

A corner is a position. If I told you to move to a corner, I'm telling you to move to a specific location. In order for God to help you fulfill your purpose, God has to position you for it. So, the stone becoming a chief cornerstone after being rejected is like you fulfilling what God has called and positioned you to do. He uses the thrust from your offender(s) to land you in the *corner*, spot, place, environment, location or position where you can carry out your vocation.

God allows people to reject you so that you can be transformed from being walked on, kicked around, thrown around and played, to being in a position were you will fulfill His will for your life. He wants you to hold things down; He doesn't want you to be held down. He wants you to be held up, not held back. A stone is unstable by itself as it gets tossed to and fro but becomes stable when it's positioned to hold walls together.

When you are involved in relationships where you are unstable and unfulfilled, God will let individuals push you away from their lives so that you can end up with others who'll help you find fulfillment. Through your newfound acquaintances, you'll discover where you fit and gain your stability. When people get *rid of you*, God uses their rejection to get you to those who have *need of you*. He takes advantage of rejection to deliver you from your *naysayers* and redirect you to your *yahsayers*.

The *Today's English Version* of Psalm 118:22 says that *"the stone which the builders rejected as worthless turned out to be the most important of all."* God utilizes rejection to get you from those who treat you like you're worthless, to those who'll treat you like you are worthwhile. He uses it as a means to liberate you from individuals who deem you as useless, placing you instead with others who'll accept you as useful.

When people treat you like you are useless, you are *used less*. But God created you to be useful, so through their neglect, He'll get you to an area, position or place—corner, and people—other "builders" where, and with whom, you're useful—*used to the full*. Your usefulness is your purpose; it's your chieftaincy title. Consider some of the chiefs of our day: commander-in-chief, chief executive officer, chief operating officer, etc. These are all positions of eminence and relevance. Like them, God created you to be prominent and relevant. If anything or anyone threatens that, God uses their threat to lead you to a safe haven where their threat will not hinder your potential.

As long as you are involved with people who deny or are ignorant of your worth, you're likely not going to know how special you are. Consequently, you will not know that you're so much better than their perception of you. You'll not be cognizant that you exceed their expectations. That's why God has

REJECTED *for a* PURPOSE

to get you out of their lives to help you discover yourself. Hence, not only does God use rejection to position you for promotion, or redirect you to a place where you'll accomplish your purpose, but He also uses it to refine and define you.

To refine simply means to free from impurities. Gold, for example, is refined by fire to free it of its impurities so that it can become the precious metal that we know it to be. Similarly, rejection is a fire that God uses to free you of the people who compromise your value. And once you've been liberated from them, the gold in you can be utilized to brighten the lives of others. As a result, the person God destined you to be will be brought to the forefront. Your preciousness is displayed to be seen. In a nutshell, you've been defined.

Not only did the stone which was rejected become the chief cornerstone, the next verse, Psalm 118:23 (AMP) says, "*This is from the Lord and is His doing; it is marvelous in our eyes.*" It's a marvelous and mind-boggling thing to discover that God uses rejection to help you fulfill your destiny. In essence, sometimes the dismissal you experienced is God's doing. And it is a marvelous thing because He is using it to direct you. He is using it to navigate you to His plan for your life; be it a project, a person, a place, or all of the above. God uses your *opposition* to *position* you. Yes, your op-position; He uses it to position you for your purpose, like the stone that was cornered as a chief—so to speak.

If you've been wondering why you were rejected, especially if—to your knowledge—you did nothing wrong, it's likely that God had something to do with it. *It was His doing.* He allowed you to be refused to ensure that the gift He placed in you would not be hindered or prevented any further from being expressed.

Chapter 2
Why Does God Use It for Us?

Let me address a question that might have come up in your mind. Although God utilizes our disappointments as appointments for us to fulfill our destiny, you might wonder why He uses rejection as a way to usher us toward our future. If that is a question brewing in your mind, let me preface answering that by saying this:

Rejection is *not* the only way God helps us find and fulfill our purpose.

Since that is the case, then what are the other ways that God employs to help us find out who we are and what we're worth? And since there are other, more appealing ways, then why does He sometimes let us go through hurt to arrive at His destination for us?

Well, I believe that Dr. Myles Munroe and Pastor Rick Warren are two out of a plethora of individuals who have done an outstanding job in helping us discover God's will for every aspect of our lives. I've also discovered that there are at least seven guidelines that can help us find our purpose, some of which reinforce and coincide with what the aforementioned gentlemen and others have already revealed in their respective books.

The seven guidelines that are noteworthy in our quest to discover our purpose are:

1. It is through God that we will find it.
2. We will have a heart for it.
3. We will have the ability for it.
4. There is a time for it.
5. There is a place for it.
6. We have expressed it.
7. People tell us about it.

In essence, in order to discover God's purpose for our lives, with "it" being our purpose, it's through God that we will find it; we will have a heart, passion or desire for it; we'll have the ability, knowledge, gifts or talent for it; there is a time for us to find and fulfill it; there is a place or environment for it; to some degree we've already expressed it; and people tell us about it. But here is the problem: unlike *Nike,* we don't always *just do it.*

Despite the Bible, which I believe is God's Word, Will, and authentic and primary resource to help us find our destinies; despite Dr. Munroe's *Understanding Purpose* series; despite Pastor Warren's *Purpose Driven Life* as well as numerous other books on the same topic; and despite the seven points I outlined previously, a lot of us still do not fulfill our purpose. We do not go ahead and do what God has called us to undertake.

I believe the best and primary way that God helps us discover ourselves and our worth is by simply telling us who we are, what we're to do, and what we're to become. He usually does this through our relationship with Him, speaking to us through the Bible, and preachers when we attend church, as well as speaking to us through family, friends, and other individuals from all facets of life. If we simply heed His voice and do what He tells us to do, we will arrive at our destinies. Unfortunately, some people choose to be disobedient. Some do not have a relationship with God and do not read the Bible or attend church. Others who do have a relationship with Him still do not read the Bible on their own; and, if they go to church, they do not adhere to what is being taught and preached.

There are some people, however, who have a relationship

with God and seek Him with all their heart. Yet, out of fear of failure or of what people might say when they do what God has called them to do, they decline to carry out God's mandate for their lives. If you are like me, sometimes it's not that we don't hear God speak to us, it's that we are not clear of exactly what He's telling us to do. We're caught between discerning whether it's God speaking, Satan speaking, or us speaking. While rationalizing about the three, we're often immobilized, and so is our purpose. In other cases, God simply does not tell you what to do; He *shows* you what to do. And sometimes He accomplishes that by making *you* the show. In other words He uses your experiences to reveal things to you.

Dr. Myles Munroe always says that to find the purpose of a product, you have to ask the manufacturer of the product. The manufacturer provides a manual detailing the function of the product and how to take care of it. This was my first point about seeking God's will for our lives. It is through Him that we will find it. He manufactured us and our purpose can be discovered by studying His manual for living—the Bible.

Furthermore, I also mentioned that we will have the ability to undertake our calling in life. We'll have the talent, gift, skills, or knowledge to accomplish our mission or ministry in life. In discovering our gifts, Pastor Rick Warren said that we need to discover our SHAPE. He used the word "shape" as an acrostic that denotes our spiritual gifts, heart, abilities, personalities, and experiences.[1]

The last word of his acrostic, "experiences," is what I'm emphasizing in this book—specifically, our experiences of rejection.

Simply obeying God will help us discover and carry out our purpose. Adhering to His guidelines in the Bible as well as the wisdom from people He placed in our lives will help us find the fulfillment we need. But what happens to those who do not know God, read the Bible, or go to church? What happens to those who believe in the wrong gods, read the wrong books, and end up with the wrong people—wrong friends, abusive parents, spouses, or significant others, as well as misinformed preachers and false prophets? What happens to those who have a relationship with God but choose to live their lives apart from Him? What happens to those who sincerely seek the Lord but are not clear of what He wants them to do, don't always understand the Bible, don't always understand His preachers, and as a result, do nothing because they do not want to fail God? Does it mean that they cannot fulfill God's call for their lives?

Just because some individuals do not believe in God and, hence, are oblivious to His directives for their lives, this does not necessarily mean that they can't arrive at their destinies. Just because some people believe in God but disobey Him, while some of the others who believe and also trust Him are scared and not sure exactly what to obey, does not mean that God cannot accomplish His will for them.

A SECRET AGENT

It is more appealing and less stressful to find our mission in life by simply listening to God and hearkening unto His voice. Some of the ways He speaks to us as mentioned before are through the Bible, through His Spirit, His Ministers, our family members, friends, and even through strangers that *He brought* across our paths. He also speaks to us through dreams and visions.

Unfortunately, some individuals will not adhere to God's will because they're either not aware of those basic resources for finding out His purpose, misguided, or simply disobedient, afraid or indecisive. God is then left to utilize another alternative. He has to use what I'll call His secret agent: rejection.

Please don't take that out of context. God does not hurt you to help you. He heals your hurt and uses it to help you. Satan is the one who loves to see you hurt, miserable, and disenchanted. He is the one who abused you. He's the culprit behind every form of pain and suffering (John 10:10). He's the one who loves to see you wallow in a low self-esteem, anguish, guilt, and regret. He condemns you. He makes you feel that you are good for nothing and that you'll not amount to anything.

He manifests His hatred for you through individuals, some

of whom might be, or might have been, church folks, your coworkers, friends, spouse, significant other, or family members. The devil carries out his schemes against you through some of your builders—individuals who were supposed to build you up, but they knocked you down, stepped on and over you, and left you for dead. They rejected you.

Notwithstanding, through their dismissal, God delivered you out of their lives so that he can treat the pain they inflicted on you and give you a "treat." Out of ignorance, fear, lack of faith, or no fault of your own, you got involved with the wrong folks. But, through things not working out with them, God *worked you out* of their lives so that you can undertake His work.

I mentioned that I believe that rejection is God's secret agent. For the sake of clarity, I believe rejection, in itself, is the devil's agent. However, the *secret* is that God gets it to work in our best interest.

If you've watched spy movies or programs on television about law enforcement trying to apprehend a suspect or a criminal organization, you'll notice that a prominent tactic that the investigators use is to try to catch a member of the organization and get him to snitch on his employer. The same holds true in movies about international espionage. A terrorist group sends a spy to gather intelligence about a country's defense and technology to use the information to attack and destroy the country. Oftentimes, the targeted nation's intelligence agency is already aware of the imminent attack and the spy. Either, they capture the spy and get him to spill the beans on the terrorist organization, or they just monitor the spy by bugging the individual's hideout, vehicle, and belongings. In so doing, they are tracking the terrorist's activities, gathering intelligence about who the spy works for, and how the enemy is planning to attack their country.

That way, they are not only protecting themselves, but also counteracting what their enemy is trying to do to them. Sometimes, unfortunately, the targeted country was attacked but able to apprehend the suspect and, through him, gather information that helps them arrest and prosecute the culprits as well as prevent and diffuse other attacks.

Similarly, rejection is God's snitch. It is the bad guy that God uses for a good purpose. Rejection was the devil's agent, but the secret is that God exploited it as Satan's traitor. In other words, what the devil assigned to bring you down, God reassigns to bring you up. What the devil designed to make you bitter, God redesigns to make you better.

God uses rejection like 007. Bible scholars have revealed that the number "7" is God's number of perfection or completion. To complete simply means to finish or get the job done. When all else has failed to help you find and fulfill your purpose, God employs 007 to get the job done! The job is to get you to accomplish God's plan for your life.

HOW TO RESPOND TO REJECTION

In essence, rejection is a wake up "call." It is an alarm clock that God uses to *wake up* your *calling.* God will not let you go through anything that you cannot handle. So if He lets you go through any form of rejection, then He wants you to benefit from it. Unfortunately, it's imperative for you to understand that being rejected does not guarantee that you will fulfill your call. You can be "called out." If you're not careful, you can "only" experience the detriments of rejection and never its benefits. Whether you fulfill your call, or get called out, depends on how you respond to rejection. If you don't respond properly to rejection, you will not successfully deal with rejection; rather, it will deal with you.

An alarm clock is designed to wake us up. The ringing of the clock is an alert for us to do something. God uses rejection in the same way. He uses it as an alert to get our attention. However, we have a choice to make when we hear the alert. That choice determines whether we deal with rejection or if it deals with us.

The right response to the buzz of an alarm clock is for us to wake up or respond to the purpose for which we set the alarm. In other words, we *use* the device for the reason for which we obtained it. The wrong response is to hit the *snooze* button. In this case, we refuse to yield to what it was designed to help us do. Many people have lost their jobs and missed very important life-changing appointments because of this.

In the same token, considering that God uses rejection like an alarm clock, when you are refused, hindered or heartbroken, do you *use* the rejection or do you *snooze* it? Do you respond the right way or do you respond the wrong way? Do you yield to the thing it was alerting you to do, or do you refuse to wake up to what God is trying to do for you? Whatever the case, it's in your best interest, that when you are disapproved, you respond the right way to the rebuff.

I encourage you to respond to any slight, neglect, job termination, breakup, divorce, or failure, with faith, hope, and love. Responding to any form of rejection with faith, hope, and love is necessary because you have at least three things to deal with when you are rejected. You have to deal with the person who rejected you, the rejection, and yourself. Faith, hope, and love, will help you counter those three. Use faith to deal with yourself, hope to deal with the rejection, and love to deal with the person who rejected you.

THE BIG THREE

When you respond to rejection with faith, hope, and love, not only will God help you successfully deal with rejection, He will also help you get a *great deal* out of it. Faith, hope, and love are the big three.

And now these remain: faith, hope, and love.... (1 Corinthians 13:13)

Usually when we are hurt, we need someone's shoulder to cry on. We need someone whose shoulder we can lean on, someone who can support and encourage us. We also need to get ourselves together. This is where faith comes into the picture. God is our best bet for restoration.

When someone *turns you down,* let this *turn you on* to God. Have faith in Him. Believe and trust that He is in control and will help you overcome the situation. Also, have faith in yourself because God has faith in you. He causes you to be triumphant and empowers you to overcome situations that you face in life (2 Corinthians 2:14, Philippians 4:13).

For every child of God defeats this evil world, and we achieve this victory through our faith. (1 John 5:4 NLT)

Having faith in God—and yourself—will help you, help yourself and overcome the situation. Having faith in God includes crying out to God and seeking God even more for help to persevere through the storm of abandonment. Use your faith in God to encourage yourself.

That, in turn, will give you hope, which will help you deal with the rejection. Have hope that being refused was for your benefit, and that things were working out for your best. Have hope that the rejection will help you be better off. While rejection tends to make us feel ashamed, hope counters that shame and turns the disappointment into an appointment for us to fulfill our destiny. Responding to the rejection with a hopeful mindset will bring this to pass for you. Hence, Romans 5:5 reads:

And hope maketh not ashamed.... (KJV)

And this hope will not lead to disappointment.... (NLT)

Such hope never disappoints or deludes or shames us.... (AMP)

Finally, respond with love toward the person who brushed you off, turned you down, or refused you.

...but the greatest of these is love. (1 Corinthians 13:13)

Loving someone who betrayed or disregarded you is a tough prospect, yet it is the most important aspect of your response to the way the person mistreated you. Responding with love to any setback is the best and strongest thing you should do. In fact, not only is love the biggest of the big three responses to rejection, it also encompasses the other two.

...but faith working through love. (Galatians 5:6 NKJV)

Love never gives up, never loses faith, is always hopeful, and endures through every circumstance. (1 Corinthians 13:7 NLT)

Treating your detractor with love is necessary for your faith in God to help you overcome your hurt. With love, your faith works, so does your hope because love bears, believes, *hopes,* and endures all things (1 Corinthians 13:7 NKJV).

You respond with love to the person who rejected you by forgiving the individual. Forgiveness is an imprint of love. It is the most important facet of love necessary for us to overcome the pain someone inflicted on us. If love was a hand, forgiveness would be its fingerprint.

Above all things have intense and unfailing love for one another, for love covers a multitude of sins (forgives and disregards the offenses of others). (1 Peter 3:8 AMP)

Hate stirs up trouble, but love forgives all offenses. (Proverbs 10:12 GNB)

There is a cost associated with overcoming and benefitting from rejection. We have to pay a price to be free of the resentment that often befalls us when we are offended. That price is forgiveness. Forgiveness is the legal tender for your freedom. It's the currency you give in exchange for your liberation from the person who broke your heart.

You can choose not to forgive. You can hit the snooze button. You can lash back and exercise your revenge by carrying out a vendetta on the person who rejected you. This way, you'll be paying the price to be miserable and chained to the agony that was inflicted on you. In addition, you are prone to be under the spell of the person who mistreated you for the rest of your life, even to the degree that the individual is clueless of your spat with him or her. Remember? You snooze... you lose.

You're too precious to God and mankind to wallow in the mud of your pain. Just because you've been castaway does not mean you should waste away. Just because you've been cast off does not give you the wherewithal to cast off your destiny. Rather, pay the price of forgiveness, which is entrenched in love. Have faith in God and this will give you hope—because faith is a substance of hope (Hebrews 11:1 NKJV).

Without hope, you will be depressed because the future will look gloomy for you. Without faith, you won't have hope. Without love, your faith won't work and you can't forgive the person who blew you off. Without forgiving, you'll be bound to the resentment you have against the person who broke your heart; and worse still, God can't really help you because He forgives us like we forgive others (Mark 11:25-27). And without God, you cannot be free from the chains of rejection.

According to Dr. Edwin Louis Cole:

Forgiveness is God's way to set us free from others' sins. Unforgiveness closes. Forgiveness opens. Unforgiveness binds. Forgiveness releases. Unforgiveness constitutes hardness of heart.

Forgiveness constitutes liberality, generosity, and freedom.[2]

Malcolm Smith echoed Dr. Cole's sentiment when he said that:

Unforgiveness hurts the unforgiver more than the unforgiven.[3]

While it is difficult to forgive, I believe that part of the reason why we find it hard to exercise this virtue is because we try to do it in our own strength. Forgiving someone is not something we can do based on our own willpower. We need God's help to do this. That's why it is so important that having faith in God is one of our responses to rejection. We should ask God for strength to forgive, and He will give you the grace to do this.

Furthermore, some of us find it hard to forgive because we don't fully understand what forgiveness is. Forgiveness is not about someone getting away with what they did to you; rather, it's about *you* getting away *from* what was done to you. Sometimes we also think that when we truly forgive someone, then we will forget what they did to us. In other words, the incident would be wiped out from our memory. On the contrary.

While the spirit of the saying, *"forgive and forget,"* means to treat someone like she never did anything wrong to you, or *don't hold things against anyone*, we literally don't forget what happened. The fact is, something happened to hurt you. True forgiveness is from the heart, and it does not hold the incident against the person. As hard as it is, forgiveness lets the situation go; however, it does not mean you don't remember what happened.

How can you forgive something that you don't even remember? The Bible says that love does not keep record of wrongs (1 Corinthians 13:5). If love does not keep a record of wrongs, then it must have been aware of the wrongs before it chose not to keep a record of them in the first place. After Jesus rose from the dead, He showed the scars in His hands and sides to Thomas, who doubted that He had risen (John 20:20-29). Well, Jesus is the perfect example of forgiveness. By showing His scars, He obviously did not forget what happened to Him on the cross. But this does not change the fact that he forgave from His heart. I think "forgive and *forfeit*" *is* a better phrase to describe forgiveness rather than "forgive and forget." Let it go.

Forgive the person. Let it go. If you don't let it go, the rejection won't let you go. It will take hold of you, hold you back and keep you in a bind. In this state, you can be hindered from fulfilling your call. Don't let that happen to you. Instead, let rejection happen *for* you—like God intended it to. Respond with faith for yourself to persevere, with hope to take advantage of the rejection, and with love by forgiving the person who dismissed you.

Dear friend, save yourself the trouble and allow God the leeway to turn your situation around by forgiving the person who broke your heart. By doing this, you'll be responding in love. Now your faith can work, and this serves as the template that gives you hope that things were working out for your best. You'll discover that you got the "right" end of the stick. You might have been someone's *outcast* but God will make you His *broadcast*—His main attraction. He'll heal you by wrapping you in His *cast* of affection and restoration, and, through your experience, He'll propel you to significance.

The movie of your life might have started or continued on a wrong note, but it will conclude with a happy ending. Your part in the screenplay of your life is to respond the *right way* to any *static* that comes against you. Your response should be of faith, hope, and love. After you've done this, you can receive, what I consider, the eight benefits of rejection.

Chapter 3
Eight Benefits of It

There are basically two ways that we can benefit from rejection. We can benefit from it 1) directly and 2) indirectly. We can gain from rejection directly when we are the ones rejected. If someone turns you down, dismisses your idea, refuses your product, your services, or your affection, you've been rejected directly. In this case, you can learn and achieve a lot from your personal experience of being passed over.

We can also benefit from rejection indirectly. There are three ways that we can experience indirect rejection. One way is when someone *else* is dismissed and you end up taking the person's place. This is where you *replace* someone who was displaced. The second way is when another individual's innovation, business, or affection is rebuffed, and that person ends up bringing his or her idea, product, services, or affection to you, and it's what you've been looking for. This is where someone who was displaced *is placed* with you. The third way we benefit from rejection indirectly is when we learn and achieve a lot from someone else's experience with being overlooked. This is where other people's experiences with rejection inspire and inform us on what to do when we're faced with the same situations they went through.

Furthermore, there are at least eight *benefits* that we can gain from rejection. They are 1) inspiration, 2) liberation, 3) preparation, 4) promotion, 5) protection, 6) provision, 7) redemption, and 8)redirection. As mentioned previously, you can receive these benefits directly or indirectly. If indirectly, then you don't have to be the one rejected to experience them. It could have been someone else who was refused, and understanding how that person overcame his hurt can help you overcome yours, too. This brings me to the first benefit of rejection.

INSPIRATION

Successful sales and business-minded people are notorious for taking advantage of this benefit. When they meet individuals who decline their product or when they encounter a snag with their project, especially when people snicker at them and tell them that they will not be able to accomplish their goals, the rejection inspires them to prove their critics wrong. They use the lack of confidence that people express about their efforts as ammunition to not only meet their objectives, but also to exceed them.

There are also people doing extraordinary things today and their accomplishments serve as inspiration for us all. Little do we know that some of what those individuals have done with their lives was facilitated by the adversities they faced. Their accomplishments range from award-winning, nationally syndicated talk shows, to songs that top the music charts, to books that end up on the New York Times Best Seller lists, and to movies that top the box office. Individuals who've accomplished such remarkable feats include Oprah Winfrey, Dr. Joyce Meyer, Pastor Paula White, Yolanda Adams, India Arie, Bishop T. D. Jakes, the late Ray Charles, and Sidney Poitier.

Rejection experienced in their broken relationships inspired some of the hit songs put forth by Ray Charles, Yolanda Adams, and India Arie. Rejection experienced in his ministry, as well as in the lives of men, women, and families under his leadership, inspired Bishop Jakes to pioneer *Mega Fest*, a family-oriented convention, and write the best seller *Woman Thou Art Loosed*, which was also produced as a movie. The rejection experienced in the form of sexual, physical, and emotional abuse also inspired the writings and teachings of Dr. Joyce Meyer, the talk-show and global ministry of Paula White, as well as the award-winning talk-show and vast philanthropic work of the media mogul Oprah Winfrey.

Many years ago, an unemployed Sidney Poitier was desperate to find any job to make ends meet. He came across a newspaper ad for an actor. Mr. Poitier decided to audition. Unfortunately for him, while auditioning for the part, because he could barely read or act, his auditor grabbed him by the collar of his shirt and the scruff of his pants and tossed him out of the audition. He told Poitier that he could not act and that he should find a job that he could handle, a job like dishwashing.

That was Poitier's *wake up call*. The rejection inspired him to improve his diction, his acting, and himself to prove his auditor wrong. Although he was tossed out of that audition, he was *thrust* to his destiny to be one of the most accomplished actors in the world. The rejection transformed Poitier from *washing dishes* to being *watched in dishes*—satellite dishes, the big screen, and other forms of media. Thanks to the dismissal, Sidney Poitier received the inspiration that helped him become the first African-American to win an *Academy Award* for Best Actor, three *Golden Globe* Awards, star in over forty films, direct nine, and write four—just to mention a few of his achievements.[1]

The very thing that Mr. Poitier was told that he was not good at was the thing he became one of the best at. Not only did the rejection inspire him to improve himself, it also helped him find himself. Not only did it help him wake up to his call, it also helped him answer his call.

The adversity that Mr. Poitier and the aforementioned public figures went through served as the platform that spring boarded them to fame. The trials they faced refined and defined them. It positioned them for their purpose. It helped them discover and fulfill their calling. It inspired the songs they sang, the messages they preached, the books they wrote, the issues they addressed, and indicated who they were to motivate, protect and care for. Those individuals have inspired and touched some, if not most, of us through their movies, music, writings, telecasts, and conferences. How they've handled, and continue to deal with, rejection is a source of inspiration for us to overcome the adversities we face, too.

In addition, just like those public figures took advantage of the slingshots of difficulty, and used them to catapult themselves to significance, you should also utilize the rockets of affliction projected at you to launch yourself to stardom. Let rejection be the storm that soars you to greater heights. Don't let its ocean drown you; ride its waves, instead.

When you utilize rejection as inspiration to better yourself, you might never win a *Golden Globe*, a *Pulitzer*, or a *Congressional Medal of Honor*. But you can still win over any adversity and become the person God created you to be. You can still win people's hearts and help them want to be better at who they are. You can still win people to God. You can still win by being a better person, husband or wife, employer or employee, pastor or parishioner, educator or student. You can be inspired to be your best and give your best.

LIBERATION

If your desires and goals in life are put on a shelf or hindered because of someone with whom you're involved, and that person does not care about you and mistreats you, when the person kicks you out of his or her life, the individual has done you a favor. The person set you free from his or her abuse and also liberated you to actualize your dreams. The person gave you freedom to express and be yourself.

Sometimes, however, some individuals will not throw you out of their lives. They keep you around as their toy and pet project. Such reprehensible treatment causes some people to leave such abusive relationships. In these cases, the rejection was an indication, a red flag or alarm for them to liberate themselves. Other people—because of fear, shame, or not knowing what to do—stay in the mess, but eventually get their freedom by seeking help and the company of those who went through and overcame similar experiences.

Furthermore, rejection, experienced in the form of prejudice and discrimination, fueled the civil rights and women's *liberation* movements. While some of the members and participants of such movements sacrificed their lives and underwent a lot of adversity, such movements were eventually able to liberate African-Americans and women of all nationalities to enjoy and experience, at present, the privileges that used to be restricted to only Caucasians and men, respectively.

In addition, when individuals who've been a thorn in your side, in your relationship, business, or ministry forsake you, you've been set free from their destructive ways.

Are you familiar with the dynamic speaker, motivator, and businesswoman who found liberation through rejection and became one of the greatest entrepreneurs in American history? Her name is Mary Kay Ash, founder of *Mary Kay Inc.* After 25 years in direct sales, being told that women could never run a business, being passed over for promotions, and having her ideas dismissed, the final straw that broke the camel's back came when a man, whom she trained, was promoted over her—at *twice* her salary.

The rebuff *inspired* her to resign as a national training director and begin writing a book that would help women gain the opportunities that she was denied. In the process, she discovered that her book was more like a business plan that would develop the talents of women and help them achieve unlimited success. In essence, she came up with an idea that would help *liberate* women to be all they could be.

With her business experience, business plan, a lot of hard work, the help of her 20-year-old son, Richard, and $5000 in savings, she birthed her idea, *Beauty by Mary Kay,* in 1963. Her company was founded on the principle of praising people to success, and on the principle of putting God first, family second, and career third. Her vision has given rise to a mega conglomerate that has made an indelible mark in American business and has blown the door wide open for women all around the world to achieve success on their own terms.

Thanks to the rejection she experienced, Mary Kay Ash was liberated to be herself, express her ideas, and liberate women from the inequalities they faced in the business world. At the time of this writing, her products were sold in 35 markets worldwide, reached $2.4 billion in wholesale sales in 2007, and had about 1.8 million Mary Kay independent beauty consultants all around the world.[2]

PREPARATION

Being rejected is a humbling experience. When you are put down, given the cold shoulder, divorced, forsaken, verbally, physically, or emotionally abused, you can feel like you're worthless, good for nothing, or an utter failure. Though humility has been described as thinking about yourself less, rejection can make you think less of yourself. Whatever the case might be, rejection tends to leave you in a humbled state. The kind of state that is ample for God's use. In other words rejection prepares you for God's use.

God purposely chose what the world considered nonsense in order to shame the wise, and He chose what the world considered weak in order to shame the powerful. He chose what the world looks down on and despises and thinks is nothing, in order to destroy what the world thinks is important. (1 Corinthians 1:27-28 GNB)

God loves rejects. He loves us all, but He tends to use rejects more than anyone else. They are ripe for His use because they've been despised, down-trodden and neglected. Therefore, they are likely to have been humbled by their experiences. They've had their heart broken and, in a sense, their ordeal has depleted them of strength and left them empty. Their emptiness serves as an opening through which God can flood His love and strength. In their humbled state, they look like a deflated balloon, but God can inflate His life in them and cause them to soar to greater heights.

And I will deal severely with all who have oppressed you. I will save the weak and helpless ones; I will bring together those who were chased away. I will give glory and fame to my former exiles, wherever they have been mocked and shamed. (Zephaniah 3:19 NLT)

Just like we are unable to handle or even do anything with a balloon already inflated and sailing in the air, God cannot do anything with people who are already inflated or full of themselves. However, in a humbled state, God can inflate us with

Himself. This way, we'll not be full of ourselves and subject to rejection again.

You see, friend, God resists the proud but gives grace to the humble. He desires that we humble ourselves in His sight so that He can lift us up (James 4:6-10). It is inherent in our nature to seek validation and recognition. God has no problem with this as long as we do not think more highly of ourselves than we ought (Romans 12:3). We should think highly of ourselves; just not *more* highly. Because if we do, we are saying that we're better than who God created us to be.

Unfortunately, when we are proud, arrogant, or conceited, we set ourselves up to be brought low. Rejection tends to do this to us. Humility is the class we need to take and pass before we can graduate with God's honors. It's a prerequisite for God to promote us.

Before destruction the heart of a man is haughty, And before honor is humility. (Proverbs 18:12)

I once heard Kirk Franklin quote Dr. Tony Evans by saying that God will let you hit rock bottom, so that when you hit the bottom you'll know that He is the Rock *at* the bottom.

One of the most intimate verses in scripture says that God is close to those who have a broken heart and to those who have a crushed spirit (Psalm 34:18).

I believe God is especially close to us when we are broken because in this condition we usually feel lonely and like no one is available to help us in our plight. We feel that the people who also might have been responsible for our melancholy have abandoned us. Therefore, the gap they created between us and God when they were present in our lives has been closed up, enabling God to get closer to us to revive and put us to use.

Besides, God lets your heart get broken so that the gifting which He placed in your heart and which was lying dormant, could be spilled out and released to permeate the lives of others. This is similar to how Mary broke an alabaster box of expensive perfume to wash the feet of Christ. The breaking of the oil and its use with her hair to wipe Jesus' feet was not just a gesture of her humility and worship, it also represented how her sacrifice touched the lives of others as the aroma from the fragrance filled the house, and, as a result, its other occupants were also privileged to bask in it (John 12:3).

She made a huge sacrifice. The oil was costly. In the same way, the anointing, ability, or empowerment that God has placed in your life is expensive. It costs God and the people whom God has appointed you to bless if you do not release your gift or talent to benefit them. God's purpose for your life goes beyond yourself. It includes others. If you're not expressing the gift lodged in your heart, you are limiting God from channeling His will through you into the lives of others.

God can, and might, use someone else to do what He assigned you to do. But He'll give you more chances than you need to do your job. He'll assist and push you to fulfill His purpose for your life by sending you reinforcement, which at times is something that gets you to pour out your heart, something like rejection. It humbles and prepares you for God's use, which is the expression of the dream that God placed in your heart.

Truth be told, at times, we have to be *broken* before we can get our big *break*. You might recall that "heart" is one of the words in the acrostic "shape" put forth by Pastor Rick Warren. According to him, when you discover your shape, you'll discover your gifts for ministry. Therefore, discovering and fulfilling your heart's desire enables you to fulfill your purpose. This is God's objective when he allows you to be broken, and this prepares you to wake up to His call on your life.

PROMOTION

God uses rejection to promote you. Before God can exalt you, if you're not already humble, He humbles you to prepare you for the promotion. At times, He does this by allowing you to be demoted in order for you to be promoted. Being demoted is a form of rejection. When you are honored and exalted by God, you've been promoted.

For promotion cometh neither from the east, nor from the west, nor from the south. But God is the judge: he putteth down one, and setteth up another. (Psalm 75:6-7 KJV)

God can promote you through divorce. This occurs if He allows you to be repudiated from a bad marriage in order to get you into a good one with a compatible spouse. The new spouse in question could have undergone an annulment, unbeknownst to him or her, to get to you, too. If a man or a woman who has been mistreating and disrespecting you in a relationship breaks up with you, and you end up with someone else who treats you like the sweetheart or gentleman God created you to be, you've been promoted. If you end up in a relationship better and more fulfilling than the one you were broken from, guess what? You've been promoted.

Sometimes God gets someone else rejected so that you can take the person's place. This is the case when someone gets fired and you're promoted to fill the person's position. In some other cases, you might have been praying to God for a job and someone gets laid off so that you can replace the person. At other times, God has to get you fired from a job you loathe or get your application declined for a job that will not employ your gifts, in order for you to end up securing the job He tailor-made for you. He gives you a job that you enjoy at a better company, with better benefits and pay, as well as a career that employs the abilities that He placed in you. God can also get you laid off so that you can start your own business which was a desire in your heart for eons of time. But the fly in the ointment of your heart was the fear of failure and losing your nine-to-five, which became your comfort zone.

But God uses rejection to get us from our *comfort zones* to our *come forth zones*. When we get there, we'll be promoted as we'll be better off doing the things God empowered us to do as opposed to the things we used to do, which left us unfulfilled.

During an interview with John Hamlin on *60 minutes*, Hilary Swank, who won an Oscar for *Million Dollar Baby*, disclosed that she was fired from the cast of *Beverly Hills 90210*. However, because she was fired, she was *freed up* to play the *leading* role in a movie for which she won her first Oscar. She was promoted, thanks to being rejected from her previous stint.

If God promotes you through rejection, He is getting you or someone else detached from an unpleasant and frustrating situation in order for you to be attached to a delightful and rewarding one.

PROTECTION

Anaj worked as the assistant manager of the flight operations department of the aviation regulatory body of a developing country. Though he was the assistant, he was also doing the work of the general manager, a role that was not filled at the time he was hired. Later on, another colleague of Anaj's was hired to assist Anaj. Anaj and his colleague both answered to a director of their department.

Both Anaj and his assistant were experienced commercial airline pilots. His assistant, however, had more pilot experience than Anaj. Nevertheless, Anaj had been hired as an assistant manager but was asked to fulfill the role of a general manager months before his colleague was brought on board to assist him. Furthermore, Anaj had been working as a general manager for about 18 months without compensation for the role.

Anaj requested that he be compensated for all the work he did as a general manager. His request was rebuffed by his director, who claimed that, because Anaj was a contract appointee and not a government appointee, he couldn't be compensated for and given the role. Like throwing egg in his face, the director promoted Anaj's assistant, who was also a "contract" appointee but who also happened to be a very close acquaintance of the director, over Anaj as the general manager.

Anaj responded to the rejection the way I've been encouraging you to. He responded with faith that God would vindicate him. He had hope that what he was going through was for the best. And he responded with love toward his boss. He had no ill will against him or against his former assistant who was now his boss. Anaj kept his head up, kept his faith, and kept his cool.

About a year-and-a-half later, there was a tragic airplane accident by an airline from the developing country in one of their airports. Not only was there a fatal airplane crash, but just a few months later, another plane from the same developing country crashed. Two tragic airline accidents within months of each other. Incidentally, Anaj's department was the branch of the aviation industry that investigated these matters.

The minister of aviation of this developing country was miffed about these developments. There were nine departments in the aviation regulatory body that he oversaw. In an effort to hold the departments accountable and ensure that those tragedies would not take place again, the aviation minister decided to clean house. He terminated all the *directors* and *general managers* of those departments. In essence, by the time the minister of aviation stopped wielding his axe Anaj was the only one left standing in his department, while his director and general manager got fired.

A new director was appointed and, about 8 months later, Anaj was promoted to the general manager position. This is my point: God prevented Anaj from being promoted because He saw what was going to happen. By allowing Anaj to be rejected, God *protected* him from losing His job and ensured that he would receive the promotion at the proper time. Anaj experienced rejection because it was not the right time for him to climb up the corporate ladder.

Prevention is a form of rejection. When God prevents you from doing or achieving something, He is either protecting you from doing something at the wrong time or preserving you for something else. If you're already involved with a project or relationship which is wearing you down, He uses rejection to get you out of it to protect you from getting depreciated any further.

You are valuable to God. If God allows you to get dismissed, He is only protecting His asset. When someone rejects you, respond to it with the hope that God is letting that happen to protect you. This kind of response reflects your faith and hope that God was preserving you from getting or keeping yourself in a mess. You should also have faith in yourself because, like I said previously, you are precious to God. So, if someone turns down your preciousness, the person is doing you a huge favor.

God could be protecting you from being, or getting, battered any further in an abusive relationship. God could be protecting you from securing employment at a company that, unbeknownst to you, is going under. God could be protecting you from getting or staying involved with something or someone that could mess up your life to the extent that you end up too devastated and discouraged to champion the cause that God designated you to carry out. Whatever the case, God utilizes rejection to preserve you for your purpose.

PROVISION

By provision I mean someone provided for a vision. For example, if you are pro-life, this means that you are *for life*. If you provided a service pro bono, this means that you did something *for free*. Similarly, if someone is supplied *for vision*, that someone is "pro-vision." This means that someone was provided for a vision—provision. If you are involved with the wrong vision, God lets you get rejected from that project to provide you for the vision He has for you. If He lets someone else get offloaded from some other venture and the person ends up with you, God just provided for your vision; He supplied you with provision.

Your vision is tied to your purpose. The vision could be for your marriage, ministry, or industry. If you are let go from a faulty relationship, or from a job, and end up with another person or employment that fulfills what you've been longing for, you've been provided for the vision in your heart. If an individual's job is terminated and that person ends up working for you and the person enhances or turns your church, business, or department around, God has provided for your vision. If a person who was dismissed from a relationship ends up with you and this individual fits the profile of the kind of person you've been yearning for, God has provided for you, and He did it by allowing the person to be released to you.

A host of individuals in America today have been able to accomplish their vision of being financially free. They were able to do this because they invested in real estate, particularly, properties that *no one wanted*. The same holds true for individuals who pioneered businesses that others *overlooked*, provided services that people *refused* to consider and invested in individuals who were deemed *damaged* goods. The *unwanted* properties, businesses, services, and castoffs served as their provisions. They fulfilled their desires by embracing other people's trash as their treasures.

Tom Szaky is a prime example of someone who, literally, turns garbage into gold. This Princeton dropout is the CEO and the founder of TerraCycle. His company develops products made of and packaged from *wastes* like vinyl records, cookie wrappers, plastic bags, and other waste materials, turns them into new products, and sells them to large retail stores. During CNN's coverage on TerraCycle, CNN reporter Betty Nguyen reported that the company takes ordinary garbage like Capri Sun juice pouches and turns them into messenger bags and pencil cases; chip bags into homework folders, and circuit boards into frames, just to mention a few. Tom Szaky receives his wastes from the likes of Frito-Lay, Kraft, schools, churches, and other groups.

During an interview with Amie Vaccaro of Green Business Innovators, Tom Szaky disclosed that his company had revenues of $70,000 to $0.5M in 2005, $1.5M in 2006, $3.3M in 2007, and projected sales of $7.5M in 2008.[3] Tom Szaky not only capitalizes on consumer wastes, but also fosters the green revolution, and facilitates an eco-friendly economy. What Tom Szaky does with *refuse* is a picture of what God does with people who have been *refused*. God redeems, restores, and reuses them *anew*.

REDEMPTION

Let's face it, we all make mistakes, and there are stakes in mistakes. When we make errors in judgment or when we do not exercise our best efforts in our responsibilities, it's to our benefit that we are made aware of them so that we can make amends. As I mentioned previously, we get rejected when we do wrong things. When we are rejected for our oversights, we're being notified that our blunders are not acceptable. We're being corrected and afforded the opportunity to redeem ourselves. It's in our best interest that we receive the reprimand and get things right. This is an occasion for personal growth.

My child, don't reject the LORD's discipline, and don't be upset when he corrects you. For the LORD corrects those he loves, just as a father corrects a child in whom he delights. (Proverbs 3:11-12 NLT)

Once we make the necessary adjustments to rectify our gaffes, we'll gain some invaluable experience and reestablish the confidence that those who brought our mistakes to our attention had in us.

While I was putting finishing touches to this book, America was going through a mortgage crises and a tanking economy. Our country's recession was due in part to fraudulent practices and bad business transactions carried out by some major financial institutions. Consequently, American taxpayers reacted by dumping their stocks and withdrawing their monies en masse from major banking institutions in the country. Their response was a reflection of their rejection and distrust of the banks. This gut reaction by the American populace also contributed to an ailing economy and forced or *inspired* the government to step in to rescue some major banks and revitalize the economy.

Interestingly, the stimulus packages and bailout monies given out by the government to restore the economy were an act of *redemption*. To redeem simply means to buy back or make something good again. Therefore, by taking control of major percentages of AIG and Citigroup, for example, and buying toxic assets from them, the American government was trying to redeem the companies and restore the economy.

Furthermore, the action of the government was also an attempt to redeem the bad image that was cast on them due to their lack of adequate oversight of the institutions responsible for the mortgage crises and fraudulent financial transactions. The cooperation of the financial institutions called to question, with the government, was also an attempt by the institutions to redeem their badly tainted credibility and restore consumer confidence.

The disapproval of banks by taxpayers, evidenced by the selling of their stocks and withdrawal of their monies, triggered a cascade reaction that almost toppled and bankrupted major banks, and this forced the federal government to intervene by redeeming the major financial institutions in order to salvage the economy.

As you can see, rejection leads to redemption. God uses rejection to point out when we are going in the wrong direction. Once we are cognizant of this, it's beneficial for us to change course. This brings me to the last benefit of rejection.

REDIRECTION

While successful sales and business-minded people thrive from the inspiration they get from being rejected, the unsuccessful ones survive rejection by being redirected by it. Their inability to make the sales quota or succeed in their business causes them to either change their approach to their business or refocus their energy into other ventures which utilize their strengths and cause them to be successful.

The lady who was asked to leave a fellowship because her previous church's leadership felt that her service in their house of worship went beyond what they felt were women's roles, ended up fulfilling her call at a different fellowship where her gifts for ministry were acknowledged and embraced. The son whom a school described as suffering from Attention Deficit Disorder became an honor roll student after his parents transferred him to another school which discovered that he wasn't suffering from that condition; rather, he just needed to be taught with an approach different from the way he was instructed at his previous school.

If we occupy and position ourselves with people and places that we have no business with, or dabble with endeavors that do not utilize our capabilities, God uses rejection to redirect us somewhere else, do something else, or be with someone else. He uses it as a detour to get us back on the right track. He uses it to navigate us to the path of our destiny.

I am reminded of a profound statement made by the British actor Bob Hoskins, who played the character of a butler in the movie, *Maid in Manhattan.* He said:

"Sometimes we're forced in directions we ought to have found for ourselves."

In this book, that force is rejection. Your destiny is the direction.

Envision that you are in a narrow corridor in a building which has five doors. You want to go out of the building, but you do not know which door leads you out of it. So at your discretion, you open one of the doors, but it leads to the bathroom. You proceed to another door, but it turns out to be a closet. You try to pry open another, but it is locked. You open the fourth, but this only leads you to the basement. The fifth, however, gets you out of the building. Rejection is like those four doors that did not let you accomplish your goal; the fifth was the path to your freedom.

During an interview with James Brown, the *Real Sports with Bryant Gumbel* correspondent (not the soul singer), Evander Holyfield disclosed that he was unable to break into his high school's football team. This caused him to focus on boxing, and, as you might know, he was successful at it. As a boxer, Evander Holyfield won the accolade of being the world heavy weight champion—four different times. He was so good at it that he found it hard to quit after he passed his prime. His rejection from football redirected him to boxing, where he proved his mettle. Similarly, God uses rejection to redirect you to individuals and ventures where your abilities will be utilized and where you'll be the success He created you to be.

Interestingly, this book was rejected by about 66 literary agents and 26 book publishers. I had to practice what I'm preaching in this work each time I opened the rejection letters that came through post or email. Just like I hoped, my writing was eventually redirected to the publisher of this work, who saw the light in my work and received my manuscript with open arms. All the other agents and publishers did not accept my work. Some said this work was not for them. One said I did not have a platform to launch the book to success, while others claimed that they were swamped with other manuscripts and didn't have time to consider my book.

While most of the publishers and agents were polite in dismissing this book, one editorial director of a book publishing company said this to me in his rejection email:

"Thank you for your inquiry. While rejection is a universal

experience I am skeptical that people would want to read about it, sadly. Thank you all the same for your approach."

Considering his opinion of my book, I trust that you can see why my book was better off with the group that took me under their wing. I'm grateful that he redirected me to another editorial director who perceived that, contrary to his opinion, the masses would want to read this book.

To be honest, the rejection I faced in trying to get this work published was a joke compared to the rejection most writers experience. Authors Mark Victor Hansen and Jack Canfield had it way worse than I did. The two motivational speakers teamed up to write an inspirational piece with the intent of publishing it within three months in 1989. Well, things did not turn out like they planned. They were first rebuffed by 33 publishers; and to make matters worse, their agent bid them good riddance after telling them that their book would never sell.

Three years and some 134 rejections later, the two relentless authors, employing efficient marketing techniques, made their *Chicken Soup for the Soul* book a best seller.[4] Now we have Chicken Soup for *every* Soul selling like hot corn bread. In a nutshell, God allows us to be rejected so that we can be *inspired, liberated,* and *prepared* to fulfill his call on our lives. He uses it to *promote, protect,* and *provide* us for a vision. He utilizes it to *redeem* and *redirect* us to our *purpose.*

Once again, just because you get rejected does not guarantee that you'll experience the benefits: Inspiration, Liberation, Preparation, Promotion, Protection, Provision, Redemption, and Redirection. How you respond to not being accepted will determine whether you'll be better off or worse off. The right way for you to deal with rejection and get a great deal out of it is by responding to it with faith, hope, and love. By responding with love, you're also forgiving the person who refused you.

Chapter 4
Wrong Timing Causes It

Envision yourself driving a vehicle on a road. You are heading to a certain place. On the way to your destination, you approach a traffic light. The light is on red, which means that you have to bring your car to a halt. The red light does not mean that you cannot drive on the road nor does it mean that you can't arrive at your destination. The red light signifies that you are to stop your car in order for the other cars on the intersecting roads to move, too. The red light flashed to facilitate and navigate smooth and orderly flow of traffic. As long as the light is red, it's not time for you to move your car.

God is the traffic controller of our lives. He often directs us in paths. He uses His paths to navigate us toward His purpose. Sometimes we might be cognizant of what our purpose is, whom to accomplish it with, and where to fulfill it. However, sometimes we do not know *when* to undertake our purpose. In other words, we do not know the right time for us to go ahead with what we believe we are to do. Worst still, we might not even know that there is a right time to undertake our mission in life. As a result, we are likely to proceed with what we believe we're to do, but carry it out at the wrong time. Hence we personify the cliché: *doing the right thing at the wrong time*. And the consequence of this is heartbreak, mistakes, and rejection!

When we do things at the wrong time, we are like the individual who runs a red light. Instead of slowing down to a halt, we accelerate to our hurt. Consequently, we end up in a wreck like scores of individuals who where unlucky to avoid the traffic coming against them. Even if we are fortunate to avoid a collision, we're likely to *pay a price* like those individuals who got caught by the police and were ticketed and *fined* for *reckless* driving.

God sometimes allows things not to go our way so that He can slow us down. This is one way He flashes His red light for us to stop. Yes, He wants us to travel the road to our destiny. But He wants us to arrive at our destinations "safe and sound." To accomplish this, He has to control the traffic of people and circumstances that affect us. He has to ensure that they cross our paths, not "cross us," crush us, or collide against us.

Unfortunately, some of us often insist on our own way and proceed to do our own thing. When we do this, we are being rebellious and playing into Satan's hands. Therefore, since we did not let God's traffic light slow us down, then we are prone to crash. If the devil has his way completely, he'll use the accident to annihilate us, but God's grace, in the least, will utilize the incident to bring us to an abrupt stop. We might suffer life-threatening injuries or heartbreak for a while, and then recover, which is a better alternative to Satan's plan to completely snuff us out.

Sometimes we might be smart enough to stop when we see the red light, but our impatience causes us to take other routes to get to our destinations faster. Do you know what can happen if we do this? We can get lost in our attempts to get to our destinations quicker. We can get so far out of God's will such that we might find ourselves lost in things we had no business getting involved with in the first place. In our attempts to take a *short cut*, we jeopardize our lives to get *cut short*.

If you run the red light and get into an accident where you incur serious bodily damage, you will need emergency medical attention. This means that you'll be taken to the hospital to be treated for your injuries. In addition, you'll be admitted to the hospital for a while until the doctor says that it's okay for you to go home. If you factor in the time that elapsed from the time of the accident to the time you recovered from your injuries in the hospital, you would realize that you wasted more time than you wanted to save when you ran the red light.

If you took another route and got lost, you would need to get a map or seek direction from someone to get you back on track. In the process, you wasted more time than you would have had you just waited patiently for the light to turn green. So, in an effort to get ahead, you got behind. This is one of the reasons why things don't happen for us as quickly as we want them to. We are trying to speed things up while God is trying to slow us down. Slow and steady wins the race; fast and unsteady gets disgraced.

There is a time for everything. Timing is very important, and it's a fundamental factor that will help you achieve success. Doing things at the right time is a necessary ingredient that will help you fulfill your destiny. It will help crown your efforts with victory. Whether you run the red light or take another route, you are still not doing things God's way. As a result, you will be rejected. Your efforts will be refused, not accepted, disallowed, or frustrated—all synonyms for rejection.

You are likely to be rejected by the person you consider your soul-mate if the individual is seeing someone else or is just recovering from a nasty breakup. You are likely to get the application for your dream job turned down if you applied to a company undergoing a Chapter 11 bankruptcy. You are likely to be rejected from dazzling the world with your God-given talents if you have not developed the character to handle the fame that your gift attracts.

Just because you know what to do, where to do it, and with whom to accomplish your purpose does not mean that you are ready to fulfill the task. Your passion for someone or something does not mean that you are prepared for that prospect or project. The right time for you to fulfill your purpose is the time when you are prepared and the circumstances are conducive for you to take advantage of the opportunity presented to you. Though you have been rejected because you tried to accomplish something at the wrong time, you are only being restricted to reestablish yourself at the proper time.

There's a right time for everything. (Ecclesiastes 3:1 MSG)

Are you familiar with Jesus' parable of the sower? This story by Christ is so profound, insightful, and relevant to our everyday lives. This probably explains why the account was written and narrated with slightly different perspectives from three different authors: Matthew 13:1-23, Mark 4:1-20, and Luke 8:4-15.

While I haven't comprehended all the insights from the parable, nor am I able to highlight all the nuances about this account, I'd like us to note something in the story that reinforces the relevance of timing to rejection. To accomplish this I'll need to give you the overview of the story.

Jesus stated that a sower went out to sow some seeds. He said that some of those seeds fell by the way side and birds from the air came and ate them all up. He said that others fell on rocky ground, and because the ground was shallow, the seeds immediately sprang up. But when the sun came up, the plants were scorched and withered away because they were not deeply rooted. He also said that some other seeds fell among thorns and the thorns rose up and choked the seeds from bearing fruits. Others fell on good ground and bore fruit.

For your personal study, I encourage you to read the parable and Jesus' explanation of it. Meanwhile, I'd like us to focus on the second ground on which the seeds fell. Let's look at the verse that specifies this scenario:

Some fell on stony places, where they did not have much earth; and they immediately sprang up because they had no depth of earth. But when the sun was up they were scorched, and because they had no root they withered away. (Matthew 13:5-6 NKJV)

Jesus explained:

But he who received seed on stony places, this is he who hears the word and immediately receives it with joy; yet he has no root in himself, but endures only for a while. For when tribulation and persecution arises because of the word, immediately he stumbles. (Matthew 13:20-21 NKJV)

A lot can be, and has been, deduced from that passage and from the parable as a whole. Notwithstanding, God is the sower, the seeds represent His Word, and the ground represents our hearts. Unfortunately, the individual whose heart represented the stony ground did not bear fruit with the word that God placed in his heart. Why? Because the seed *immediately sprang up*. It came up too quickly. It wasn't time!

The plant came up ahead of time because the ground from which it sprouted was shallow. It was not deeply rooted. In other words, the individual was not prepared, ready, or mature enough to handle the seed of God's word in his heart. Therefore, when the sun, which represents the trials of life, came up, the individual stumbled. The person did not have the depth or substance to handle adversity.

Similarly, God has planted seeds of purpose in us. In order for those seeds to come into fruition, manifesting as us fulfilling our destinies, we need to be properly trained and developed so that we can have the maturity to handle our gifts and abilities.

One way God ensures that we do not jump the gun in answering His call on our lives is by Him restricting us through authority figures in our lives, be it parents, teachers, pastors, counselors and other forms of leadership. A traffic light flashing red is like an authority figure stopping your progress. This is done for your safety and to ensure that you proceed with your mandate at the right time.

CATERPILLAR TO BUTTERFLY

I once heard a version of a story that was attributed to the writer, Henry Miller. The tale was about a butterfly trying to break out of its cocoon. A man was watching the insect as it exercised efforts to come out of its enclosure. Its efforts paid off after it forced an opening in the cocoon and tried to push itself out of the hole. After struggling for a while, it appeared that the butterfly could not go any further. The man who was watching the whole action assumed that the butterfly was unable to break out of its shell, so he decided to help the insect out. He took a pair of scissors and cut open the cocoon, and the butterfly came out easily.

Unfortunately for the butterfly, it was unable to fly. It had a withered body and shriveled wings. Unbeknownst to the man, the butterfly needed to beat its wings against the restricting cocoon so that the resistance it encountered with its shell would force fluid from its body into its wings so that it could fly once it was out of the cocoon. Since the butterfly got out *ahead of time,* thanks to the unsolicited help of the unassuming stranger, the butterfly was crippled for life, unable to fly, and it eventually died.

The main point that I'm trying to convey from that story is that the butterfly died because it came out of its cocoon at the *wrong time.* It was unable to takeoff because it was not ready to fly. Its body was not prepared, neither were its wings. The purpose of the cocoon was to provide the resistance that would help develop its body and the muscles of its wings so that, when it broke out from its shell, it would be able to fly.

Caterpillars metamorphose into butterflies. Their cocoon facilitates the process. Their cocoon *protects* and *prepares* them to fulfill their destiny of becoming butterflies. This is how God designed their life. This is also how God orchestrates our lives, too. Just like the stone became a chief cornerstone, caterpillars become butterflies, but the transition is *inspired* and influenced by opposition or resistance, which is a form of rejection.

Rejection is a cocoon that God uses to force the fluid of potential in us to strengthen our wings of purpose so that we can fly into our destiny *at the right time.* God uses rejection as a safeguard. It's a protective coating that God utilizes to ensure that we emerge into our significance. It's also a double-edged sword. On one hand, it inspires and forces out our abilities, gifts, and talents. On the other hand, it also prevents us from expressing them until we are mature enough to handle them.

If we don't experience the restriction necessary to help us grow "our wings," we can end up like the butterfly, crippled and unable to fly to our destiny. We can stifle our potential which can lead to the demise of our God-given ambitions and endeavors. God allows us to be rejected for the purpose of fulfilling our destiny at the right time. He uses the opposition to ensure that we are positioned and properly postured for our callings.

IT'S TIME FOR YOUR "BABY" TO COME OUT

Let's go back to the traffic light analogy. I mentioned that if we run a red light we can get into accidents. But do you know what is fascinating about our encounters with traffic control? Sometimes, we don't run the light. Sometimes, the light runs us. By this I mean that in some cases, perhaps due to us getting ourselves distracted, we find ourselves still waiting with our cars even after the light has changed from red to green. And, we only move after we hear the blaring honk of the car behind us.

Every once in a while, God does not only use rejection to slow us down, He also uses it to *start us up*. He employs it not only to stop us, but also to push us. Like the sound of the horn of the car(s) behind us which *wakes us up* from our trip to la-la land to get our vehicles moving, after we were unintentionally holding up the progress of the vehicles behind us, God uses the green light of rejection to get us moving forward.

Although God utilizes resistance to prevent us from carrying out our purpose at the wrong time, He also uses it to prod us to answer our call at the right time. This is necessary because while we are prone to do things that we are supposed to do at the wrong time, we also have the tendency to be complacent about *not* doing what we are supposed to do when it's time for us to do it. In other words, there are times that we do the right thing at the wrong time, but we also do the wrong thing at the right time. By right thing, I mean expressing our God-given abilities. By wrong thing, I mean not exercising them. By right time, I mean the period that we are supposed to express our God-given abilities.

Leadership expert Dr. John Maxwell said it best in what he describes as the law of timing:

The wrong action at the wrong time leads to disaster;
the right action at the wrong time brings resistance;
the wrong action at the right time is a mistake;
the right action at the right time leads to success.[1]

Oftentimes, obstetricians have to induce labor in a pregnant woman so that she can give birth to her baby. This is usually done when it is time for her baby to come out, but for whatever reason, the baby doesn't. Therefore, to push the baby out from overstaying his welcome in his mother's womb, the doctor induces labor.

Along the same lines, God, The Great Physician of our lives, wants us to give birth to "our babies" when it is time for them to come out. He wants us to birth the potential, visions, dreams, ideas, or ambitions that He placed in the wombs of our hearts. If we do not do this (the wrong thing) when we are supposed to (the right time), He induces us to push them out. Rejection is an *injection* that God uses to induce labor in us to push out our purpose.

Sometimes we are not just the woman pregnant with dreams and schemes; sometimes we are the pregnancy. But like the baby that does not want to come out, we do not want to come out of our shells. Some of us are comfortable in a rut. Some of us are content in living within manmade limits. Some people don't want to come out of their wombs of mediocrity. Like a baby that is limited to the *fetal* position in her mother's womb, some of us are limited to the *fatal* position in the womb of relations, associations, and affiliations that we need to come out from.

Just like a baby is limited to the nourishment of his mother, we are restricted to the nourishment of the companions, companies, or communities with whom we are involved. Unfortunately, at times, what we might perceive as nourishment from those holding us in a bind can actually be malnourishment. But God needs you and me out! He wants us to be *liberated* to fulfill our destiny.

If we don't come out of those uteri that hold us back, He gets the uteri to *contract* and push us out. He uses the very people who were supposed to protect you to reject you. He uses them to dismiss you. If He does not get you out voluntarily, He gets you out kicking and screaming like a baby that has just been birthed. And like that baby, you will cry. You will wail. You will be distraught. But be of good cheer! You might weep at night but your joy will come in the morning

(Psalm 30:5). You might cry and throw tantrums like that baby, but you will be filled with joy like the mother of the baby when you discover that your baby has come out and you are free to be yourself.

God wants you to birth your baby. If this is being hindered from happening by people you might be involved with, God uses rejection to *deliver* you out of their lives like a baby is delivered from his mother's womb.

Please don't misunderstand me. The people from whom God has to deliver you don't always have to be mean to you. They can be very loving and accommodating to you. And, in an effort to protect you from failing in an endeavor that *they think* that you cannot accomplish, they can inadvertently dissuade you from carrying out a worthy ambition that God placed in your heart. Their actions for or against you might have been well-meaning but can end up being demeaning to you and your dreams. Without God ejecting you out of their lives through their disapproval or other conflicts with them, their counsel can *cancel* you. What they meant as *advice* for your purpose could turn out to just *add vice* to your purpose.

Besides, just like it is beneficial and life-preserving for a mother and her baby, to induce the mother to immediately give birth to her baby who was overstaying her welcome in her womb, sometimes it's also to your advantage and to the benefit of the people from whom God liberated you for you to be removed from them. Especially if they are family members.

Due to wrong mindsets, misinformation, and ignorance, people with whom we are involved can live unfulfilled lives. However, when God delivers us from those associations and gets us with other individuals who can help us reach our potential, the results of our endeavors will not only benefit us but can benefit the people who originally dismissed us.

Moses sensed that he was supposed to deliver the children of Israel from Egypt. Unfortunately, he unwittingly tried to accomplish the task at the wrong time. As a result, he ended up killing an Egyptian. To make things worse, he was rejected by one of his *own people* whom he was trying to help in the first place. Then he had to run for his life when he discovered that the murder he committed was known (Exodus 2:11-15; Acts 7:25).

Moses had to find God, first, and get proper direction and preparation from Him on how to fulfill his purpose before he embarked on the tedious task of liberating Israel.

Joseph shared his vision with his family and was rejected by both his father and brothers. It was not the right time for Joseph to lead his family, neither was he in the right place. Joseph also needed to grow up. His maturity and eventual migration to the place where he was to fulfill his destiny was facilitated by his brothers, who rejected him by selling him into slavery (Genesis 37, 39, 40 & 41).

Joseph and Moses did not err with regard to what they believed they were to become. They only missed the mark because they tried to fulfill and disclose their God-given tasks at the wrong time.

So, how will you know when it is the right time for you to embark on your mission? Well,

1. You will have a desire to carry out your mission.

2. You will have enough preparation for your mission.

3. People and opportunities will *come to you* to undertake the mission.

The people who will come to you to help you fulfill your purpose are individuals or organizations that have the resources to support and launch you into your destiny.

At least these three guidelines must be in place before you fulfill your call. God looked for Moses at the burning bush and then sent Aaron to him. God equipped him with the staff in his hand and showed him signs and wonders. When Joseph was in prison, he interpreted the dreams of the Egyptian king's butler and baker, both of whom were tossed in prison with him. He asked the butler to mention him to Pharaoh to get him out of the cell. The butler quickly forgot about him once he was out of prison. I don't think the butler suddenly developed amnesia; I believe that *it was the Lord's doing*. It was *not time* yet for Joseph to emerge; it was two years later (Genesis 41:1).

The right time for Joseph to fulfill his purpose was evidenced by the fact that the Pharaoh *summoned for him.* Joseph had tried to get the butler to put in a word asking Pharaoh to release Joseph from prison. The truth is that Joseph was trying to make things happen on *his own strength.* But his effort proved to no avail as the butler forgot about him. The time came when *an opportunity came to* Joseph to interpret the dream of the Pharaoh. The opportunity came; the butler remembered Joseph; the Pharaoh called for him; it was time! The rest is history.

Chapter 5
Feeling It vs. Dealing with It

S usan was on her way home from the hair salon, sporting a brand new hairdo that she hoped would get a very positive reaction from her husband, Jack. She wanted to get home so quickly that she almost got into an accident. Thankfully, the truck driver hit the brakes, barely missing her BMW SUV as she ran the red light. When she arrived at her drive way, Susan took a quick peek at the interior front mirror, ran her fingers across her forehead and flicked back strands of her brunette curls, perfectly streaked with blonde highlights.

She walked briskly to the entrance of their condo but slowed down once she got to the door to catch her breath. She opened the door, stepped on the marble floors, and called out to her husband, alerting him in her most sensuous voice that she was home. Jack who was in his study in the basement frowning over some figures on his desktop, responded with a grunt.

Susan descended to the basement, bubbling with enthusiasm. When she got to the entrance of her husband's study, with her hands on her shapely hips and with a slight pose, she lingered a few seconds in the doorway smiling expectantly at her husband. A few seconds after Susan realized that her presence had not made her husband look up from the computer, she greeted him again—this time with an inviting smile across her face.

Jack looked at her briefly for a few seconds, and said, "Hi honey." He then turned right back to his computer. Susan's smile disappeared and she stormed off to her room with tears welling up in her eyes. Ten minutes after she left, Jack suddenly got up, grabbed his car keys, ran out of the house, and headed to the nearest drugstore.

He came back home fifteen minutes later, and half-ran and half-skipped to his bedroom to see his wife. She was lying on her side of the bed in the fetal position, still robed in the outfit she wore to the salon. Her back was facing him. Jack slid slowly and deliberately on the bed toward her saying, "honey," in a low tone. He tried to touch her, but, as if on cue, once his hand touched the back of her shoulder, she brushed it off, got off the bed, stormed to the bathroom and locked the door.

As she headed for the bathroom, a bewildered Jack wondered what he had done this time. As usual, he did not have a clue. Feeling upset, he wondered for the umpteenth time if their marriage was going to make it. Susan, sobbing in the bathroom, wondered the same thing. She wondered if there was another woman in her husband's life. He didn't even comment on her hair. She felt rejected. So did Jack. He wished he never got the *Viagra* that he ran out to get.

What Susan did not know was that when her husband saw her at the entrance to his study, her new look did turn him on, although his reaction was delayed. That was why he ran out of the house to the closest pharmacy to solicit the services of Dr. Viagra.

Unfortunately, Susan was upset with him, and he could not figure it out. Evidently, Susan had a secret that he needed to discover and resolve before he could get any closer to her. Susan's secret was that she *felt* rejected by her husband. Jack had a secret of his own; he felt rejected, too. But the truth is that Susan was not rejected by her husband. She only "felt" rejected by him.

There is a thin line between feeling rejected and being rejected. You can *feel* rejected without *being* rejected. This happens when people don't respond to you like you want them to. In Susan's case, all she wanted was for her husband to acknowledge and compliment her on her new look; and, of course, she was in the mood to reward his compliment in the bedroom. But, he didn't compliment her, at least, in the way she expected him to. Consequently, she felt he was not interested in her and she began to rationalize why he didn't want her by assuming he had a mistress.

Jack was enthused with his wife's new look. Unfortunately, he did not respond to her like she expected him to, which gave Susan the impression, the feeling, that regardless of what she did, he was not impressed. That was far from the truth. The feeling of rejection that Susan experienced was really the fruit of miscommunication between her and her husband. To avoid that from happening again, Susan would need to communicate her feelings to her husband. Conversely, Jack would need to understand her feelings and learn to articulate his affection and attraction toward her immediately. This is a practical way that they could resolve their conflict.

Oftentimes, we think we are being rejected when we feel rejected. Just because people do not acknowledge you the way you expect them to does not necessarily mean that they do not like you. Just because someone addresses you sharply does not mean the person despises you. Like Jack, the person's mind might have been in la-la land. The individual's response to you could be influenced by what the person was thinking at the time, or it could be influenced by the individual's personality.

A common mistake that a number of us make is judging someone based on how other people treat us. We might have friends or acquaintances that are very affable and outgoing. They go out of their way to acknowledge and shower us with words of appreciation. In our humanity, we are prone to gravitate toward such individuals. In contrast, some people are reserved and more conservative. They will not say anything to you even if something is dangling out of your nose. Ok, that's an exaggeration, but you catch my drift.

It's unfair to individuals who are not as personable as we'd like, to be to be blacklisted because they don't respond or interact with us as personably as some other people. I'm not be-littling the fact that people do indeed dismiss us. When people ignore you, you will feel rejected. But just because you feel like someone does not care about you does not always mean that the person actually dislikes you.

Before we write anyone off, it's in our best interest that we rightly discern whether we are being rejected or just feeling re-jected. We can obtain the wisdom that will help us differenti-ate between the two from God.

If you feel rejected, before you conclude that someone dis-likes you, you want to make sure that is the case. If someone rebuffs you, usually, you would know. Until someone deliber-ately frustrates you such that it is clear that he or she does not want you around, or the person disapproves of you, it is not fair for you to conclude that the individual dismissed you. I do know that people can disguise their hatred for you. Even so, having the attitude that thinks the best of the situation is necessary. That attitude is love.

DON'T TAKE IT PERSONALLY, TAKE IT TO GOD

You are never wrong when you operate in love toward oth-ers. When you feel rejected, I encourage you to view your re-jection from the eye of love. In doing so, you are in a better position to discern whether you were feeling rejected or actu-ally were rejected. Love believes the best of situations. Again, Love...bears...believes...hopes...and endures all things.

1 John 4:8 states that God is love. Therefore, in order to ensure that you are not overreacting to the way someone treats you, operating in love toward the person who you felt of-fended you helps you consider other factors that might have caused the person to treat you badly. Your discretion will also help you ascertain whether prevailing circumstances in your life or experiences you had from your past lured you to think that you were rebuffed when the person did not actually brush you off. The things that you were dealing with, or negative memories from your past, might have made you feel that you were refused.

That is why it is important for you to believe the best of the situation by approaching the issue objectively from a perspective of love. In essence, since God is love, when you deal with rejection, *don't take it* personally; *take it* to God. This is how I've been able to deal with, and overcome, my feelings of rejection.

I have had my share of bouts with rejection. Knowing that God was with me and taking my feelings of rejection to Him have proved most fundamental to my dealing with it and getting a great deal out of it. It has helped me to be more considerate of other people and has, no doubt, contributed to this writing.

I'm amused at the thought that I started writing seriously after I felt rejected. Like I mentioned earlier, my first book, *While You Are Single...* was birthed shortly after a lady I was interested in declined my feelings for her. Quite naturally, I felt rejected. But I overcame it, knowing that God was with me, and realizing that there was a bigger purpose behind her dismissing me. Part of that purpose was for me to take a good look at myself to discover whether I was suitable for her. Evaluating myself and gathering information that would help me become the right person for someone else gave rise to the book. Basically, she rejected me for my purpose, and that was the best thing that ever happened for me. I used to be just a waiter. After she declined my advances toward her, I wore another hat; I became a more accomplished person: an author.

I survived my feelings of rejection by not taking them personally but taking them to God. In doing so, I took her feelings into consideration. Just like she did not want to have a relationship with a guy she did not have feelings for, I didn't want to be involved with a lady I was not interested in, either. This didn't mean she despised me or had anything against me, it just meant that she did not think I was the best for her. She may have been right. By rejecting me, she did us both a favor, by preserving herself for the kind of guy she desired, and by redirecting me to the right lady who would accept me.

GO STRAIGHT TO THE TOP
Let's consider a lady who approached Christ to help deliver her daughter from a severe demonic possession. While she beseeched the Lord to help her with her plight, she endured and

overcame rejection. Read the encounter below, and I'll explain further.

And behold, a woman of Canaan came from that region and cried out to Him, saying, "Have mercy on me, O Lord, Son of David! My daughter is severely demon-possessed." But He answered her not a word. And His disciples came and urged Him, saying, "Send her away, for she cries out after us." But He answered and said, "I was not sent except to the lost sheep of the house of Israel." Then she came and worshiped Him, saying, "Lord, help me!" But He answered and said, "It is not good to take the children's bread and throw it to the little dogs." And she said, "Yes, Lord, yet even the little dogs eat the crumbs which fall from their masters' table." Then Jesus answered and said to her, "O woman, great is your faith! Let it be to you as you desire." And her daughter was healed from that very hour. (Matthew 15:21-28 NKJV)

Here is a lady seeking Jesus for help with her daughter, and He ignores her. At this juncture, a number of us would have cursed Him out. We would be upset that the so-called Minister, Preacher, or man of God was insensitive and full of himself. To add insult upon injury, Jesus' disciples urged Christ to send her away. How insensitive. Take note that Jesus' disciples, His "leadership," those closest to Him, encouraged Him to dismiss her. Simply put, they asked Him to reject her.

Jesus then responded to the woman by telling her that He was sent to the lost in Israel. Despite the rebuff, she pressed on. She worshipped Him. She still had *faith* in Him. She humbled herself even more for the sake of her tormented daughter. She asked Him to help her. But again, Jesus responded to her by saying:

...It is not good to take the children's bread and throw it to the little dogs.

Whoa! At this point, those of us who might have taken Jesus' first response to our plea for help with a pinch of salt would have lost it. We might have had no qualms with letting the Lord have one on His lips, then asking Him for forgiveness later. He implied that helping her was like throwing food, meant for his Israelite children, to little dogs. Basically, he called her a dog to which food is *thrown*, not given.

Yet again, the lady responded to Jesus' apparent disrespect by saying, *Yes Lord....*

She said that even the little dogs eat the crumbs which fall from their master's table. Jesus then exclaimed at her faith. He was impressed. In essence, she aced the test. According to her desire, her daughter was healed. Her faith in Jesus did not waiver after He appeared to have rejected her. Her proper response to the rejection by faith enabled her to obtain the victory she desired.

If we had been in the lady's situation and Christ treated us like He did her initially, we'd have felt insulted. The Canaanite woman likely felt the same way, but she was not really rejected by Christ. I believe that, despite feeling restrained, she was able to prevent her possible feelings of rejection from hindering her faith in the same person from whom she experienced the rejection. I believe a key to her victory was her knowledge of who Jesus was. By calling Jesus the "Son of David," she must have known enough about Him to believe that He could deliver her daughter.

We can learn a valuable lesson from the disciples' suggestion to Jesus to send the woman away. They must have thought that they were doing the Lord a favor. They probably thought they were protecting and shielding him from a nagging woman. Did you notice that it was those closest to Christ who encouraged the Lord to discard the woman? Oftentimes, we judge leaders based on their followers. Perhaps an associate of an authority figure rejects you. Maybe you've been rebuffed by your pastor's assistant, your boss's subordinate, a friend's best friend, or a Christian, an ambassador for Christ. If this is the case, there is the tendency for you to assume that the pastor, boss, friend, or God has rejected you, too.

We are prone to assume that people like pastors and their leadership, board of directors, and their CEOs, managers, and supervisors who work closely together and hang out together, all share the same values. That might be true in the context of their religious and professional affiliations, but that is not absolutely true.

For example, God has been given a bad name by too many of us who profess to serve and represent Him. Scores of individuals have evaluated God based on the conduct of Christians. The logic behind their assessment makes sense, except that they have it backwards. People should evaluate Christians or Christianity based on Christ, not the other way round. I believe the Canaanite woman understood this concept and used it to her advantage.

My imperfections have no doubt contributed to some people's misconstrued notion of God. By faith in God, I strive to conduct myself responsibly in line with His precepts. Even so, it is grossly inappropriate to evaluate God based on my actions. Out of bitterness, ignorance, or fear, I might mistreat an individual, but that does not mean that God mistreats the person, too. It's sad to say that too many people have missed out on what they could have obtained from God because a so-called believer offended them. In their bitterness, they wrote God off. Similarly, individuals have missed out on their pastor's counsel and blessing, their employer's bonus and promotion, or a friend's listening ear and encouragement because someone close to each of those respective individuals offended them.

Just because Judas stole from and betrayed the Lord does not mean that Jesus was a thief and a betrayer. Just because Peter denied the Christ does not mean that Jesus was two-faced. Just because David was an accomplice to murder and committed adultery does not mean that God is a murderer and an adulterer (Mark 14:10-11, 66-72; 2 Samuel 11). People do what they do because they, like us, are free moral agents. Our individual actions do not always reflect the values of those who have been placed as authority figures over us. Therefore, we should not judge leaders based on our interactions with their subordinates.

A lady should not miss out on becoming the next CEO of the company she works for just because a male colleague who works closely with the board of directors claims that a woman will never get that position. A married couple should not boycott a five-star hotel just because they had a fallout with the hotel's manager, without consulting with his or her employer. A guy should not write off a particular church because he got cursed out by the church's parking lot attendant, without speaking with the fellowship's leadership about the issue.

The Canaanite woman did not let the disciples deter her from getting her need from the Christ. She also did not let the Lord's claim that His abilities were for His lost children in Israel stop her from getting her blessing. She knew that He was a descendant of David. She might have obtained that knowledge from prophecies and manuscripts she had read, or she simply just heard about Him. This further suggests that she also knew that He was sent to the lost sheep of Israel as He claimed. In addition, she must have known something that Jesus did not mention in his brief interaction with her.

That information probably emboldened her to solicit his help despite Jesus dragging His feet. She must have known that the Lord would also bring justice and be the light for the gentiles. Gentiles like her, me, and other non-Jews (Isaiah 42:1, 6-7).

In essence, her resilience to overcome possible feelings of rejection was because of her knowledge of who the Christ was. She let her faith in who He was, and is, overcome her feelings of rejection. In the same way, we can overcome feelings of rejection by placing our faith in God. If we are going to succeed in life, we have to conduct ourselves by faith, not by feelings. Besides, we should not write off anyone because we feel the person rejected us. If we really don't know the person like the Canaanite woman knew Jesus, then it is unfair for us to conclude that the person does not like us, not unless the individual blatantly dismisses us.

In Jesus' case, I'm led to believe He was testing the woman. Jesus' encounters with other people who also needed some form of deliverance led me to believe this. Unlike the others who needed God's help, the Canaanite woman was the only person who Jesus appeared to have refused to assist. I hold the view that Jesus did that for our sakes. He wanted us to learn from the lady.

Amongst other things, He wanted us to learn how to overcome feelings of rejection by faith, learn that we should not assume that a leader rejects us because the leader's subordinate rebuffs us, and get to really know someone to avoid making misguided conclusions about the individual. If a leader's assistant attempts to hinder you from your goal, before you conclude that the leader feels the same way about you, it's in your best interest to check with the leader, first. In a nutshell, like the Canaanite woman, go straight to the top!

Chapter 6
It Leads You to the Right Person

In Tyler Perry's hit movie Diary of a Mad Black Woman, there was a scene at the beginning of the screenplay in which a husband suddenly asked his wife for a divorce and asked her to leave his house. He made this demand on their wedding anniversary and right after he revealed to his wife that he had a mistress, who coincidentally emerged from behind him when he made his outrageous request. In the same breath, his wife also discovered that he had children by his mistress.

While his flabbergasted wife was trying to make sense of what was going on, the husband got violent. He *dragged* her out of his house, through the entrance doors of their mansion, ruining the elegant evening dress that she was wearing, a dress that she thought her husband bought for her, but he instead bought for his mistress'. He then tossed her, sprawled on the ground, in front of a young, attractive U-Haul truck driver whom *he hired* to pack her belongings and get her out of his life. All this drama took place while his mistress looked on.

What an atrocity! The husband's act was despicable, to say the least. Nevertheless, what he did to her—or, *for* her, is what I am trying to convey to you in this book, particularly in this chapter.

The estranged wife eventually ended up in the arms of the younger U-Haul truck driver, who treated her with respect and dignity, unlike her husband, who mistreated her with disrespect and hostility. But how did she end up with the younger man? Her husband pushed her into his arms. Her husband dragged her into his life. Her husband rejected her to the right person.

She did not end up with the better man immediately, though. She had to settle her differences with her husband first. She had to learn to *forgive* him for what he did to her. Being rejected by her husband opened up a new world of opportunities for her. Although it was painful for her to navigate through her hurt to find hope and love again, she eventually wounded up better off away from her husband. She was afforded the opportunity to discover herself and fulfill her desires, which had been repressed and left dormant while she was married to her husband.

Her response to her husband's animosity against her was the key to her finding happiness. She responded by forgiving him and still loving him as a person, even when he did not deserve it. She still went on with the divorce, to the dismay of the husband who found out too late that he did not want her to leave. After she and her ex *reconciled* their differences, she accepted the proposal of the finer gentleman whom her husband hired to drag her out of his life.

Dear friend, sometimes God has to *drag* you into His blessings. If you are involved with someone that God does not approve of, God will allow that person to throw you out of his or her life so that you can land in the arms of someone who is better for you.

You are God's investment, and God is the investor. Since God has your best interest at heart, He is not going to sit back and relax and watch you squander the potential he vested in you. He expects you to yield a good return. He expects you to bear good fruit. He expects you to fulfill your purpose. If you are with the wrong "company" or companion, God will allow you to be withdrawn from that relationship in order to invest you in a relationship where you will be all He wants you to be. The way God accomplishes this, sometimes, is by rejection.

An example of how rejection gets you to the right person is

found in the life of one of Jethro's daughters. Jethro, also
known as Reuel, was the priest of Midian, and he had seven
daughters. They often went to a well to draw water to water
their father's flock.

*Now a priest of Midian had seven daughters, and they came
to draw water and fill the troughs to water their father's flock.
Some shepherds came along and drove them away, but Moses
got up and came to their rescue and watered their flock. (Exodus 2:16-18)*

Jethro was caught by surprise when his daughters came
back home from watering his flock earlier than usual. He inquired from his daughters as to why they came home ahead of
time. Their response to their father was triggered by the experience they had at the well on that fateful day. But before I
go any further, I'll need to draw references from John 4:6-14,
which will help us to better understand the relevance of
Jethro's daughters' experience by the well as it relates to my
discussion on rejection.

That reference reveals Jesus' encounter with a Samarian
woman by a well. He asked the woman to give him water to
drink, but she asked him why he talked to her since He was a
Jew, and the Jews did not interact with Samarians. In response,
Jesus told her that if she knew who she was talking to, she
would have asked of Him, and He would have given her, living water. She answered Jesus by telling him that the well was
deep and that He had nothing to draw with, so she asked Him
about where He was going to get the living water? She also
asked Him if He was greater than Jacob who not only built the
well but also drank from it with his family, as well as watered
his flock from it. Jesus told her that if she drank the water
from Jacob's well she would thirst again, but if she drank the
water that He gave, she would never thirst again.

The main point that I'm drawing from that account is that
Jesus referred to himself as a source of water supply. In
essence, He was a well—a spiritual well. The Samarian
woman, in talking about the water in the well, was referring
to the physical nourishment necessary for our life on earth;
but Jesus, in talking about the living water in himself, was re-

ferring to spiritual fulfillment that lasts to eternity. With this in mind, I'll continue my discussion on Jethro's daughters. Bear in mind that when I discuss the well that Jethro's daughters drew water from, don't just think of it as a physical source of water necessary for our natural sustenance; also look at the well as symbolic of God, The Supplier of the living water necessary for our overall wellbeing.

Jethro's daughters told their father that the reason they came home earlier than usual was because someone delivered them from the opposition they faced from certain shepherds who drove them away from watering his flock. Basically, some shepherds frustrated these women in their efforts to water their father's flock. The first part of verse 17 mentions that shepherds came and "drove them away." This is a form of rejection. These women experienced rejection by the well.

As a guy, I know that if a man is trying to get involved with a lady, the least he would do is be nice to her, even if he was only trying to sleep with her. But that was not the case with the shepherds. Apparently, these guys did not like Jethro's daughters. This is suggested by the fact that they drove his daughters away from watering his flock.

In responding to their father's inquiry about the reason for their quick trip to and from the well, the fact that the ladies told their father that they were delivered from the shepherds suggests that being frustrated by those men was a frequent occurrence. This means that the women usually came home late because they had to wait for those chauvinists to water their flocks and leave the vicinity before they drew all the water they needed to take care of their own flocks, too.

However, on the day they came home early, they had help; hence, that was the reason they got home earlier than usual. The water, of course, was for their physical nourishment as well as for the flock. But let's look at the water from the spiritual standpoint I established earlier. You know friend, water is a source of nourishment. It's life-giving. It's our sustenance. But those women where rejected in an environment where they were supposed to receive fulfillment. The same thing happens today.

A lot of us go through the very thing those women went through. The same place that we go to draw "water" is the same place that we get hurt. Considering the rate at which couples break up, it is sad to say that the place where they were supposed to receive healing from the wounds they suffered from their breakup is sometimes the same place where they got hurt in the first place. The place I am referring to is what we often refer to as church, a place of worship, a place where God resides, a place of spiritual supply for our overall wellbeing. I'm referring to church as a place in which "the well" is situated.

What we often refer to as church should be an environment where we experience and fellowship with our "well of life." Just like those women were rejected around the well's vicinity, some of us experience rejection in church, too. The same place where Jethro's daughters went to draw water was the same place they experienced rejection. Similarly, scores of individuals face the same animosity in church, where they were supposed to receive encouragement. Sometimes, they receive discouragement instead.

It is unfortunate that the place a lady or a guy is hoping to find a suitable mate is the same place the individual gets rejected. In some cases, an individual embarked on a relationship with someone at his church. The person he got involved with turned out to be bad news, or things just did not work out. In addition to the pain of the breakup, the jilted individual also had to deal with seeing the person in church. The rejected person now finds it difficult to receive from the pulpit. What usually happens after this takes place? Just like those women found it difficult to draw water from the well because those shepherds were in their way, the individual rejected in church finds it difficult to draw from the water of God's word shared by the pastor or any other speaker.

The presence of the ex-prospect or spouse frustrates the rejected individual from drawing the "living water." It is a bitter experience to see the person who broke your heart in the same place where you go to get your heart fixed. The sight of the individual, or a hurtful exchange with the person in church, further aggravates your pain and makes it more difficult for you to receive your healing from God. As a result of this, too many people have left church; worst still, they left God, all because they experienced rejection in the place where they were supposed to experience acceptance.

But that's exactly what the devil wants. The devil uses rejection to get you away from God (the well) so that you can fall into his trap. God uses rejection to deliver you from the devil's trap into His will.

IT HELPS YOU FOCUS ON GOD FIRST

Jethro's daughters responded differently to the rejection they faced from the shepherds. They did not stop going to the well; they kept going to it. Despite the animosity, despite the frustration, despite the disdain they experienced from the shepherds, they kept going to the well. Why? Because they *needed* the water. They could not do without the water. They needed it for their physical nourishment as well as for their father's flock. They could afford not to chitchat and cultivate camaraderie with the shepherds, but they could not afford not to have the water from the well.

How they responded to rejection reinforces how we should respond to rejection, too. We should keep going to our well (God). We should have faith in Him and depend *more* on Him than on people. Sometimes, God uses rejection to expose the fact that it is better to depend on Him than to depend on people. They will let you down in a heartbeat.

It is better to trust in the LORD than to put confidence in man. (Psalm 118:8 NKJV)

Likewise, you can afford to be rejected by individuals but you cannot afford to let the way someone treated you stop you from having a relationship with God. Leaving God because someone left you is never the right move. You are supposed to do the opposite. You are supposed to move closer to God. You are supposed to let Him fill the void created by the person who left you. God will do a better job with the space in your heart vacated by your ex-love interest, as well as mend your broken heart. If your relationship with God is suspect, or if your purpose is being hindered by the person with whom you are involved, God will allow the person to reject you in order for you to get back on the road to your destiny.

Because they were rejected by the shepherds, the women only went to the well for water. Any hope of having those shepherds as potential suitors was shattered by the way the shepherds treated them. Hence, they were restricted to the well. Their focus was the well and the water in it. Considering Jethro's daughter's odds of getting hitched with any of the shepherds they met at the well, can you fathom the odds of finding a suitable mate in church? It appeared that their options of getting espoused were limited to those shepherds.

Perhaps, if you are unmarried and seeking a mate, you can relate to this predicament. It seems like our best options are limited to the people we see in our respective churches. Some of us hope to get hitched with someone in our houses of worship but, considering the times we live in, the odds of finding someone who is genuine at church, coupled with the fact that the few potential suitors or single ladies might not like you nor want you, this sometimes makes finding true love in the house of God look like an unlikely feat.

Finding a prospect in church is good and well, but we should not lose focus on why it is most beneficial for us to go to church in the first place. Like drawing water from a well, we should be going to church to draw closer to God. We are to draw from the water of His Word to make it in life. He provides everything else we need. So the key is seeking God for who He is and not just for what His hands can give us.

It's in our best interest for us to go to the well of life for His living water and get the nourishment we need from now till eternity—and for now and eternity. The minute we lose sight of this, we are prone to getting rejected—*re-ejected* back to focus on God. Seeking just what God can give us is like getting wet with water, but seeking God wholly is like drinking water. You can get wet without drinking water, but you can't drink water without getting wet. Do you want to get wet with water, or do you want to drink water? Put another way, we can stand apart from God and only try to get what His hands can offer, or we can jump in His arms, getting all of Him, with His hands wrapped around us rubbing us over, with the stuff in his hands.

Sometimes, we get sidetracked and caught up in a person, and God uses the disappointment of that person blowing you off to redirect you to focus on Him—and Him only. Jethro's daughters went to the well for only one thing, the water in the well. The rejection they experienced from those shepherds made very sure of that.

IT HELPS YOU END UP WITH THE RIGHT MATE

Despite the pain, Jethro's girls kept going to the well. Then, one day, their resilience paid off! I really can't say much more about all of Jethro's daughters, but I can say more about one of them. Her name was Zipporah. You see, since those shepherds rejected her and her sisters, and since they kept going to the well regardless because they needed the water, guess what happened for Zipporah? She found her husband—by the well. Do you get the picture? Zipporah was granted the opportunity to end up with Moses because the shepherds rejected her. Zipporah was rejected to Moses. She was rejected to the right mate.

Moses agreed to stay with the man, who gave his daughter Zipporah to Moses in marriage. (Exodus 2:21)

When those shepherds tried to act up, the Bible says that Moses:

1. Stood up for them;
2. Helped them; and
3. Watered their flock.

Then the shepherds came and drove them away; but Moses stood up and helped them, and watered their flock. (Exodus 2:17 NKJV)

Dear reader, someone may have stood you up, but God will use the rejection of you being stood up to lead you to someone who will *stand up* for you. Someone may have neglected you, but God will use the neglect to get you to someone who will *help* you. Someone may have drained you of your strength, drained you of your emotions, and drained you of your resources; but God will use their "drainage" to flood you into the arms of someone who will water you with affection, water you with encouragement, and water you with support. Someone who will water your flock—so to speak.

Do you know where Zipporah found Moses? She found him *sitting by the well*. I don't know how long Zipporah and her sisters went to the well. I don't know how long they dealt with those shepherds and the frustration they experienced from them. But Zipporah did not let that stop her from going to the well. In fact it helped her focus more on the well, since none of the shepherds liked her. I don't think she expected to find her man at the same well where all the men that rejected her drew water. Zipporah's commitment to the well was compensated when she found her man by the well.

Do you see why you should not stop going to the well even though you experience hurt there? The answer for all your problems is by the well, not away from it. You will be worse off leaving your relationship with God. Keep your commitment with God and soon enough you will end up with the right person. Keep attending a good Bible-teaching church despite any rejection you might have faced from a member or members of that same fellowship. You didn't go there for them, you went there for your fill of living water, water that God flows through your pastor and any other speaker who delivers the Word to you.

Bear in mind that God is your source. Whether you end up with the right person at your church, some other fellowship, or at the grocery store, know that the person comes from God. You will find such an individual in a relationship with God just like Zipporah found Moses by the well. He was not standing by the well; He was *sitting* by the well. This suggests that he was *resting* by the well. He was not in a *hurry*.

From a spiritual standpoint, Moses resting by the well signifies a man who is fellowshipping with God, a man who has a genuine relationship with God. What was he doing sitting by the well? Resting, of course, from his long journey from Egypt and quenching his thirst with water from the well.

"Are you tired? Worn out? Burned out on religion? Come to me. Get away with me and you'll recover your life. I'll show you how to take a real rest. Walk with me and work with

*me—watch how I do it. Learn the unforced rhythms of grace.
I won't lay anything heavy or ill-fitting on you. Keep company
with me and you'll learn to live freely and lightly." (Matthew
11:28-30 MSG)*

If you stop going to the well because you were rejected near
the well, you will be jeopardizing your chances of finding the
person God has for you. The well is never your problem; it is
those who come by it that pose a problem. Church is not the
problem; it's usually church *folks*.

Zipporah did not miss out on Moses because she kept going
to the well. In fact, do you know what Moses' name means?
It means "drawn out." Pharaoh's daughter gave Moses the
name because she drew him out of the river (Exodus 2:10). So
by drawing water from the well, despite the difficulty, she
"drew her husband out." Amongst other things, I believe that
this signifies someone drawing a mate or whatever they need
from God. When we draw *to* God, we can draw *from* God.

When we draw to God in times of disappointment, hurt
and setbacks, and then draw from Him, He'll eventually hook
us up. God will let us get withdrawn from a relationship so
that we can draw to Him and draw the best person He has for
us, out of Him.

The person you end up with in a relationship is determined
by where you draw the person from. You will end up with a
Godly mate if you draw the person from God. You'll draw an
ungodly mate if you draw the individual apart from God.
You'll end up with a mate who epitomizes what the night life
is all about if you draw the person from a night club. You are
prone to having a relationship short-lived if you draw your
prospect from a one-night-stand.

If you do not have an idea of the kind of person God wants
in your life, let's take a look at the man Zipporah found by
the well. His character gives us a glimpse of the kind of person God wants in your life—especially if you're a woman.

First off, Moses stood up for Jethro's daughters. He protected them from the shepherds, even at the expense of his
physical wellbeing. Note that Moses was one person standing
against shepherds who were more than one person. He must

have been a tough or very courageous guy, willing to take a beating to help the women. That is the kind of man God wants to give you. Someone who makes up for all the people that rejected you. Someone who is willing to give his life for you. That is what true love is all about. That is what "till death do us apart" means.

They answered, "An Egyptian rescued us from the shepherds. He even drew water for us and watered the flock." (Exodus 2:19)

Secondly, Moses helped water their flock. He made the women's job much easier. While they rested and watched, probably in amazement, they saw this God-sent angel draw water for them and water their father's flock. Mind you, Jethro had seven daughters. Have you ever seen shepherds with their flock? If you haven't, I have. Usually, the flock of sheep outnumbers the shepherds. There were seven women. How many sheep do you think they brought with them to the well? Let's just assume that they each had one sheep. That is seven sheep that Moses watered, not to mention the water he drew for each of the women—women whom he did not know.

Moses, in my opinion, is the male equivalent of Rebecca, who gave water to a stranger and his ten camels to drink when the stranger was looking for a wife for Isaac (Genesis 24). Just like Rebecca ended up as the right mate for Isaac, so did Moses end up as the right mate for Zipporah.

By watering the flock, Moses was not only a blessing to the ladies but also a blessing to their father. The right mate for you will be a blessing and an asset to your family. God wants you to end up with someone who not only protects you and makes up for those who rejected you, but also someone who helps you draw closer to God. The right person will be someone who draws the living water for you, someone who facilitates your relationship with God, someone who quenches your thirst with the water of God's Word (Ephesians 5:26).

The third thing that characterizes the kind of person that God desires for you is that the person will speed things up for you. The person will make life easier for you. The person will help you accomplish things faster. You'll not need to work as hard and as long as you usually did. Because Moses stood up for Zipporah and her sisters, they were able to have their father's flock watered on time, while the shepherds who used to pester them were kept at bay. That was why they got home earlier than usual.

In a nutshell, the kind of person God wants for you is someone who will protect, provide, and propel you. Even your parents can be impressed by the person God has for you. When Jethro heard what Moses did for his daughters, he almost rebuked his girls for not asking him home to sup with them. Moses was then invited to their house, he was content to live with them, and Jethro gave him Zipporah to marry. Moses then took over the shepherding business. Hence, Zipporah and her sisters' time was freed up to tend to other chores—another benefit of being involved with the right person.

Needless to say, the person who God will like to bring to your life will be someone who has a relationship with Him. Is it not interesting that Rebecca was found by a well? Moses was found by a well. Rachel, Jacob's "main-squeeze," was found by a well (Genesis 24; 29:1-11). The Samarian woman who had been through five annulments and an illicit affair, found Jesus, the answer to her problems, by a well, too (John 4:6-14). Jesus is the well of life. You will not find a Godly man or woman apart from Him. If you have been seeking love away from the well, you are likely to be disappointed. Let your disappointment lead you back to the well. It is the right place for you to find the fulfillment you need.

God's best is a person that will propel, protect, and provide for you. Jesus told the woman at the well that if she drank from her well, she would thirst again. But if she drank from His well she'd never thirst. The woman had mentioned that Jacob gave them the well. You see, Jacob's name means *supplanter*. This means *deciever*. I believe one thing among other things that we can grasp from Jacob's well is that his well represents the society's way of doing things. In this dog-eat-dog world, the idea is to connive, cheat, outdo others, *decieve* to get ahead or get into a relationship. The idea is to try this and try that to find fulfillment.

Well, if we drink from the deciever's well (Satan, father of deception), we will continue to be thirsty. We'll never be satisfied. We'll be going through the same frustrations over and over, like that woman going back and forth to draw water in the well. But if we draw from the water of life—we don't need a bucket. We don't need to go back and forth. Once and for all, we'll be fulfilled. He's inside of us and will guide us every step of the way. He'll lead us to everything we need: wholesome relationships and our purpose in life.

Friend, sometimes the only way we can end up drinking from God's well, is for us to be rejected from drinking other "manmade" wells.

IT LEADS YOU TO THE RIGHT PLACE

Why do you think Moses ended up by the well? Simple— he was rejected! You might recall from the story of Moses that he was raised as the Pharaoh's daughter's son. This is why we consider him as the Prince of Egypt. When Moses was 40-years-old he decided to visit his Israelite people. He saw an Egyptian maltreating one of his countrymen, so he avenged his compatriot by killing the Egyptian (Acts 7:23-24; Exodus 2:11-12).

A day after that incident, Moses went out again only to see two of his countrymen fighting. He tried to reconcile them both but the person who was at fault in the fight said to Moses:

The man said, "Who made you ruler and judge over us? Are you thinking of killing me as you killed the Egyptian?" Then Moses was afraid and thought, "What I did must have become known." When Pharaoh heard of this, he tried to kill Moses, but Moses fled from Pharaoh and went to live in Midian, where he sat down by a well. (Exodus 2:14-15)

Moses ended up by the well in Midian after he fled from Egypt. It was while he was trying to mediate between two of his countrymen that he was rejected. One of them rebuffed his help to reconcile them. It was through the rejection that he realized that the murder he had committed was known. As a result, he ran from Egypt and ended up in the right place, Midian, by the well. It was there that he met Zipporah. After relocating to Midian, he also encountered God at the burning bush, where he was mandated to fulfill his purpose of delivering the Israelites out of Egypt. After Moses was rejected to the right place, he discovered his wife and rediscovered his purpose.

Previously, I talked about not leaving your church because someone there rejected you. When I said that, I took for granted that you understood that your church should be centered on God and not the people who fellowship there with you. Nevertheless, if you are experiencing animosity and being malnourished in a particular fellowship, it is understandable for you to go somewhere else where you can receive the fulfillment you need from God.

Adversity in church might not be your problem. Your problem might arise in your workplace, college dorm, or area of residence. Sometimes the issue does not arise in any of those places; it could arise in you. Sometimes the issue *is you*. When you end up in a vicinity where you are not supposed to be in the first place, or overstay your welcome there, you set yourself up to be a prime candidate for disappointment. God, however, uses the conflict to lead you to a better place where you can experience peace and find love like Moses did. In essence, God uses rejection to get you to the right place, especially when you ignore every other means He employed to get you to relocate.

Chapter 7
It Leads to Your Acceptance

I once heard a tale about the seven-cow woman. The story is told of a land far, far away (without Shrek) which had a custom which stipulated that if a man wanted to marry any of the women from the land, he had to pay a dowry. Usually, the dowry was a reflection of the woman's worth. The price that every man was required to pay in order to betroth and marry any of the women in their town was at least one cow. The highest number of cows ever paid to marry a woman from the land was three cows.

There was a lady in that land who nobody wanted to marry. She was the ugliest woman in the land. While all her peers got married, no one paid attention to her. She was deemed unattractive and unwanted. One day, however, a wealthy man came from out-of-town to the land. He spotted the lady who no one wanted and liked what he saw in her. He approached her father and asked him what he needed to do to receive her as his wife.

To the father's delight and surprise, he told the man that all he had to do was give him a cow. The wealthy man said he would adhere to the woman's father's request. In fact, he did not pay one cow for her; he paid seven cows for her. Everyone in the town was shocked at the man's generosity. Little did they know that he saw something in her which no one else saw. The price he paid for her was a reflection of the value he saw in her.

As a result, the woman that nobody wanted, who was treated like a reject, became the most beautiful woman in that land. Her self esteem went through the roof. Her radiance, which was locked up inside due to the way she was neglected, was released to illuminate her glamor. Her inner beauty became reflected on the outside, too, thanks to the man who saw her heart. He accepted her for who she was and that inspired her to reflect her true virtue and beauty.

All the men who rejected her only preserved her for the man who accepted her. She was too good for even three cows. No wonder the men didn't recognize her value. She was so much better than what they could handle. Therefore, when the man who had the substance to handle her worth came, he knew she was the one for him and spared no expense in making her his.

Likewise, when someone looks down on you or passes you over for someone else, the person is rejecting you to be accepted by some one else better for you, someone who sees your heart, someone who recognizes and appreciates your value. You were refused to be received by someone else.

As I mentioned before, one of the reasons people reject us is because we exceed their expectations. You might not know how precious you are, but God who created you knows. He ought to; He created you. He knew what He placed in you that the person who refused you doesn't. Since God is trying to hook you up with someone who will appreciate you, He will prevent you from ending up with someone who will depreciate you.

If you are a sweetheart or a gentleman and individuals still turn you down, especially when you feel that they are cognizant of your virtue, valor, and integrity, don't be disappointed. They are helping you out. They are doing you a huge favor. Thank them for refusing you. You are too good for them. I don't mean to sound arrogant, nor do I mean to encourage you to be conceited, but when someone does not recognize your worth, then the person does not have any business being with you. God does not want you to be involved with someone like that.

The Bible admonishes us not to give what is holy to dogs or cast our pearls before swine, because they will trample them under their feet and turn and tear us apart (Matthew 7:6). You are God's jewel. God does not want you to end up with a pig or someone who will dog you out. It's not His desire that you end up with someone who'll mess up your life or treat you like dirt.

If you think about it, if you had a precious diamond and, somehow, a pig slopped over it, even if you retrieved it from the animal and washed away the hog's slop from it, you are likely not to look at your jewel the same way you perceived it before it got messed up by the swine. In the same way, when someone dishonors you, you're likely to develop a low self-image based on how you were mistreated and not how you were before the agonizing experience. God wants you to be pure; He doesn't want you to be treated like you're impure.

If you end up with someone who treats you like you're worthless, God uses the rejection to get you out of that relationship to get you to someone who will give you the affection and attention that everyone deserves. God uses rejection to refine and define you. He uses it to free you of impurities or those who made you feel impure and insecure.

IT'S A BRIDGE THAT GETS YOU FROM BEING TREATED AS WORTHLESS TO BEING TREATED AS WORTHWHILE

There is a true story similar to that of the seven-cow woman. Though, this time around, nothing about cows or *Shrek* was mentioned. The biblical account reveals an Israelite man named Elimelech who left Israel with his family because of a famine that plagued his homeland. He and his family migrated to Moab. When they got there, Elimelech's sons, Mahlon and Chilion married the Moabites, Ruth and Orpah respectively. Years later, Elimelech, Mahlon and Chilion died. Consequently, Naomi, Elimelech's wife, was left with Ruth and Orpah. When she heard that things were much better in Israel, Naomi decided to go back home. Reluctantly, she allowed Ruth to tag along with her while Orpah remained in

Moab (Ruth 1).

Ruth's story gets interesting when she ends up working in the field of a prominent, affluent, and opulent man known as Boaz. Naomi suggested to Ruth that she get close to him so that he would marry her. Ruth adhered to her mother-in-law's instruction. She sought out Boaz and found him sleeping at the threshing floor where Naomi told her she would find him. She lay beside his feet and, at midnight, Boaz woke up and discovered her lying beside him.

He inquired from Ruth as to the reason why she was lying by him. In response, Ruth told Boaz that she wanted him to take her under his wing. In essence, take her to be his wife. Boaz was willing to grant Ruth her request but he mentioned to her that there was another relative who was next in line to marry Ruth before him (Ruth 2 & 3). The custom in Israel was that if a man died without children, the brother closest to the deceased man was to marry his wife (Deuteronomy 25:5). A term they used to describe this process is "redeem." Therefore, when a man marries his deceased brother's wife, he was redeeming her and buying back all the inheritance that belonged to her deceased husband.

Since Elimelech and his sons had died, the closest relative to them was the one who had the right to buy back their land and preserve Elimelech's lineage. Boaz was a close relative, but there was a closer relative ahead of him next to marry Ruth. Boaz was next after him. Boaz told Ruth that he would ask the close relative to perform his customary duty in marrying Ruth in order to restore her inheritance from her marriage to Mahlon back to Ruth. The inheritance or property in question was Elimelech's land. Boaz told Ruth that if the close relative refused to redeem Ruth, he would take her up on her offer. Of course Ruth wanted Boaz, and Boaz wanted Ruth, too. But Boaz had to follow their custom. Boaz approached the close relative and presented him with the opportunity to obtain Ruth's inheritance and marry her.

Then he said to the close relative, "Naomi, who has come back from the country of Moab, sold the piece of land which belonged to our brother Elimelech. And I thought to inform you, saying, 'Buy it back in the presence of the inhabitants and the elders of my people. If you will redeem it, redeem it; but if you will not redeem it, then tell me, that I might know; for there is no one but you to redeem it, and I am next after you.'" And he said, "I will redeem it." Then Boaz said, "On the day you buy the field from the hand of Naomi, you must also buy it from Ruth the Moabitess, the wife of the dead, to perpetuate the name of the dead through his inheritance." And the close relative said, "I cannot redeem it for myself, lest I ruin my own inheritance. You redeem my right of redemption for yourself, for I cannot redeem it." (Ruth 4:3-6 NKJV)

When Boaz told the relative to redeem Elimelech's land, the relative accepted the offer. But, Ruth was also connected to the land. So, in order for the deal to be sealed, he was required to redeem the property from Ruth and marry her, too. But he changed his mind when Boaz mentioned that he had to buy the land from Ruth. He declined to redeem the property because he was required to buy it from Ruth. In essence, he rejected Ruth. He wanted the property, but he did not want Ruth. He wanted her field, but he didn't want Ruth. He wanted her inheritance, but he did not want her.

That is similar to what happens in relationships today. Many men want women's inheritance, but they don't want the women. Many men want what women inherited from their mamas—their bodies—but they don't want the person housed in the body. Many a man wants a lady's hips, lips, and fingertips—her inheritance—but a number of such men could care less for the woman.

The same holds true for men and their inheritance, too. Some women are only after what men can give them but shun the men. Some women only want to bask in a man's ability to provide for their needs, while they ignore the man and his needs. Such relationships are like getting milk for free without buying the cow.

God does not want you to be exploited in a relationship where someone only wants you for your body. If you are involved with someone who exploits your body, your money, or any of your other inherited possessions, and you don't see that you are not supposed to be in such a relationship, God will assist you by allowing the person to reject you.

The close relative rejected Ruth. In doing so, he did her a favor because he relinquished her to Boaz. This account also suggests that *if* God places a desire in your heart for someone (who is not married), but someone else is ahead of you in getting hitched with the person, or blocking you from being involved with the individual you have feelings for, God will work the situation out for you. He will help you end up with the person he placed in your heart.

According to the Israelite custom, the close relative was first in line to marry Ruth. In our day, there is an unwritten rule or custom which says, "First Come, First Served." You should not try to get involved with someone who is already seeing someone else even though you have a soft spot for the person. Some other person might be going out with the person you have feelings for, and there is nothing you can do about it, except to give the situation up to God. If God, *indeed,* impressed upon you a desire for the person who is in relationship with someone else, God will bring the person to you. It might be that your heartthrob would be rejected to you like Ruth was to Boaz despite the fact that the close relative had the opportunity to espouse Ruth, first.

...The race is not to the swift.... (Ecclesiastes 9:11)

So then (God's gift) is not a question of human will and human effort, but of God's mercy. (It depends not on one's own willingness, nor on his strenuous exertion as in running a race, but on God's having mercy on him). (Romans 9:16 AMP)

If someone wants you strictly for what they can gain from you, the person is treating you like you are worthless. The person acknowledges that you are worth something, but what the person acknowledges as your worth is just that part of you that he or she wants to exploit. To the person, your worth is limited to your body or your money. If this is the case, the person thinks you are worthless. The individual is only interested in part of you, which is less of the whole you. Hence, you are being treated like you are worth *less.*

Some other times, your significant other might treat you like you are worth something until they find someone else; then, the person starts to treat you like you are worth *less* than the other person that they hooked up with. You should not be treated like this. You are worth *more*; you are worthwhile. Therefore, God will allow you to get rejected to someone who appropriately acknowledges your worth and treats you with respect and dignity.

Ruth 1 and 2 gives us an idea of who Boaz and Ruth were. We know where they come from. We know their background, and we can draw conclusions on their character and status. Boaz was influential and very wealthy. Ruth was virtuous, hardworking, kind and considerate, based on how she supported her mother-in-law. Yet, we do not know anything about this close relative other than the fact that he was next to redeem Ruth. We don't even know his name.

Who was he? What was he about? All we know about the guy who was next to marry Ruth was that he was a close relative. We know Ruth and Boaz's names but we do not know the close relative's name. Since we do not know his name, I believe this signifies that he depicts someone with no "calling." I also believe that he represents an individual with no identity and no purpose. God does not want you to be in a relationship with that kind of person. He does not want you to be involved with someone with no vision, no identity, and no calling—no name.

IT GETS YOU FROM A HELPMATE TO A HELPMEET

Boaz and the other individual who had first preference to redeem Ruth were both close relatives. The close relative was related to Boaz. He was connected to Boaz. He was similar to Boaz. But—he was *not* Boaz. Just because you meet someone who is "closely related" to the image of the person you consider as your true love does not mean that that person will truly love you. The person might be a nice person, a Christian, attend church, be involved in the community or some kind of ministry, and appear to lead a Godly lifestyle. These are all good character traits of God's best for you.

Nevertheless, that does not necessarily mean that the person is *best suited* for you. The person could be putting on a facade. In our best interest, God prevents us from being in relationship with people who are phony. If you do not heed God's attempt to caution you from being involved with someone who you think is "the one," you leave God with no choice but to allow you to get turned down.

Someone does not always have to breakup with you to reject you—at least initially. The person can disrespect, ignore, and mistreat you. Anyone who only helps him or herself to your assets is mistreating you.

In some cases, the individual whom you consider to be someone closely related to the image of the person whom you consider to be your soul mate could actually be genuine. The person could be Godly, and the individual's conduct testifies to his beliefs. However, not every person is compatible with you. When God created Adam, He decided to make him a helper comparable to him. God did not make Adam a helper; He made Adam a helper *comparable* to him.

There is a difference between a helpmate and a *helpmeet*. A helper and a helper comparable to you are not the same. A helpmate just gives you help; a helpmeet not only gives you help, but also meets your help, or gives you the kind of help you need. A person might be helpful, but not helpful to you. Sometimes when people try to help you, they make things worse because they are not *suited* for the kind of help you need. An individual can be an icing on a cake, just not the icing on *your* cake. You know what I mean? God desires to bring you someone who is suitable for you. Someone who fits you—not someone who gives you fits.

There are some remarkable and admirable single individuals ideal to make good spouses. But not every single person is comparable, compatible, and complementary to you. If you ever wondered why someone you admired and respected rejected you, someone who you thought was God-sent, especially when you did not do anything wrong to the person, and you are a nice person like Ruth, it is likely that God allowed you to be dismissed in order to save you for someone else better suited for you. Someone like Boaz, whose name means "strength." God is leading you to a strong Godly person.

The close relative was willing to help by redeeming Ruth's field, but he wasn't interested in helping Ruth. He was interested in helping himself; he was not interested in helping her. The close relative gave up Ruth to Boaz. Ruth was rejected by a no-name person to a big-name person. She was rejected by a nobody to a somebody. The minute she met Boaz, he wasted no time in building her up. He called her blessed, virtuous, and kind; he acknowledged her worth. He gave her gifts; he provided for her. He did not help himself at her expense; he helped her in the expense of himself. He had her best interest in mind. Boaz depicts a helper comparable to Ruth. He was Ruth's helpmeet. As a result, he married her and assumed marital relations with her, which led her to give birth to a baby, something she was unable to do for at least ten years in her previous marriage to her deceased husband (Ruth 1:4-5; 3:10-11; 4:13).

You might recall, when I deliberated on Moses and Zipporah, I mentioned that God wants to bring someone in your life who will speed things up and help you accomplish things faster. Boaz did not just enrich Ruth's life with his wealth, but also through God's empowerment, he was able to enrich her life with a child. He helped her accomplish something that was difficult for her to do before. He rekindled her pride through motherhood. He provided, protected, and propelled her.

God blessed Ruth's union with Boaz, and she bore Obed, David's grandfather. Ruth's name is also etched as one of the books in the Bible, and history notes her as one of Jesus' great grandmothers.

Chapter 8
It Opens Doors for You

It was in a side room in a red brick church building with a white steeple on top that we were having a young men's fellowship. This building served as the facility to conduct services for the youth of the congregation I was serving when I resided in Richmond, Virginia. It was in one of the side rooms in the building that some youth and other young male adults and I fellowshipped over some Krispy Kreme, Kool-Aid, sodas, wingettes, chips, and other junk food. We were discussing the subject of pride, and I referenced the story of Esther.

The story began about a king, Ahasuerus. He threw a party for his royal guests and, in his euphoria, he asked that his queen, Vashti, grace the occasion. He wanted to impress his royal friends and acquaintances with his wife's beauty. But, Vashti rebuffed his request. I mentioned to the young men that her action was a reflection of her pride. And as the saying goes, *pride comes before a fall*. After consulting with his royal advisers, Ahasuerus dethroned his queen and banished her from the royal palace (Esther 1).

When I said that, one of the young men in the group asked me if that meant that Ahasuerus divorced his wife. Until the lad made that remark, it never occurred to me the magnitude of the king's action toward his wife. I responded to the youngster by telling him that Ahasuerus divorced his wife.

Scripture doesn't elaborate further on Vashti after that unfortunate episode. Nonetheless, based on what was revealed in the Bible, it seemed like King Ahasuerus' reaction to his wife's response to him was harsh. He just stripped Vashti of her royal position and banished her from his presence. In essence, he rejected her, too. The fact that he sought another queen to replace Vashti suggests that he not only banned her from his palace, but that he also divorced her.

Like God, I hate divorce. I hate it because God hates it. I hate it because it negatively affects children of divorced parents. I hate it because it causes division among family and church members of congregations in which the pastor underwent an annulment. Despite my contempt for divorce, it's still very paramount in our society. Notwithstanding, I hope my discussion of Ahasuerus' separation from Vashti would be a source of encouragement for divorcees.

God's mercy and grace evidenced in the success of some second and, perhaps, third marriages has led me to believe that being divorced is not the end of the world, certainly not the unpardonable sin.

RECONCILIATION CLOSES THE BREACH

I stand corrected, but it *seems* to me that God was the first Person to divorce. Divorce means separation. It means death in a relationship. God "divorced" Adam and Eve when they transgressed in the Garden of Eden. Like Ahasuerus banished Vashti, so too did God banish Adam and Eve from the garden. Ahasuerus looked for another queen; God got another Adam—Jesus (Romans 5:12-21; 1 Corinthians 15:45-49).

God told them that if they ate fruit from the forbidden tree, they would die. They did. They died spiritually. Their bond with God was broken. There was a breach in their relationship with God. *They* caused their separation from God by *their* disobedience. God enforced their dismissal from the Garden of Eden. Sounds like God divorced them. What do you think?

That breach extended to you and I. We are recipients of Adam and Eve's sin. However, God gave us a way out, which should be the first option to resolve divorced people. Reconciliation. Through Jesus we are reconciled to God (2 Corinthians

5:17-19). I'm totally for reconciliation.

Furthermore, I gathered that reconciliation in its most basic form means to settle differences. You can settle your differences with your ex without remarrying your former spouse; however, you can't remarry your former spouse without settling your differences. The key word is *reconciliation*. Reconciliation also means to accommodate, to adjust, harmonize, be friendly again, to coordinate and to *forgive*. I'm sure spouses of successfully blended families will concur that they had to forgive their former spouses, and adjust, accommodate, harmonize, be friendly and coordinate their activities to foster peace between them and their respective exes.

I don't know if you noticed but reconciliation does not mean *remarriage to your ex*. When we believe in Jesus Christ and receive Him into our hearts, we are reconciled with God. The breach between Him and us has been closed up. However, we don't *return* to the garden, and this does not undermine the fact that we've been reconciled. God has called us to peace. For a relationship to be successful, individuals in that relationship have to be in *agreement*. They have to be *at peace* with each other. If not, the relationship won't make it.

Can two people walk together without agreeing on the direction? (Amos 3:3 NLT)

Divorce as we know it is really a physical manifestation of a spiritual separation. In a sense, Adam and Eve being dismissed from the Garden of Eden was a physical manifestation of their spiritual separation from God. Even if a husband and a wife don't divorce legally, their ongoing and *constant* disagreements, contempt, disdain, war with each other, and *unwillingness* to make the relationship work, can be a sign that they are spiritually divorced. They are not at peace. But God has called us to peace (1 Corinthians 7:15).

I agree that what *God* has put together let no man put asunder (Mark 10:9). Notwithstanding, I also believe that what *man* has put together God *can* put asunder. God hates divorce; *not* divorcees—and He doesn't like bad marriages, either. Especially the ones He did not setup in the first place.

Be that as it may, Vashti was dethroned after she slighted her husband. I can't say much more about Vashti, but I can say that her rejection of her husband was the best thing that ever happened for Ahasuerus. Vashti basically re-ejected him to another woman. This is the case with all the *successful* second marriages. Rejected spouses got re-ejected to a better, friendlier, peaceful, and compatible spouse. Or, divorced spouses learned from the mistakes they made in their first marriages and applied them to their second marriages. In essence, being rejected caused them to find out where they went wrong and helped them make the necessary adjustments in themselves, and adjustments for their second or subsequent marriages.

In Ahasuerus' case, he sought out another queen, and he ended up with Esther; he ended up with a star (Esther 2:1-18). Vashti was beautiful, as her name reveals; but Esther was a star. The name "Esther" means "star." Ahasuerus was re-ejected from someone beautiful to someone who was a star—Es-ther. Not all beautiful people are stars, but all stars are beautiful. A door was opened for Esther because Vashti was rejected.

SOMEONE'S DEMOTION COULD BE YOUR PROMOTION

What King Ahasuerus gained from being rejected by Vashti is by no means limited to Esther's youthful beauty and stardom. I encourage you to read her story in the book coined after her name, and you'll gather that in addition to her loveliness and purity, she was humble, courageous and godly. She was a worthy example for women to follow—men, too. The king gained a submissive wife; a woman who sought him with the right approach, not one who slighted him and left him with reproach.

In addition, had Ahasuerus not been re-ejected to Esther, he would have met with his demise. Two of the king's doorkeepers were displeased with the king and connived to take him out. But Mordecai, Queen Esther's cousin, a wise man who raised Esther as his daughter after her parents' death, discovered the plot against Ahasuerus' life. He intimated his discovery to Esther who, in turn, told the king. The culprits were apprehended and hanged (Esther 2:21-23).

Because of Ahasuerus' relationship with Esther, he had access to Mordecai, whose wisdom and insight contributed to his wellbeing. Being rejected to Esther gave king Ahasuerus longevity. Not only did he gain an outstanding wife, he also gained an outstanding adviser in the person of Esther's cousin. King Ahasuerus' life was spared because Mordecai found out ahead of time about the plot to kill him.

Furthermore, Ahasuerus gained a better administration with Queen Esther and Mordecai on his side. The king had promoted a man named Haman above his princes (Esther 3:1). Haman turned out to be a disgruntled element who was furious at Mordecai because Mordecai refused to bow down before him. Haman plotted to kill Mordecai and instigate a mass genocide against the Jews (Esther 3:2-6).

Once again, Mordecai's vigilance, diligence, and persistence paid off when he encouraged Esther to do something to thwart Haman's conspiracy against the Jews. Esther humbled herself by going on a fast for three days in order to have favor with her husband when she approached him about the issue. She had to approach Ahasuerus the right way because anyone who approached the king in his court without being summoned to him was subject to death. The only way one would avoid death was if the person found favor with the king. If the individual found favor with the king, the king would hold out his golden scepter toward the person (Esther 4).

Esther found favor with the king since she prepared herself by fasting (Esther 5:1-2). Her courage to go before the king was also reinforced by the fasting of her people and her maids' fast. She organized two banquets and invited the king and Haman to both. It was during the second feast that she revealed to Ahasuerus Haman's plot of anti-Semitism. The king was enraged and got Haman hanged in the place that Haman originally prepared to hang Mordecai. By that act, Ahasuerus ridded himself of the bigot, Haman, from his regime (Esther 7:1-10).

I believe he also gained respect from the Jews and God's blessing. I believe God's blessing was on Ahasuerus not just because of his queen, Esther, or her cousin, Mordecai, but because God had promised Abraham that He would bless those who blessed Abraham and his people (Genesis 12:1-3). The Israelites were Abraham's people since they were his descendants. Esther, Mordecai and the Jewish people were Israelites. So, Ahasuerus' defense of them was a blessing to them and therefore God blessed him, too.

Not only did Ahasuerus gain from being rejected by Vashti, but Esther, Mordecai and the Jews gained from his rejection, too. Evidently King Ahasuerus was grieved after Vashti slighted him. She hurt his feelings and probably crushed his ego. Even so, God used his rejection for good. The rejection opened the door of his heart to Esther. In essence, rejection offered Ahasuerus a better life with a better wife and a better administration. Rejection opened the door for Esther to rise from obscurity to authority; it transformed her from a peasant to a princess. Rejection opened the door for Mordecai to advance to King Ahasuerus' cabinet. He became a trusted ally to the King of Persia and Israel's liaison, an ambassador for righteousness. In a nutshell, rejection saved the life of the Jews and gave them hope.

Judging from the story of Esther, a proper response to rejection leads us to achieve exponentially more than we lost or thought we lost before we were rejected. Whether you've been rejected by your spouse, your significant other, your company or your church, I assure you that when you respond with the understanding that God is working something good out of your rejection, you will end up better off than you ever envisioned had you still been involved with those who rejected you.

Chapter 9

It's not a Setback; It's a Setup

Years ago, when I was living in Nigeria, I went to a party with two of my friends. I thought my friends were cool, and by the way they carried themselves, I think they thought so, too. However, I didn't think so about myself, especially when I was around them. In fact the only reason I knew them and occasionally got to tag along with them was because they were my neighbors.

We were all about the same age, lived in the same neighborhood, grew up together, played soccer together, rode bicycles together, practiced Michael Jackson, Hammer, and New Edition dance moves together, as well as shared tips with each other on how to win girls. Actually, they shared the tips; I used the tips. They never worked for me, though. The only tips that worked for me were the ones that I stuck in my ear. Don't they feel good?

Furthermore, my friends went to renowned and cool high schools. I went to an unknown and "uncool" high school. The main thing that was cool about my friend's schools, other than the fact that they were popular in Nigeria, was that they were co-ed schools. I went to an all-boys boarding school—so not cool.

At the school I attended, we were banned from having assorted haircuts. Every student's hair was supposed to be plain.

No box, trapezium, pentagon or high-top cuts. With this in mind, what we, the students, usually did was wait till a few days before the school semester was over before we had our hair cut into whatever style we wanted. That way we'd look nice when we got back home for the holidays.

As usual, I had one of those Carl Lewis-type cuts about two days before we dismissed for school break. The next morning, during morning assembly, for whatever reason, our Vice Principal went on a "hair-hunt." I was one of the victims of his unexpected raid. I felt my confidence dashed to pieces like my hair, which was falling before my eyes as the Vice Principal drove his scissors through the middle of the top of my head like a dump truck driving its forklift into a building. Talk about having a bad hair day.

Consequently, I had to get all my hair cut off. In the early nineties, at least in Nigeria, that style was not in vogue. I'm amused that in the 21st century, despite the competition from cornrows, close cuts are still holding strong, at least for African-American males. Even so, my oblong head does not hold close cuts well.

Be that as it may, I was back home from school two days after my bad haircut. Once I got home, my friends informed me of a party that was going to take place and I decided to go along with them. We caught a cab and went to the area where the party was taking place. It was a house party, and, by the way, we weren't invited. We were going to crash the party. My friends were decked in Bugle Boy shirts, stonewashed jeans, and Timberland boots. Their haircuts, swagger, and wardrobe helped them look like Bobby Brown. The way I was dressed made me look more like Charlie Brown. My friends looked like they were dressed in 90's garb. I looked like I was dressed in 60's garb.

I got half of my wardrobe from my dad: a white, gray, and green striped, long-sleeved shirt, and a "square" navy-blue, woolen tie, which was way out of fashion. Was it ever in fashion? I also wore black, baggy, gabardine pants. My pants were so baggy that you could fit two of me in them. The material for my slacks felt silky, and they were so shiny that a lady could use my pants as a mirror to put on makeup.

I was sandwiched between my friends when three attractive teenage girls approached us, and I could feel the butterflies in my stomach. My anxiety was fueled because of a bad experience I had—or never had—with one of the girls. I had a crush on her, and I made a fool of myself in trying to go out with her. Well, she rejected me. (I told you the tips never worked.)

One of my two friends and I had escorted one of the other girls in the trio to her house. She used to live in our neighborhood, too. Though we never chit-chatted, I knew who she was, and she knew who I was, too. The third girl was a mystery to me and to my friends, too. That mystery was quickly dispelled when the girl that my friend and I had escorted introduced my friends to the unknown lady. Again, I reiterate, she introduced my friends to the mystery girl; I wasn't introduced.

My friends did not bail me out, either. I just stood there embarrassed and moping while the girls engaged in a conversation with my friends. Shortly after, I found myself standing alone like the Statue of Liberty, watching my friends and the gals stroll away together toward the house where the party was taking place.

They just left me like I was not there. I was devastated; I felt rejected. My party ended before it started. I managed to pull myself together to go to the party. I wasn't there long when one of the hosts of the party felt that the guys outnumbered the girls. So he decided to start bouncing unwanted guests. Yeah, you guessed it; I got bounced!

I found myself staring at a steel gate which stood between me and the party. I held on to two of the bars of the gate with my head sticking through the bars like an inmate probably once did in Alcatraz. I didn't really do that—but, can you feel my pain? Fortunately, another friend of mine who also crashed the party kind of bullied and sweet-talked the bouncer to get me back in the party. I appreciated his help, but my party was finished after I felt snubbed by my friends and the ladies who took them away from me.

It wasn't too long after I got reinstated into the party that

I saw my two friends and some other ladies get into a car and leave the party. They left me behind. To be honest, I was happy they did. I did not attempt to stop them because I was not in the frame of mind to handle any slight, especially in front of the girls that they had with them.

I had to borrow money from some other friends, who I followed, to catch a bus that would take me home. And to catch the bus, you would have to have the skills of an NFL wide receiver because in Nigeria, "some" of the transportation was such that you'd have to take a dive to catch the bus—still in motion. With that in mind, I was successfully able to pull a Terrell Owens to catch the bus that was going toward my house.

Once I reached my stop, I signaled to the bus conductor, the guy responsible for collecting the bus fare, and alerted the driver to stop the bus. Once I disembarked from the bus I saw a cab also come to a halt at my stop. An attractive young lady stepped out of the cab, paid her fare, and seemed to be heading in the same direction as I was. Coincidentally, I had seen her before. She was one of the prettier girls that I scoped out at the party I had just come from.

All of a sudden, the butterflies began to dissipate. The flies disappeared, but they left the butter; in other words, I felt I had some flavor or "flava". Charlie Brown was given his marching orders, and in came Bobby Brown. With the proper etiquette, I approached the lady, introduced myself, and confirmed that she came from the same party that I just left.

I reasoned with her that since we were heading in the same direction, I hoped she didn't mind if I tagged along with her. She obliged. I don't know if she accepted my request because it was late at night and she felt secure with an escort, or she was just being friendly with me; the bottom line is that I got the hook up. My party finally started. We had a friendly and meaningful conversation on our way to our respective homes. In fact, I escorted her all the way to her house before I went to mine. It was about a 30-minute walk to her house and 20 minutes from her house to mine. I don't recall if I got her number, but that's beside the point.

My point is that the setbacks I faced with my friends at the party set me up to meet the lady in question. The rejection lured me away from my so-called friends and placed me on the path that led me to someone who accepted me and made my day. This is kind of how God uses rejection to benefit you.

I felt rejected by my friends. Since we lived and grew up in the same neighborhood, in a sense, they were like family to me. I still consider them as such. In fact, I don't hold the incident against them. I was emphasizing more on the rejection I had to deal with. Though my day at the party started out sour, it turned out to be sweet. My friends, both the males and the females, perhaps unbeknownst to them, clouded me with disappointment, but the pretty girl I met on my way home handed me the silver lining.

Sometimes rejection is a strategy that God uses to get you out of a family that is holding you back. Family for you might be your friends, parents, siblings, church family, coworkers, in-laws, classmates, or teammates. At times, being around them could be detrimental to your purpose. They could undermine your potential and limit your ambition to theirs, if they have any. In order for God to help you achieve the things He's placed in your heart, if the people who are family to you are hindering that from happening, God will have to get you out of their lives. One way He gets to accomplish that is by letting them reject you. Why they reject you is really beside the point, as long as you get removed from them, God uses their setting you back to set you up.

IT HELPS YOU REALIZE YOUR DREAMS

Even those closest to you—your parents, brothers, relatives, and friends—will betray you.... (Luke 21:16 NLT)

Some people feel intimidated being in the presence of individuals who have visions and goals for their lives as well as others who are successful, attractive and exceptional, even when the standouts did nothing against them. They feel insecure because when they compare themselves to the purpose-driven and successful individuals, they "feel" like they do not measure up to their expectations and aspirations. As a result, some of these insecure individuals "hate" on them, usually by speaking against them, talking down on their accomplishments, or keeping them at arm's length. That should not be the case, but that's how some people behave.

Regardless, we should not let other's perceptions and their rejection of us stop us from being who God wants us to be. In fact, when they come against us because of what we aspire to be, they are only assisting us to arrive at our destination.

Joseph is a prime example of someone whose vision was not received by others. It so happened that the people he disclosed his dream to were his family members. Joseph shared his dream with them, but they made fun of him and rebuked him for implying that he would be a leader over them. Even his father, who bestowed more love on him than his brothers, chastised him for the implications of his dream (Genesis 37:5-10). It's sad to say that those closest to us could kill our dreams if we let them. That being the case, it stands to reason why God takes advantage of them not accepting us to redirect us to a place were their beliefs, misguided thoughts, and ignorance does not undermine our importance.

Joseph's brothers conspired against him; they stripped him of his coat of many colors, threw him in a pit, and sold him into slavery in Egypt. Little did they know, nor did Joseph know, that they were sending him to the exact place where he was destined to actualize his dreams.

When people refuse us and God has His hands on us, they are actually isolating us to a place where our full potential will be realized. Being in a relationship with the wrong person, ignorant family members, or close-minded business firms can hinder us from realizing our potential. They often slow down our progress by their traditionalistic, religious, and antiquated ideologies. They put us in a box. But, God wants us out of the box. He does not want us to be caved in. He wants us out and about His business of saving, healing, restoring, and empowering lives. I found it profound that after Joseph was sold to Egypt as a slave, he ended up serving Potiphar, and the Bible said that God was with him (Genesis 39:2). Wow!

Scripture doesn't tell us that God was with Joseph when he was with his family. With his family, he was loved by his father but despised by his brothers. He wore a coat of many colors, but there was nothing said about God being with him. Of course God was with him, however, it appears that God's presence with Him was even more pronounced in his slavery where he must have felt alone.

Actually, he was isolated alone with God. Hence, he was in a position where he could learn from God without his father or brothers adding their contrary two cents. Joseph's administrative skills were realized in Egypt, not with his family. Joseph's rejection got him to a place where he could actually be himself. Sometimes familiarity is a comfort zone. As the saying goes, *familiarity breeds complacency.* Joseph's brothers probably only saw Joseph as their little brother and their father's beloved. Their skewed perception of him blinded them to his potential. Jacob perhaps only saw his favorite son as the fruit of his deceased first love, Rachel. This also might have distorted his perception of Joseph.

In Egypt, Joseph's role was no longer limited to what his father and his brothers thought of him. Though in isolation, he was positioned to introspect, withdraw from himself, and express the gift that God had deposited in him. Abilities that had been lying dormant all the years he was with his family.

Potiphar's house was the launching pad for his ministry and industry. He was so good at his job that Potiphar placed him in charge of all his affairs. Joseph probably got comfortable realizing his potential. He was doing his thing. But, God wanted more. This was not all God *brought* Joseph to Egypt for. God had a bigger vision. This vision was the reason why God allowed Joseph to be rejected by members of his family so that he could end up in the area where he would fulfill his purpose.

Potiphar's wife also contributed to Joseph's rejection. After all Joseph had done for Potiphar, here comes his spouse trying to mess things up. She was drawn to Joseph's looks, and she tried to seduce him to sleep with her. Joseph refused her advances. She kept on pressuring him until, one day, during his struggle to resist her, he ran out of the house leaving his cloth in her hand. She falsely accused Joseph of trying to rape her. Her husband then put Joseph in prison (Genesis 39:7-21). Can you imagine how Joseph felt? After all he did for Potiphar, his master incarcerates him based on a false accusation from his wife. The ripple effect of this episode fascinates me.

Joseph rejected Potiphar's wife's advances toward him. In essence, he pushed her back to her husband. Potiphar's wife, in turn, lashed back by falsely accusing Joseph of trying to violate her. Consequently, Joseph was sent to lock-up. Joseph must have felt rejected. He must have felt déjà vu. He managed his master's affairs with the utmost integrity. He did the right thing by rebuffing Potiphar's wife's seduction. Yet, in essence, they rejected him just like his brothers did.

But, guess what? Once again, the Bible says that God was with him in prison (Genesis 39:21). That really fascinates me. Joseph is incarcerated and, again, we hear that God was with him. Bearing this in mind, I want to encourage you by letting you know that if you are facing any form of rejection, God is with you, too. He is right smack in the middle of your pain. He is right in the dungeon with you. In fact the reason you still have your sanity is because of the grace He's given you to persevere in your situation. In addition, He is using your *opposition* to *position* you for your destiny.

And we know that God causes everything to work together for the good of those who love God and are called according to his purpose for them. (Romans 8:28 NLT)

God will cause your rejection to work for your good if you love Him. And He'll use it to help you fulfill your purpose. Sometimes prison is the pathway to our freedom. "Why?" you might ask. Well, the situation you are going through is not just about you; it's bigger than you. As you might already know, what Joseph went through wasn't just about him. It was about his family, the Egyptians, and the rest of the world.

Similarly, what you're going through is also for other people. It could be for your family, community, ethnicity, company, or country. Besides, in prison, you'll get to see those who are there and help bring them out. In other words, by experiencing what other people are going through, you'll be able to help them overcome their trials just like God is helping you overcome yours. This is why God is with you—to bring you through the ordeal to achieve a great deal. In the process, He'll use you to bring other people out of their hang-ups, bondage, or prisons. People like your family, friends, coworkers or acquaintances, some of the very people who wrote you off.

In prison Joseph meets Pharaoh's baker and butler. Both men displeased Pharaoh and were sent to prison. In essence, they were the Pharaoh's *rejects*. While in prison, the baker and butler each had dreams. Their dreams left them in distress as they did not know what their dreams meant. Coincidentally, the interpretation of dreams was Joseph's forte. The baker and the butler turned out to be in the right place as Joseph was available to help them interpret their dreams. Joseph told the chief butler that his dream meant that he would be restored to his rightful position as the king's cup bearer. Unfortunately for the chief baker, Joseph told him that his dream meant that he would be executed.

Joseph's interpretation came to pass as the chief butler got his job back while the chief baker was executed. After Joseph interpreted the chief butler's dream, Joseph asked him to refer him to Pharaoh and get him out of jail. Well, the chief butler forgot about Joseph once he got out of jail (Genesis 40). Nonetheless, about two years later, the Pharaoh had a dream that disturbed him, and no one in his empire could interpret the dream. A light bulb and a wave of guilt probably swept through the chief butler when he suddenly remembered the guy who interpreted his dream when he was incarcerated.

Perhaps you can relate more to the chief butler when he was in prison than with Joseph. Maybe you used to hold a prestigious position. You might have owned your own establishment, been a vice president of a thriving company, been a chief officer, been an associate of a pastor, been in some form of leadership or a position that offered you the privilege of rubbing shoulders with upper management. Unfortunately, everything came crashing down and the bottom fell out on you when you lost your business, got demoted, or got fired. Like the chief butler, you lost everything. Management gave you a vote of no confidence. Your boss showed you out the back door of the company. Human resources handed you a pink slip. You were suddenly dismissed, and you didn't know any legitimate reason why that was the case. Maybe you did. Either way, like in the case of the chief butler, it's for a purpose.

I believe that getting sent to prison by the Pharaoh was just an excuse that God used to get the chief butler to prison so that he could meet Joseph. God used the chief butler to be a witness and a reference for Joseph's ability. He was the link that God used to get Joseph to the Egyptian king. He was also restored to his position as the king's cup bearer. Similarly, it's possible that God allowed you to be demoted or fired in order to get you around someone who needs your help.

So, open your eyes and look around you. Who is that individual, or those individuals, whom you've been bumping into since you were axed from your previous position? It could be that God wants to use you to help him, her or them, and, in the process, you'll get yourself restored to your former position, if not a better position. If this applies to you, I believe you'll know the person you are supposed to assist. Do that and see what happens for you.

The chief butler was Joseph's *provision*. He was provided for Joseph's vision or dream of becoming a leader. Furthermore, Joseph was also Pharaoh's provision. Joseph underwent rejection for the purpose of interpreting Pharaoh's vision or dream and making arrangements to ensure that Pharaoh was prepared to handle his vision when it came to pass.

The chief butler told Pharaoh about Joseph, and Pharaoh summoned Joseph to come before him. Joseph interpreted his dream marvelously. Pharaoh was so impressed with Joseph's insight that he made him Egypt's vice commander-in-chief. He also dressed Joseph in garments of fine linen, took off his signet ring, put it on Joseph's finger, and also put a gold chain around his neck (Genesis 41:1-46). In addition, Pharaoh made Joseph ride in his second chariot, the archaic version of the royal Bentley, Rolls Royce, Benzo, or whatever tickles your imagination.

What an honor. Second only in command to Pharaoh, Joseph was the man. He was the head honcho, the governor of Egypt. Joseph, who was sold as a slave and tossed like a *stone* to Egypt by his brothers, became *a chief cornerstone*. He fulfilled his destiny. A huge famine in Canaan necessitated that his brothers went to Egypt for food. Unbeknownst to them, their brother, Joseph, whom they discarded, was the one administrating the distribution of food supplies since he was in charge of everything in Egypt. That's how they ended up meeting him. Eventually Joseph reconciled with his brothers and father and assured them that all was well as they were afraid that he would carry out his revenge on them for what they did to him.

"Come closer to me," Joseph said to his brothers. They came closer. "I am Joseph your brother whom you sold into Egypt. But don't feel badly, don't blame yourselves for selling me. God was behind it. God sent me here ahead of you to save lives. There has been a famine in the land now for two years; the famine will continue for five more years—neither plowing nor harvesting. God sent me on ahead to pave the way and make sure there was a remnant in the land, to save your lives in an amazing act of deliverance. So you see, it wasn't you who sent me here but God. He set me in place as a father to Pharaoh, put me in charge of his personal affairs, and made me ruler of all Egypt. (Genesis 45:4-8 MSG)

Joseph did not retaliate because he realized that God used what they did to him to get him to Egypt, to become the nation's governor, Joseph's function and position. Like a cornerstone, he held things together. In essence, Joseph realized that all he went through was the Lord's doing and it was marvelous in his eyes, my eyes and hopefully, yours, too.

Joseph was transformed from being a dreamer to an individual who actualized his dreams. He matured from a boy to a man. He went from being despised by his brothers to being revered by them and an entire nation. He was transformed from just being papa's boy with a coat of many colors to a governor with several garments of linen, wearing a gold chain around his neck, Pharaoh's signet ring on his finger, riding Pharaoh's second chariot and married to the priest of On's daughter (Genesis 41:37-46).

Like Joseph you could have been rejected by your family. Even so, realize that God is with you. As long as He is with you and you with Him, and you understand that He is working out something good for you, you will end up where you belong. Those that dismissed you actually drove you to your destiny. They rejected you for your purpose.

You might not feel like you've gotten to that special place or found that special person or position, but you're on your way. You might be like Joseph as a slave in the prison of your circumstance. Be encouraged. You're in transition. Enjoy the journey, embrace the journey, and enlighten yourself during the journey. Stick with God. Like Joseph, conduct yourself responsibly regardless of the prevailing circumstances you're faced with. Say the right thing, say it the right way, and God will be with you every step of the way.

Chapter 10
Even if You're Setback, You're Still Set!

During a football game, when a quarterback is trying to throw a touchdown pass, he usually takes a few steps back before he throws the ball. He does that to position himself properly to project and direct the ball accurately to reach his target receiver. In other words, he sets himself back to build the leverage he needs to throw the ball in a way that will enable his receiver to catch it and score a touchdown. But in order for this to take place, he has to take a few steps back; he has to set himself back.

Similarly, in an airport, a pilot has to taxi a plane back to the beginning of the runway to prepare for take off. The pilot sets the plane back to its starting point to position it to launch. And even before the plane takes off, the plane *tilts back* just a tad little bit before it lunges forward. Likewise, when you get set back, have the mindset that you're only being positioned to score a touchdown for your life. You're being set to take off! You might be set back, but you're still set!

People, friends, or family members might set you back, but God utilizes their plans to set you up for your destiny. In their efforts to cause you to fail whether intentionally or accidentally, they're helping you to succeed. Like a plane set to take off, you're being set to launch into your purpose. Like Joseph, you're being positioned in the place where you need to be in order to proceed with God's mandate for your life. God is using your opposition to position you.

Bishop T.D. Jakes observed:

*Like an arrow caught in a bow most people go backward before they shoot forward.... Those of us who have experienced setbacks in life often release and shoot farther **because of** the setback and not **in spite** of it.... Sometimes what makes us insecure and vulnerable becomes the fuel we need to be over-achievers....The antidote for a snakebite is made from the poison, and the thing that made you go backward is the same force that will push you forward.*[1]

Do you know something that first baffled me, but later enlightened me, about Joseph's plight? It was his dreams. I don't know if you ever thought about this, but Joseph did not interpret his dreams. His brothers and his father did. When Joseph told them about his dreams, they were the ones that got upset with him because of the implications of *their* interpretation of his dreams (Genesis 37:5-11). This seems to suggest that Joseph was not the only one who could interpret dreams. His brothers could, too, at least the ones responsible for rebuking him for implying that he would rule over them.

With that in mind, could it be that his brothers were neglecting a gift that God gave them, too? Could it be that they regarded their gift the same way they regarded Joseph? They did not take it seriously. They might have overlooked the gift of dream interpretation; and, perhaps had Joseph not been removed from his family, he would have developed the unproductive generational habit, too.

I believe it's possible that Reuben, Joseph's eldest brother, had the gift. But maybe because his father, Jacob, who also interpreted Joseph's dream, never encouraged him to pay attention to and apply the gift, he took it for granted. Simeon, his brother after him, following his older brother's example, also overlooked the gift. Then Levi, the third-born, only propagated the pattern. And the habit continued all the way down to Joseph. At this point, I believe God said, *enough*!

If that was the case, I can understand why God had to get Joseph out of his family to prevent him from doing exactly what his family members had been doing. But how do you tell a seventeen-year-old to leave a loving father who dotes over him? How do you tell one of the youngest members of a family who is secure and comfortable in just being the apple of his father's eye to leave his family? You probably can't pull that off. However, if you can't get him to leave his family, you can get his family to leave him—or, like in Joseph's case, get rid of him.

God allowed Joseph to be ostracized by his brothers in order to get him to fulfill the dream that *they* interpreted. God did not want Joseph to be a man who was just wrapped in a coat of many colors; God wanted him to *show* his "true color." Likewise, God does not want you to be flash with no substance—a coat of many colors. He wants you to be substance, not flash. He wants you to display your true color—your purpose, not many colors—many misguided labels that other people placed on you. Have this mindset if you're experiencing rejection from your family. They might be setting you back, but you're still set to take off and score touchdowns in your life, and enhance, sustain and brighten the lives of others just like Joseph did for his family, his people, and the Egyptians.

IT HELPS YOU SAVE LIVES

The movie *Happy Feet,* which won an *Oscar* and a *Golden Globe* award, adequately illustrates how being rejected can be the best thing that ever happened for you. The screenplay also reinforces the fact that those who dismiss us can be our own family members, be it our immediate family or extended family. In addition, the main reason why we've been rejected by our kinfolks often eludes us and is usually bigger than the reason why our family thought they dismissed us. Responding with faith in God, faith in ourselves, hope that everything will work out for the best and loving our detractors by forgiving them, will enable us to discover, understand, and fulfill the real purpose for which we were castoff.

I acknowledge that everyone who viewed the movie could have drawn insights from it that differ from mine. In fact, the objective of those who wrote, produced and directed the movie could also be in sharp contrast to what I'm about to reveal. Notwithstanding, the movie suitably depicts how we can be rejected for a purpose.

The main character in the animated feature was a young penguin named Mumble. Unlike all the other penguins, he could not sing. He could tap dance instead. And, he usually did this when he was happy, hence, the name *Happy Feet*. Unfortunately for Mumble, he was treated like an outcast because he tap-danced instead of sang. His own father dissuaded him from tap-dancing. Mumble was rejected because of his unusual gift. In fact, the *leader* of the penguins known as Noah, the elder, claimed that they were cursed because of Mumble.

The penguin community to which Mumble belonged was dealing with a scarcity of fish. And as far as Noah, the elder, was concerned, the food scarcity was the curse pronounced on them because of Mumble's dancing antics. Isn't it interesting that the main antagonist against Mumble was the leader of their community? Do you recall that the stone which the builders rejected has become the chief cornerstone? If we apply this passage to the movie, Noah would be the builder and Mumble would be the stone. And Mumble became the chief cornerstone for their community. Let me elaborate.

Things got so bad for Mumble that Noah, the elder derided him and banished him from their community. Mumble's father, Memphis, wasn't adequately supportive of his son. He'd always restrained his son from tap-dancing. Despite being declared a persona non grata by his own kinfolks, Mumble responded with faith, hope, and love. Mumble was inspired to prove that he was not responsible for the scarcity of fish. With courage and the help and support of some friends from another penguin species known as the Amigo penguins, Mumble embarked on a fact-finding mission on why they could not find fish to eat in their ecosystem.

Mumble was able to discover that the reason there was scarcity of fish was because humans were fishing in their area. While humans were fishing, Mumble found himself in the wrong place at the wrong time and ended up getting caught up in the net with an abundance of fish which were supposed to be feeding his community. Trapped in the net, Mumble was siphoned away from his habitat and ended up at an aquarium far from home. He was distraught. But in his dejection, he leaned on one thing he'd always known from birth. His feet.

His groove eventually caught the attention of his captors. They were captivated by the penguin's tap-dancing and wondered if there were other penguins like him. So they strapped a device on him, released him back to the area from which he was caught, and followed him to discover his homeland.

When the humans discovered Mumble's habitat, as an incentive to motivate the community of penguins they found in the area to tap-dance, they brought lots of fish. Thanks to the grand prize, everyone who previously pointed accusing fingers at Mumble started to tap-dance, river dance, and break dance so that they could eat. Even Noah, the elder was cutting a two-step—or was it a quadruple-step? To cut a long story short, Mumble saved his community.

The one who Noah, the elder claimed brought a curse, was the one that brought a blessing. The one held responsible for the scarcity of food turned out to be the one responsible for bringing an abundance of food. Mumble's gift of tap-dancing, which Noah claimed was going to cause their community to be extinct, was what made Mumble distinct, and the thing that drew the attention of the humans to their plight. The stone (Mumble) which the builder (Noah and other leaders including Memphis, Mumble's father) rejected had become the chief cornerstone (the rock, building block, pillar of strength, savior or hero of the penguin community).

In light of what this book is about, Mumble was rejected for the purpose of saving his community. His dance moves, which were rebuffed, turned out to be the bait which lured humans to their habitat to realize the damage they were doing to their species and ecosystem. Mumble saved the day. He saved his penguin community from starvation, saved his habitat from degradation, and ultimately saved his species from extinction. And his transition from zero to hero was facilitated by the rejection he experienced.

So how does that animated feature apply to you and me?

Well, like Mumble, your own family members might be keeping you at arm's length. Some of the people you look up to, people who are supposed to support and build you up, people who are supposed to be family to you, your own blood, might be dismissing, deriding, and disrespecting you. Furthermore, they might be doing so because of something distinct about you. In *Happy Feet's* case, it was because he couldn't sing, but tap-danced instead, which, was not the norm for their species.

Maybe you are not gifted or adorned with abilities that perpetuate your family tradition. Perhaps you have a different gift. Mumble was dismissed for his happy feet. Maybe yours is a happy smile. Maybe it's the color of your pupil, the pigmentation of your skin, or the way you talk. Maybe it's the texture of your hair, the way you think, the way you work, or the way you approach issues. Or, maybe it's just because you have plans, dreams, and visions for your life different than what your kinfolks expected from you. Whatever it is, it's likely not the norm for the folks in your neck of the woods. Your vision is probably bigger than the environment you're in. As a result, you're being treated like an outcast.

If that is the case with you, be encouraged. Respond the right way. Respond with faith, hope, and love. Respond like *Happy Feet*. Don't respond with an *unhappy fit*. Sometimes, in order to make a difference, you have to be *different*. Have this in mind when people label you as different and give you the cold shoulder for it. They are only liberating you to champion your cause, the purpose for which you are being rejected. If you haven't realized this, the reason you are being rejected is one of the ways that God helps you find your purpose.

What is that particular gift, endeavor, or peculiarity about you that different people at different times in your life have criticized you about, hindered you from achieving, or told you that you could not do? The thing, be it an attribute, an ability, a gift, your style, is likely your purpose or linked to your destiny. While Mumble was ostracized because he danced, Joseph was questioned about leading his family. Well, he led his family after all. Moses was questioned: *Who made you a ruler and judge over us?* by his own fellow citizen, his own brethren (Exodus 2:13-14). Well, he turned out to be their ruler and judge. Jesus was taunted: *"All hail king of the Jews!"* Well, he turned out to be the King of Kings (Mark 15:17-18). Just like Joseph's brothers interpreted Joseph's dreams, family members, leaders and friends, through their criticism, cynicism, and antagonism against you, can inadvertently *interpret your dreams for you.* They can unknowingly reveal and confirm your purpose. This is one of the ways that God helps us find our mission in life.

When he was a child, Bill Wilson was walking with his mother down a street and then they stopped and sat down to rest for a while. His mother told him to wait for her to return while she went somewhere else. *Three* days later, Wilson was still waiting for his mother at the exact spot that she told him to wait for her. A man had noticed him waiting there for the past three days. The man came to Wilson's assistance, picked him up and took care of him. The pain of the abandonment that Bill experienced fueled in him a desire to help children suffering everywhere, offering them hope and love, while combating issues like poverty, child prostitution, hunger and AIDS awareness.

The pastor, author and speaker began his mission in 1980 as president and founder of Metro Ministries International. His organization is considered the world's largest Sunday school, serving over 42,000 children worldwide with Sunday school services, child sponsorship, special programs, and personal home visits every week. Metro's mission is to find and rescue inner-city kids living in urban environments often plagued with drugs, poverty, violence, crime, and hopelessness. Metro offers programs that help prevent kids raised in such unfavorable settings from being mere products of their environments.

Metro operates programs for urban children at 200 sites in New York City as well as in the Philippines, Romania, and South Africa. Their program was identified as a factor in the reduction of crime in the Bushwick community, which was considered one of the roughest neighborhoods in Brooklyn, and is also the area where the organization is headquartered.

The success of Metro's programs even led President George Bush Sr. to appoint Pastor Bill Wilson to serve in the National Commission on America's Urban families in 1991.[2]

Without a doubt, we can see the result of what happened to Pastor Wilson as a child. God used what he went through to help him find and fulfill his purpose of saving children's lives.

AT TIMES, IT IS A BETTER OPTION THAN ACCEPTANCE

Well-meaning family members can be your worst enemies (Matthew 21:36 MSG).

Several years ago, in Waterloo, Iowa, a seventeen-year-old Caucasian teenage girl was impregnated by an African-American male. This took place around the early seventies. During that era and in that small mid-western town, not only was having babies out of wedlock a taboo, so was having cross-cultural relationships. The young lady told her parents about her pregnancy. Her parents gave her two options. They told her to either abort the baby or be disowned by them. The teenager chose to be rejected *for the purpose* of keeping and *protecting* her baby boy. Not only was the young lady rejected by her biological father, she was also abandoned by the baby's father when she was eight months pregnant.

The young lady moved to San Diego, California. Things got worse for her as she started taking drugs and was declared an unfit mother by the State of California. One day, while walking on the street, a Hispanic lady drove by, parked her car, and approached her. The Good Samaritan encouraged her and helped her realize that she made the right decision by keeping her baby. She then gave her a Bible and introduced her to Jesus Christ. The Hispanic lady also gave her a place to stay until she gave birth to her baby and made a living for herself.

The teenager began to read the Bible, which gave her the inspiration for her son's name. Later on she met a remarkable man whom she married and, together, they raised her son. Her baby boy grew up to be an outstanding young man. He travels around the world, offering hope and inspiration to people through his music. The author, worship leader, recording artist, songwriter, producer, arranger and composer's music has garnered a few Stellar and Dove awards, a Soul Train, and two

Grammy awards. He has worked with the likes of Cece Winans, Martha Munizzi, and Donnie McClurkin, and performed at events such as the Promise Keepers and the NBA All-Star week.

The young man's mother allowed her family to disown her in order to protect her son's life. Not only did she protect him from being aborted, she also protected his purpose from being aborted. She was inspired to name her son *Israel* due to the frequency of seeing the name in the Bible. Her son's full name is Israel Houghton, and he also co-founded the internationally acclaimed band, *New Breed*.[2]

Interestingly, sometimes we find ourselves in situations where we only have two options. There are times that we may have to choose between being accepted and being rejected. Obviously, we all want to be accepted. We all want a sense of belonging. We all want to be part of a family, be it a nuclear family, a country club, a sport's team, a group of friends, "the in crowd" or a local church. At times, unfortunately, choosing to be accepted simultaneously leads to the abortion of our destiny. On the other hand, choosing to be rejected leads us to fulfill our purpose, and like a domino effect, it enables us to help others accomplish God's plan for their lives, too.

Chapter 11
It Puts You in the Spotlight

Carissa Phelps repeatedly ran away from home, away from an abusive stepfather and a mother who could not protect her. She was one of eleven children, and she couldn't stand continuing to live in the cramped and dysfunctional environment. Feeling tired and helpless in raising Carissa and dealing with her rebellion, her mother dropped twelve-year-old Carissa off at the Fresno County Juvenile Hall lobby and left her there. Carissa stayed there for three days, but they could not admit her because she had not committed a crime. Finally, they sent Carissa to a group home, which she disliked and ran away from.

Foster care ignored Carissa, and the juvenile justice system failed her. The pattern of running from group home to group home and being homeless began to be Carissa's norm. This lifestyle eventually landed her on the streets, and she ended up in the thick of child prostitution.

The end of Carissa's downward spiral and its reversal toward *redemption* and her destiny began when she stole a car at the age of thirteen. Her crime netted her six months in Fresno Juvenile facility, which ran an experimental program that included group therapy. It was there that she met Ron Jenkins, a former Fresno State Football player who was a counselor at the facility. He saw her pain, and he saw her potential. He noticed that she was intelligent, and he encouraged her to get an education, telling her it would help turn her life around. Another person who was instrumental in encouraging Carissa to rise up from her pitfalls was her high school math teacher, Mrs. Weggeman, who also encouraged her to achieve her goals.

Although Carissa was pushed to the streets by her family, she was redeemed from the streets by her *other* family of mentors, counselors, and teachers. This new family informed and inspired her to be the best she could be, and boy, did she turn her life around. Even while roaming the streets at twelve years old, she had an inkling to overcome her situation and then comeback to rescue other children trapped in the web of homelessness and child prostitution.

Carissa went on to college at the University of California Los Angeles (UCLA), where she graduated with *both* a law degree and an MBA. After graduating from school, she began to fulfill her dream by becoming a community organizer and a national speaker on youth homelessness for Virgin Mobile's RE*Generation campaign. She even gave up a lucrative position as a private equity analyst in Los Angeles to pursue her cause. She went back to Fresno where she developed a community economic development fund.

Carissa also teamed up with her classmate from UCLA, David Sauvage, to produce a documentary, *Carissa*. This documentary tells her life story of homelessness and prostitution and puts a *spotlight* on what an estimated 300,000 American children under the age of eighteen are going through. She is also lobbying Congress to fight against youth exploitation. Carissa is using her ordeal of homelessness and prostitution to achieve a great deal in bringing people out of it. The rejection she experienced from her family inadvertently led her to her *mission* of giving a voice to children who are on the streets.[1]

David also exemplifies an individual who was rejected by his family. Fortunately, this turned out well for him. God dethroned Saul from being king of Israel. In order to replace him, God sent the prophet Samuel to go to the house of a man named Jesse to appoint one of Jesse's sons to be the next king (1 Samuel 16:1-5).

Samuel was revered. He was an important dignitary well known in Bethlehem, the city in which Jesse resided. On hearing that Samuel was coming to town, the elders of the city trembled. Samuel was highly respected and recognized as the man of God, the prophet of the Most High. When Samuel spoke, what he spoke came to pass. This was the case because he spoke the oracles of God. The fear of the elders of Bethlehem was fueled because when a prophet came to a town, it usually meant he had a Word from God. Sometimes the message he had from God was one that pronounced judgment on individuals or an entire town.

The elders must have been relieved to discover that Samuel was in their vicinity to appoint a king for Israel. Samuel invited the elders, Jesse, and his sons to a sacrifice where he was going to anoint the next king. Jesse was no doubt elated to assume that one of his "seven" sons was going to be the king—though Jesse had eight sons. Wow, I bet he was excited and proud. Jesse summoned all his kids—except his youngest child, David—to come before the prophet. I imagine that he groomed his seven sons, sparing no detail in ensuring that one of them would be picked to assume the throne of Israel.

Even the usually flawless prophet of God, Samuel, concurred with Jesse's conclusion. When Jesse came to the sacrifice with his sons, on seeing Jesse's eldest son, Eliab, Samuel could not help but exclaim that he would be the one that God wanted to be king. The man of God actually said, "Surely, the Lord's anointed is before him!" (1 Samuel 16:6 NKJV) But, boy, was he wrong. Even God had to correct him. God had to make him aware that in choosing an individual, He looks at the heart and not at the outward appearance of the person. As you might know we can put on facades. But God does not look at our "mask-aras." He looks at our hearts, our motives, and our attitudes, and makes His choice based on them.

God told Samuel that Eliab was not the one He chose to be king. Jesse then brought Abinadab, Jesse's second born, and he was rejected, too. Jesse then presented Shammah, the third born, and he met the same fate. In fact, Samuel gave the other four brothers the same spiel he gave the first three.

Thus Jesse made seven of his sons pass before Samuel. And Samuel said to Jesse, "The LORD has not chosen these." (1 Samuel 16:10 NKJV)

I find this interesting: Jesse *made* seven of his sons pass before Samuel. It seemed like Jesse was trying to tell God who should be the king. Jesse was making a conscientious effort to help the prophet out. It was like Jesse was saying that if any of his kids were going to be king, it had to be one of his first seven. Reading that he *made* his kids come before the prophet almost sounds like they were reluctant to come forward.

After seeing that their eldest brother, Eliab, the most likely candidate for the kingship by looks, birth rite, and Jewish tradition was refused, the remaining six brothers must have realized that their chances of being chosen were next to impossible. The embarrassment of being rejected from being king like their eldest brother probably made them reluctant to come forward. But Daddy made them come before the prophet. Even so, the prophet told them that neither of them was God's chosen.

God knew all along whom he wanted to be king. Why did He then waste everybody's time in going through the motions of scouting out Jesse's first seven sons knowing fully well that He did not want any of them to be the king? Perhaps God did that to help Samuel, Jesse, his sons and us see how our approach to choosing leaders differs from His. Possibly because God wanted them and us to see that without His wisdom and insight, we are always going to make misguided decisions. Maybe He was trying to let all of us know that we would save a lot of time by seeking him first for direction and doing things His way, rather than waste time and effort trying to do things our way. Or, maybe God was just displaying His sense of humor.

Whatever the case, God did not choose any of the sons Jesse presented. As a result, He must have set up every one present with a big question mark in their heads— the question of who was to be king if not those seven?

And Samuel said to Jesse, "Are all the young men here?"
Then he said, "There remains yet the youngest, and there he
is keeping the sheep....And the LORD said, "Arise, anoint
him; for this is the one!" Then Samuel took the horn of oil
and anointed him in the midst of his brothers; and the Spirit
of the LORD came upon David from that day forward. (1
Samuel 16:11-12 NKJV)

The son that Jesse did not think would be king turned out
to be the one God chose for the position. This sounds like "the
stone which the builders rejected has become the chief cornerstone." Jesse did not even consider David as one destined
for kingship. That is evident by the fact that he brought David
to the sacrifice but left him aside to look after the sheep, while
he presented his other sons before the prophet. When Samuel
asked Jesse if he had any other sons, Jesse responded by saying "...there he is keeping the sheep...." This suggests that
David was close by, but not in the exact area where his father
and brothers were observing the sacrifice. They left him with
the sheep. In Jesse's mind, that was his place...to tend the
sheep. That is rejection.

Can you imagine your own father not believing in you? Perhaps, you do. If this is the case, please, accept my sincere
apologies. I did not mean to lead you to bring up painful memories. However, I do want to let you know that regardless of
how your father, mother, siblings or other family members disregarded you, that does not mean that God will not fulfill his
purpose for you. They might not know how valuable you are,
but God does.

Your worth is your value and part of who you are. God
placed that value in you. When people do not recognize your
worth, they devalue you. They treat you like you are worth
less. But you are worth *more*. So, by rejecting you they are actually pushing you to other individuals who would see that
you are worthwhile.

By leaving David with the sheep, Jesse unknowingly was
doing David a favor. He actually left David in the spotlight of
God. Maybe that was why Samuel had to go through the motions of checking each of the seven sons out before he could

find the right candidate. I believe God was not even in the exact place where everyone gathered for the ordination. God was waiting *beside* David and the *sheep* for Samuel to come and anoint the man He chose.

The fact that David was left with the sheep speaks volumes. Do you recall my earlier discussion about the Canaanite woman who overcame Jesus' test of rejection when she approached him to deliver her daughter (Matthew 15:21-28)? Do you remember that Jesus told her that He was sent to the lost "sheep" of Israel? God refers to his children as sheep. So, David being left to look after the sheep was symbolic of him overseeing, protecting, and guiding God's people. David was in the right place tending to the sheep. In a way, he was the *king of the sheep.* No wonder God gave him the *kingship.*

God's excellent choice of David as king was further evident when David slew Goliath. It was not long after David was anointed as the king of Israel that there was war between the Israelites and the Philistines. Jesse's first three sons were part of the Israelite army:

The three oldest sons of Jesse had gone to follow Saul to the battle. The names of his three sons who went to the battle were Eliab the firstborn, next to him Abinadab, and the third Shammah. David was the youngest. And the three oldest followed Saul. But David occasionally went and returned from Saul to feed his father's sheep at Bethlehem. (1 Samuel 17:13-15 NKJV)

I suppose God knew something Samuel, Jesse, and even his sons did not know when He rejected all the sons Jesse presented. That passage reveals that the three eldest sons *followed* Saul. I understand that they followed Saul pertaining to the war. But I also believe that "and the three oldest followed Saul" could mean that they were following after Saul's footsteps. They followed Saul's ways, which also implies that they were prone to conduct themselves in the manner that caused God to dethrone Saul. Therefore, why should God elect another king who would do the same thing his predecessor did?

In contrast, David "occasionally" went to Saul. I believe he went to Saul as a sense of duty, since he was Saul's harpist and

armor bearer (1 Samuel 16:21-23). So, why did David visit
Saul occasionally and come back home? According to the
scripture, David returned from Saul to *feed his father's sheep.*
Yes, the verse is talking about Jesse's sheep, but let's not lose
a revelation here. David returned from Saul *to feed his father's
sheep.* I believe this reveals the heart of a man committed to
feeding the father's sheep—God's children. Saul was not
David's priority; David's "father's sheep" were.

In the course of the war, Jesse sent David to find out how
his brothers were doing as well as to bring food for them and
the captain over them.

*So David rose early in the morning, left the sheep with a
keeper, and took the things and went as Jesse had commanded
him.... (1 Samuel 17:20 NKJV)*

David arrived at the camp where his brothers were sta-
tioned. He greeted them, and while talking with them, he
heard Goliath mouthing off about what he was going to do to
the Israelites. That was how David got wind of what was
going on. His curiosity was aroused and he inquired about the
ensuing battle between the Israelites and the Philistines. His
ambitious juices were definitely given a boost when he heard
that the man who could kill Goliath would be rewarded with
great riches, the king's daughter (Saul's daughter), and that his
family would be exempted from paying taxes (1 Samuel
17:25).

On hearing that, David was ready to take up the challenge.
But his eldest brother was upset with him and questioned him:

*When Eliab, David's oldest brother, heard him speaking
with the men, he burned with anger at him and asked, "Why
have you come down here? And with whom did you leave
those few sheep in the desert? I know how conceited you are
and how wicked your heart is; you came down only to watch
the battle." (1 Samuel 17:28)*

Here again, David is rejected by his own brother. He was
just trying to help, and yet his own blood disdained him. His
brother accused him of being prideful and rudely reminded
him of his place with the sheep: ...*And with whom did you
leave those few sheep?....*

Does that sound familiar to you? When you try to accomplish a feat that is unprecedented, something that has never been done before, sometimes even your family members will reject your efforts. They will claim that you cannot do it. And in an effort to convince them that you can, because you believe in yourself and your God to help you, you try to prove it, although they belittle you. They become angry with you and claim that you are being arrogant.

Sometimes they will remind you of the mundane tasks they've known you to do in the past. They might even remind you of your past mistakes or things you tried to do in the past that did not work. They remind you of your "few sheep"— your small accomplishments—and they'll tend to limit you to doing only those "small things" you did in the past. They do not know that the principles you applied to your small achievements are also applicable to help you achieve bigger things.

Eliab, perhaps still jealous, envious, and furious that his youngest brother was ordained instead of him, discouraged his little brother. But, of course, David did not relent. He began to exemplify why God chose him to be king. David was not trying to prove his brother wrong. That is so petty. He was trying to protect his "father's sheep." He was trying to defend and prevent the name of Israel from being embarrassed by Goliath. David more than any other man, including his brothers and Saul, who was the king then, knew who he was and the strength of his God to defeat the Philistines.

Courageously, David approached Saul and told him that he would fight Goliath. Initially, Saul was reluctant to let David fight the giant because, according to Saul, David was too young and inexperienced. But David told Saul that he could handle Goliath. David did that by reenacting a past experience he had. You know, Eliab was right. David should be watching the sheep because it was David's experience with the sheep that afforded him the courage, the wisdom, and the leadership to handle Goliath. I believe it was his faithfulness to the sheep, the animals that his father and brother charged him with, that led God to choose him as king.

David told Saul that while he was looking after his father's sheep, a lion and a bear took a lamb out of his flock. He then mentioned how he killed the lion and the bear and delivered the lamb out of their mouths (1 Samuel 17:34-37). He said that God helped him then and that God would help him treat Goliath like the animals he slew. David, in his wisdom, drew parallels between Goliath and the lion and the bear that attacked one of his sheep, with Goliath representing the animal trying to attack the father's sheep, Israel.

According to John 10:10, the devil comes to kill, to steal, and to destroy. But Jesus came to give life. Also, the devil is like a roaring lion looking for whom he might devour. The devil is an assassin out to steal, kill, and destroy God's children. Therefore, David protecting the sheep from the mouth of the lion and the bear is representative of someone protecting God's people from the devil—*the evil* one.

Like a roaring lion or a charging bear is a wicked man ruling over a helpless people. (Proverbs 28:15)

David saving his lamb from the lion and the bear was indicative of him delivering God's people from the wickedness of men, men like Goliath. With that being said, Saul allowed David to take on Goliath, and take on Goliath he did. He took him out. With God's help, David killed Goliath and cut his head off. By that accomplishment, he no doubt displayed why God chose him to be king.

The child that got rejected by his father and brothers turned out to be the Lord's anointed. His family thought less of him. They limited him to being with the sheep. Little did they know that they restricted him with the responsibility that developed his strength. It was with the sheep that he developed his craft. It was with the sheep that he experienced the power of God. It was with the sheep that he learned how to trust God, how to be patient, how to guide, how to lead, how to feed, and how to protect, all job descriptions of a man that God chooses to lead his people. David's family helped David out by keeping him with the sheep.

By killing Goliath, not only did David save Israel from being embarrassed and enslaved by the Philistines, but he also saved his family. He made them rich and exempted them from paying taxes, his reward for overcoming the giant. That was part of what God was trying to do for David's family.

Let me draw some more important points from a previous passage:

So David rose early in the morning, left the sheep with a keeper, and took the things and went as Jesse had commanded him.... (1 Samuel 17:20 NKJV)

That scripture depicts David's response to his father's request when Jesse asked him to take food supplies to his brothers and their captain. Did you note that David never forgot about his father's sheep? He placed them in the hands of a keeper and went on to carry out his father's errand. Despite being anointed king, David did not gloat at his brothers, neither did he disrespect his father. He did not treat his father resentfully because his father did not consider him for the throne. He did not get back at his father or brothers for ignoring his abilities to oversee Israel. He treated them like he was never anointed king. He still respected them. He still loved them. He still treated them like his family. This is evident by the fact that he responded to his father's request with no qualms, and he took supplies to his brothers.

Similarly, you should not disrespect your family after you achieve the success that they did not expect you to obtain. Even though you made it on your own, despite your family's lack of support, you should still support them. As a matter of fact, God allowed them to reject you so that you would not be limited by their success or lack of it. God wanted you to discover your worth apart from your family. He wanted you to discover the gift he placed in you without your family tampering with it. He wants you to cultivate it and to be productive. By so doing, you are in a position to accomplish things that your family could not accomplish. Things you could never have realized had you still been limited by their unproductive ways.

There are things that God is trying to do for your family but, for whatever reason, they could not receive those things. However, God saw that you had the antenna to receive his blessings. The blessings are for you and your family. So, you are a conduit through which God can channel his blessings to them. But, first, He has to get you out of their thinking, their misguided philosophies, and sometimes dream-killing traditions. One way He gets to do that is by letting them push you out of their lives so that, apart from them, He can first, heal, restore, and nurture you. He will then bring you across the paths of other individuals who will believe in and inspire you to be the person God purposed you to be. After you have established yourself, then you should go back and at least, allow your family to partake of the fruit they would not have received had they destroyed your dreams and aspirations.

Jesse rejected the thought of David being king because, in his ignorant thinking, David did not meet the expectations of a king. Eliab rejected David because, in his spitefulness and lack of understanding, David did not meet the expectations to even be on the battlefield. Saul initially rejected David from fighting Goliath because David did not meet the expectations of a soldier, much less one who would fight Goliath. God allowed all of them to reject David so that David would *meet* His expectations of being the king of Israel. David benefited from Saul's eventual rejection from the throne because it opened the door for David to become king.

Chapter 12

It Helps You Start Your Own Ministry

U sually, the word "ministry" is often limited to church work. This should not be the case because, although ministry is work, it's not just church work. Ministry is any form of work that you render to help people. Synonyms for ministry include bureau, office, department, organization, and agency. Your ministry is your industry; it's your profession, and it's to serve others. A doctor is in the ministry of health. A lawyer is in the ministry of law. A janitor is in the ministry of hygiene, a chef is in the ministry of hospitality. A married, stay-at-home-mother ministers as a wife and mother. Even a dog ministers as man's best friend.

With that in mind, even though I'll be drawing points from scriptures that highlight rejection in the ecclesiastical ministry, please do not limit my discussion to only conflicts in church. You can also apply them to *your* ministry.

Pastor John Osteen was a prominent pastor and was on the state board of the denomination he served in Houston, Texas. When one of his daughters was born with a birth injury, rather than complain and blame God, he was driven to seek God even more. In the process, he saw God in a new way. He saw God as a loving, healing, and restoring God. Inspired by this reve-lation, while exercising his faith in God with his wife for their daughter's healing, he decided to share his discovery through his messages to the congregation that he served.

Unfortunately, he ruffled the feathers of some of the members of the fellowship. What he preached was not received by them. They gave him the cold shoulder for his newfound sermons. In fact, the church took a vote to decide whether they wanted him to stay or leave their congregation. Although Pastor Osteen secured enough votes to stay, he was mistreated and disrespected by some of his parishioners. In essence, they rejected him! As a result, Pastor John Osteen resigned from the church denomination.

Despite this setback, his daughter was healed, and, because he left the denomination, he was *liberated* to start his own ministry. On Mother's Day in 1959, with the help of about 90 people, he turned a small, rundown, filthy "abandoned" feed store into the Lakewood Church.[1]

Approximately 50 years later to the time of this writing, this church, which is currently under the reigns of his son, Pastor Joel Osteen, according to *Nielsen,* is the largest congregation in America. The congregation is so huge that it had to purchase and occupy the area where the Compaq center used to be situated in Houston, Texas.

The way Pastor John Osteen responded to the rejection he faced in ministry set the stage for the church which now occupies the former home of the Houston Rockets Basketball franchise. It enabled him to blaze the trail that ignited his son to turn the Compaq center into a center where people from all walks of life can "come pack" or fill up to congregate and cultivate their relationship with God.

Furthermore, even the acquisition of the Compaq center was facilitated by a rejection that Pastor Joel Osteen experienced. While listening to him give a sermon that dealt with learning to do things God's way, I recall him revealing how he ended up being interested in the former sport complex. His congregation had outgrown its former church facility and, as a result, he decided to seek a new location to accommodate the growth of his parishioners.

He was excited about a large site not too far from his former location. For about four or five months, he negotiated acquiring this property but, to his dismay, the property was sold right out from under him. He was disappointed about the sudden and unexpected turn of events. He felt that that property was going to be the new location for his church. *Fortunately,* he was given a rude awakening, which turned out to be a *good awakening.* Better still, a *great awakening.*

About six months later, the Compaq Center was up for sale, and, as you might know, he ended up acquiring the 17,000 square-foot facility. Talk about a *promotion.* Being refused from obtaining the property he had had his sights on *redirected* him to the current location of the ministry under his care. The former Compaq Center became the *provision* for Lakewood Church.[1]

Bernie Marcus also experienced rejection. In April 1978, a flood of accusations were lodged against him. The next thing he knew he was thrown out of his office and his files were ransacked. On that fateful and painful day, for the first time in his life, Marcus was fired from being the CEO of Handy Dan Home Improvement Center. Even his vice president of finance, Arthur Blank, was given the boot.

The word was that Marcus' debacle was orchestrated by his boss, who disliked him. Marcus was upset and angry at the way he was maltreated by his boss, and he decided to get even with him. So, he filed a lawsuit against his boss. Meanwhile, Sol Price, the founder of Price Club, which now is a part of PriceCostco, invited Marcus for dinner. While dining, Marcus discussed his plight with his host.

Marcus mentioned that he was suing his boss for about $1 million, which was the worth of his contract with the company he ran. But, his boss severed the deal by firing him. Therefore, to get back at his boss and to regain his entitlement, Marcus explained that he had filed a lawsuit. Price, however, advised him to do otherwise.

Price took Marcus to an empty room virtually devoid of furniture. In the room, he showed Marcus stacks of papers that represented a lawsuit which had taken about three years of his life. In fact, it was during the litigation that Price started Price Club; and he had his son run the retail outlet since the lawsuit consumed most of his time and energy.

In an effort to prevent his friend from going through the ordeal he went through, Price acknowledged Marcus' business astuteness. He advised Marcus not to waste his hard-earned money and young life accumulating depositions like he did, dissuaded him from going on with the lawsuit, and encouraged him to move on with his life.

Marcus heeded his friend's advice. After he got back home, he called his lawyers and asked them to drop the lawsuit, and he moved on with his life. He dug deep within himself and withdrew the dream that had been lying dormant in his heart. For years, Marcus had had a vision of opening his own store. Now that his employment had been terminated and he had put behind him the injustice he suffered, he decided to pursue his dream.

In June 1979, fourteen months after their unceremonious dismissal from Handy Dan, Bernie Marcus and his former VP of finance, Arthur Blank, started their own ministry—they opened their own store in Atlanta, Georgia. While the establishment they were terminated from went out of business, their creation went on to become a household name and the largest home improvement retailer in the United States.

You might have heard of Bernie Marcus' and Arthur Blank's profitable venture. At the time of this writing, their business employed over 209,300 workers; had over 2200 branches in the United States, Canada, Mexico, and China; generated just over 71 billion dollars in revenue and a net income on the up side of $2 billion. Their company has also graced the pages of *Forbes* and *Fortune* magazines. In case you didn't know, their establishment goes by the name *Home Depot.*[2] Furthermore, at the time of this writing, Arthur Blank was CEO and owner of the NFL's Atlanta Falcons.

As you can see, although they were dismissed, Bernie Marcus and Arthur Blank were projected to success. Their ordeal led them to achieve a great deal. They ended up better off away from where they were. They were disowned from working for a hardware company and went on to eventually own their own business which redefined the hardware industry. All this did not happen automatically, though. Mr. Marcus, thanks to the sound advice from his friend, Mr. Price, responded properly to his dismissal. Basically, he was encouraged to respond with forgiveness—not to get even with his boss, but to become his own boss and fulfill his destiny.

Entrepreneur Harvey MacKay articulated it best when he said:

Going out to "fix" someone isn't the best way to fix yourself.[3]

In the same token, when you get dismissed, castoff or fired like the business mogul, forgive your detractor and move on with your life. Like Mr. Marcus, make something of yourself. Envision your ordeal as an opportunity for you to achieve a great deal. Refuse to lash back, but strive to make a come back. Don't try to get even, keep believing—and hoping that things are working out for your best. Have faith in yourself and have faith in God.

In addition, if you get rejected, seek out someone who you respect to help you manage the situation. This individual should be someone who will help you make a good sense of the situation, a person who has common sense, not someone who will cause you to do nonsense. Bernie Marcus had Sol Price. You should also find someone who will uplift and stir you in the right direction. If there is no one, there is always God. He is always present in times of trouble. He is always available to help you come out on top. You are never alone. Remember that He is close to those who have a broken heart. If you make your bed in hell, He is with you, how much more if you got thrown into hell—so to speak (Psalm 139:8).

As long as we exist in this life, rejection is inevitable. Overcoming the experience is contingent on how we respond to it. If we snooze we lose; if we use, utilize or take advantage of rejection, we win. With God, we can do all things (Philippians 4:13). He'll cause us to overcome anything.

IT EXPANDS YOUR MINISTRY

Sometimes God allows you to be rejected as a way to draw you away from your detractors to get you to start your own ministry. Not only does He utilize rejection to lead you to pioneer an establishment, He also uses it to expand your ministry. Before I go any further, join me by reading the following passage:

Sometime later Paul said to Barnabas, "Let us go back and visit the brothers in all the towns where we preached the word of the Lord and see how they are doing." Barnabas wanted to take John, but also called Mark, with them, but Paul did not think it wise to take him, because he had deserted them in Pamphylia and had not continued with them in the work. They had such a sharp disagreement that they parted company. Barnabas took Mark and sailed for Cyprus, but Paul chose Silas and left, commended by the brothers to the grace of the Lord. (Acts 15:36-40)

Paul and Barnabas were a ministering team, and they went about evangelizing together. Unfortunately, they got into a serious argument. Their rift was over their assistant, John. Their disagreement about him got so contentious that they parted ways. These two men who had been ministering together for a while separated because of their subordinate.

Their conflict started when Paul rejected John because John had left him and Barnabas during a previous ministry trip. Barnabas did not agree with Paul's decision to leave John behind and, as a result, they split. Barnabas stuck with John while Paul chose another assistant called Silas.

That was an unfortunate development. However, such things happen in ministry. Church, business, and other industry leaders often disagree on the direction they think their ministries should go. Along with that also come disagreements about those who should be on their staff and so forth. John was at the center of Paul and Barnabas' contention. It is possible, however, that Barnabas' insistence to hold onto John was prompted by the fact that John was his cousin (Colossians 4:10).

I wonder how John felt when Paul refused him. Paul completely wrote him off. Paul did not even give him a chance to redeem himself. That sounded harsh. John must have felt hurt, so was Barnabas, his cousin. Paul, one of the foremost leaders of their day, rejected them both and took Silas instead to continue his ministry.

The situation between Paul, Barnabas, and John appeared to be a disappointing conclusion to the work that was carried out by the trio. The ministers parted ways, continuing the ministry separately. Having examined their rift more closely, it occurred to me that their separation turned out to be a win-win situation.

Let's look at what happened shortly after Paul and Barnabas disassociated from each other. Paul and Silas went to an area in Macedonia. During their ministry there, Paul exorcised a demonic spirit that aided a girl in fortune-telling. As a result, she was not able to give divination, and this cost her employers their fortune-telling business. Therefore...

...they seized Paul and Silas and dragged them into the marketplace to face the authorities.... the crowd joined in the attack against Paul and Silas, and the magistrates ordered them to be stripped and beaten. After they had been severely flogged, they were thrown into prison, and the jailer was commanded to guard them carefully. (Acts 16:19-23)

No, I am not saying that Paul and Silas ended up in prison because Paul rejected John and his cousin. However, my point is that Paul and Silas were a better team to handle the opposition that befell them after they departed from their brethren. In retrospect, Paul's decision to dismiss John was on point. Paul might have appeared harsh, but he must have discerned that John was not ready for the persecution that came along with his ministry. He must have reasoned that if John deserted him before, he was likely to do it again when things really got bad.

Whoever was going to be with Paul during his trials would have to be someone with a strong internal fortitude. Paul's initial desire to have Barnabas with him implies that Barnabas was the kind of person who could handle adversity like Paul. But because Barnabas chose to stick with his cousin, Paul had to seek another option. That option was Silas. Silas was given an opportunity to have his name etched in history because his predecessor, John, was fired.

Silas had proven himself in times past as a faithful minister.

He had also been recommended by the apostles. Therefore Paul couldn't have had a better person with him in prison. His competence to be with Paul in prison can be deduced from his reaction to their incarceration. In harmony with his boss, he prayed and sang.

For Paul and Silas, being tossed into prison was a form of rejection. But unbeknownst to those who rejected them, and perhaps to Paul and Silas, they had a purpose in prison. They were rejected for a purpose. Their plight wasn't for them to have choir practice, night vigil, or a revival service in the pen. Their purpose in prison was to help the prisoners and facilitate the salvation of their jailer and his household.

About midnight Paul and Silas were praying and singing hymns to God, and the other prisoners were listening to them. Suddenly there was such a violent earthquake that the foundations of the prison were shaken. At once all the prison doors flew open, and everybody's chains came loose. The Jailer woke up, and when he saw the prison doors open, he drew his sword and was about to kill himself because he thought the prisoners had escaped. But Paul shouted, "Don't harm yourself! We are all here!" The jailer called for lights, rushed in and fell trembling before Paul and Silas. He then brought them out and asked, "Sirs, what must I do to be saved?" They replied, "Believe in the Lord Jesus, and you will be saved—you and your household." Then they spoke the word of the Lord to him and to all the others in his house. At that hour of the night the jailer took them and washed their wounds; then immediately he and all his family were baptized. The jailer brought them into his house and set a meal before them; he was filled with joy because he had come to believe in God—he and his whole family. (Acts 16:25-34)

I believe God allowed Paul and Silas to end up in prison to show those individuals already locked up how to get out of prison. In addition, they ended up in prison to liberate the person who imprisoned them. Not only did he get saved, but his household did as well. Paul and Silas were rejected for a purpose—to set the captives free and to seek and save those who were lost (Luke 4:18-19; 19:10). Paul and Silas ending up in prison was a blessing to the other prisoners and the jailer.

Though their feet, and perhaps their hands. were shackled, Paul and Silas' hearts were not. Their faith in God and belief in Him to deliver them from the prison was not shaken. Rather, what got shaken were the prison doors, the chains, and the man charged to keep them in prison. When Paul and Silas worshipped God, not only did the door to their jail cell open and their chains break, but also the doors and chains of the other prisoners. Paul and Silas' responded to their imprisonment by praying and singing to God. By doing so, they set themselves and their fellow inmates free. ... *all the prison doors flew open, and everybody's chains came loose.*

On realizing this, the jailer was about to commit suicide, but Paul stopped him in time by letting him know that no one had escaped. Whether the other prisoners eventually seized the opportunity to escape remains to be known. But, the most important thing that we can learn is the way Paul and Silas responded to their predicament. By worshipping God, they acknowledged His presence with them and expected something good to come out of their situation.

My friend, that is another example of how to respond to rejection. That is another example of how to get the best out of being rejected. Prior to their incarceration, they only delivered one lady. After their rejection, they delivered the prisoners, the jailer, and the jailer's household. Their ministry was *expanded*. They accomplished more after they were rejected. In fact, being banished to the prison assisted their cause.

I want to report to you, friends, that my imprisonment here has had the opposite of its intended effect. Instead of being squelched, the Message has actually prospered. All the soldiers here, and everyone else, too, found out that I'm in jail because of this Messiah. That piqued their curiosity, and now they've learned all about Him. Not only that, but most of the followers of Jesus here have become far more sure of themselves in the faith than ever, speaking out fearlessly about God, about the Messiah. (Philippians 1:12-14 MSG)

The prison keeper was so astounded by what happened that he could not help but ask the men of God what he had to do to be saved. In response, Paul told him that all he and his household had to do was believe in Jesus Christ. They did, and they got saved. The other prisoners listened to Paul and Silas as they sang to God. Then God's power manifested by shaking the *foundations* of the prison, resulting in the opening of the doors to their cells and the loosening of their chains. The prisoners discovered firsthand what the apostles did to set everyone free.

Drawing nuggets from Paul and Silas' response to their imprisonment, we can also set ourselves free from any prison rejection places us in. Not knowing what to do when you are rejected, or responding inappropriately to it, will leave us hopeless and bound like the other inmates already locked up prior to Paul and Silas' brief visit. By listening to Paul and Silas praise God, the other prisoners found out what they could have done to liberate themselves from their predicament.

In the same way, I hope you've been listening to what I've been saying to you through this discourse. Responding with an attitude of gratitude toward God and believing that He will deliver you will acquit you from any form of rejection you face. God can move heaven and earth to shake the foundations of the prison of rejection designed to hold you down. Did you notice that the foundations where shaken? You see, God will deal with the root of your problem—the core of your rejection. Now when He shakes "it," be ready to deal with it properly, discard it, and then move on with your life. Walk in the liberty that God has afforded you.

Just like Paul and Silas ended up in prison to show the other prisoners and the jailer how to liberate themselves from prison, whether it is a prison made of bars of iron, bars of emotional or psychological bondage, or one built out of alienation from God, God uses how other individual's successfully overcame rejection to help you overcome yours, too.

The prisoners discovered how Paul and Silas responded to their plight. Similarly, there are people bound by their problems. As you will see in a subsequent chapter, you might be the test case to help set them free. You might be the one God allowed to experience their pain so that, through your faith in

God to overcome the situation, you can give hope to others experiencing the same thing and help them be released from their affliction. Paul and Silas ending up in prison facilitated God's agenda in helping the prisoners, the jailer, and his family. Ending up in prison expanded Paul and Silas' ministry.

Julia Stewart started out as a waitress at an International House of Pancakes (IHOP) restaurant close to her home in Southern California. She spent about twenty years, primarily on the marketing side of the dining industry, including tenures at *Burger King* and Stuart Anderson's Black Angus and Cattle Company Restaurants. Her desire was to run a company, and she knew that she had to have experience in operations as well as in the profit and loss side of the restaurant business. With this in mind, she quit her marketing job and opted to start out as an assistant manager at a *Taco Bell* store.

Julia Stewart rose up through the ranks, and, seven years after joining Taco Bell, she was placed in charge of 5600 chains of the franchise. It was at this point in her career that she was hired by Applebee's International as the president of their domestic division. For three years, she worked for Applebee's International. But in 2001, she resigned from the company when she discovered that she was being *passed over* for their CEO position. She didn't get upset for being overlooked for the top job. She was grateful for her experience working for them, and she was even more *inspired* to pursue her goals for the hospitality industry.

In 2002, *IHOP* hired her as their president and CEO. With Julia Stewart at the helm of the restaurant, coupled with the help of her management team, they helped revitalize the dining chain, which was not doing too well. Julia Stewart exemplifies someone who gained from being rejected. At Applebee's, she was just a president of a domestic division. At *IHOP,* she ended up securing a position that added *CEO* to her previous title, and this is just the tip of the iceberg.

In the summer of 2007, *IHOP* successfully placed a bid to acquire Applebee's. Guess who was already positioned to head up America's largest casual dining chain? Yep, you guessed it—the same person who was overlooked for the job six years before. It seems like Julia Stewart got *double* for her trouble. She emerged as *both* president and CEO of *both* IHOP and Applebee's, the combination of which is now known as *DineEquity*.[4] Her ministry was *expanded*. This *promotion* probably contributed to Julia Stewart being named the 49th most powerful businesswoman in 2007 by Fortune magazine.[5]

Chapter 13

It Helps You Find Your Niche

One day in 1998, early in the wee hours of the morning, I was sitting on my couch in my townhouse apartment, watching Dr. Joyce Meyer though a thirteen-inch black-and-white TV. During her telecast, which was then titled *Life in the Word*, she mentioned that if you're seriously struggling with an undertaking, it's likely that God did not call you to it.

That was it! That was what I needed to hear in order to bid good riddance to medical school. I was a biology student in college, aspiring to be a doctor. But I was not enjoying my course of study. In fact, in 1997, I had enrolled in a medical program in the Medical College of Virginia. My performance in the program was fair but not anything to be excited about. Besides, I did not like it. I loathed the cadavers, their formaldehyde smells, and I slept through Dr. Sybel's class about 95 percent of the time. The class felt like a movie theater, since the surgical genius switched off the lights and ran slides of the intricate details of human muscles.

After I received as confirmation what Dr. Meyer said, I knew exactly what I was called to do. Dr. Meyer had also mentioned that you would have a passion for what you were supposed to do. And what I knew I was to do, I had a strong desire for it, alright. There was no question whatsoever in my mind what my calling was. I felt like kicking myself. I should have known

144

all along what my destiny was. And thanks to the Bible teacher, it was brought to my attention. I was going to be a professional *soccer player*. Yipeeee!

By the way, I came to that conclusion after two unsuccessful walk-on tryouts for the Virginia Commonwealth University's (VCU) men's soccer team. After my divine revelation, I went for tryout number three. Approximately five days a week, about fifteen to twenty minutes each day, with the Rocky song, Eye of the Tiger, playing in my head, I jogged about two miles around the block where my apartment was. I also worked on some ball control and ball joggling skills.

In the fall of 1998, yours truly went for my third tryout. With my newfound inspiration, determination, and experience from my first two tryouts, I played my heart out to make it to the team. About forty-five minutes later, with my left knee grazed and bleeding from a nasty contact with the artificial turf, my muscles screaming for oxygen, my chest burning from exhaustion, I sat on the turf with my legs apart like the letter "v," with my hands barely able to hold my aching body up, amid five other formidable contestants and about a dozen onlookers.

The head coach of the VCU Rams soccer team whispered into the ears of the team's Canadian goal keeper-trainer and ex-Rams goalie who assisted him with the tryout, and he walked off. My body was telling me that if this was what it felt like playing for VCU, count me out! But my pride said otherwise. My ego was hoping that I would be picked. After three tryouts and telling everybody from my friends to my parents that soccer is my calling, they had better pick me, I thought.

The goalkeeper coach pointed to two other guys as a gesture to let them know that they were picked for the squad. He also nodded in my direction and thanked the others who did not make the cut for their efforts. The goalkeeper trainer told me and the other two guys who passed the walk-on test when to come and join the team. I limped home with joy galore, but my enthusiasm was short-lived.

Training was no laughing matter. It was business! Other than a friendly introduction from our freshman goalie, who through a twist of fate was charged with the humongous task of being the starting goalie, I did not get any welcome-to-the-team pleasantries from most of the other squad members. Instead, I was welcomed with cold stares and an overdose of adrenalin. During practice, my ankles were met with crunching tackles, my ears were bombarded with expletives when I gaffed on the football pitch, and my body frequently kissed the grass when I got bumped.

Passing the tryout was phase one. Trying to break into a team shirt was phase two, not to mention a position "on the bench." Because the season had already started, I could not officially play for my school. About a week after I joined the team, thanks to the rigorous training and the mandatory "red shirt" the other two walk-ons and I had to wear, it wasn't long before I was the only walk-on left. The other two guys *quit!*

I was made the team manager, a fancy name for the guy who oversees the team's laundry, soccer balls, training equipment, and ensures that there is drinking water in the two, giant, green and black plastic kegs with the Gatorade logo. This was not what I bargained for, but I kept my head up, trained hard and continued to pay my dues. I was the team manager and not an "official" teammate throughout the fall 1998 season.

The NCAA Division One soccer season was usually in the fall, so in the spring of 1999 we just trained. I was still with the team, pursuing my "calling." We were given a break for the summer, but our head coach demanded that we be in shape when we got back in the fall.

During the summer, I hit the gym and ran miles every other day, even in the muggy, blistering, scorching heat. Our assistant coach, who also doubled as our fitness expert, required that each member of the team be able to run two miles in fourteen minutes. I did it in twelve.

Prior to getting back with the team for the fall season, I browsed our website to check the new players and confirm that my name was finally on the roster of the VCU Rams. It wasn't. I cannot begin to tell you my disappointment and feelings of rejection.

I refused to accept the implications of the roster. I still

showed up with my teammates for the mandatory team meeting that we were to have before we commenced training for the fall season. After the meeting, my coach called me aside and apologized that I was not on the squad. One of the new players on the team had eligibility issues and my coach reasoned with me that if things did not work out with the player, I would be the first consideration to take his place.

The player was not eligible; I still wasn't given his place. My place was still in the laundry room, overseeing my teammate's jerseys and hoses. Serving my teammates in lieu of playing officially with them was a very humbling experience. Equally humbling was my experience at a hotel booked for our team for a tournament away from our school. Due to some miscommunication, there were not enough rooms booked for our team. Actually, they were one person short. Guess who? So, I had to bunk with two "fresh men." The hotel improvised by providing a rollaway bed as an addition to the twin beds in the room that was booked for them. As a "senior" student and the fact that I had been with the team a "year" longer than the two freshmen, I did not think that we had to play a game to determine who got the beds and who ended up on the rollaway. Though I did not share my conviction with the fresh-out-of-high school kids, they did not share my sentiment, either. The freshmen decided that we should play "scissors-paper-rock" to figure out who ended up on the rollaway. I lost the game—but I won the rollaway. I did not tell my other teammates, though. I kept it to myself, just like I kept the feelings of rejection of not making it on the squad.

My school upset the University of Maryland on their home field, and, despite our coach's caution to us not to be careless in our next match, we were upset in the next game by American University. We felt the wrath of our coach during training the next day after the loss.

With all that I had stomached for the past year, and feeling that I should no longer kiss the dirt, get knocked down on the soccer field, cramp, pull muscles, press through rigorous training, and occasionally drive the team van, while going to school full-time and holding down a part-time job since I did not make the team, I approached my coach after the training and handed him my resignation papers. Funny thing was...I was never officially hired.

Please don't get me wrong, I was no Pelé, Samuel Eto, Lionel Messi, Christiano Ronaldo, Ronaldinho or Landon Donovan. I could not *bend it like Beckham*, but I could still bend the ball—even though it might end up outside the stadium. All the same, I was as good as some of the players on the team. Furthermore, my unofficial tenure with the team wasn't all doom and gloom. I built camaraderie with the team, and despite being the "team manager," I enjoyed the perks: free sports gear, hotel accommodations, Golden Corral, and the numerous slices of Papa John's pizza that served as our dinner after playing away-games, washed down with cans of Pepsi...yeeaaaah baiiiiibey!

Thanks to my unsuccessful stint with the soccer team, I had more time to dedicate to attending Bible study at my college. Interestingly, the Bible study was organized under the name *VISION*. So, being rejected from the soccer team led me to vision. I was provided for vision—provision; I was also led to God's vision for my life. That was where I fit.

In addition to attending my church and cultivating my personal time with God, going to Bible study was where I began to discover and express my affinity for the gospel. It was my fellowship with other students that emboldened me to minister. It was in the session that I was given a voice, granted an audience and had my first speaking engagement. It was also in Bible study that I received my first leadership position as the president of VISION and experienced relationships and learned reasonable amounts of information that contributed to my messages and my books—this one included.

In Bible study, I was not required to serve; I volunteered to serve. I set the room before our sessions and cleaned up after. I was treated like a teammate. I was embraced, appreciated, and encouraged. I was depended upon; at times I was treated like the *go-to* guy. I did not feel like a fringe player like I did with the Rams. I felt like a major player. I enjoyed it; God made me good at it, and I was called for it! I was not supposed to be in the ministry of football (not NFL); I was supposed to be in the ministry of the gospel. Soccer was not my niche; scripture was.

I still play the game of *futbol* for recreation and to keep myself in shape. Nonetheless, I had no business playing the game professionally. Not being able to break into the college team made that crystal clear, and that helped *redirect* me to what I'm doing now. And for that I'm grateful.

Friend, that is how God uses rejection. He uses it to get you from where you do not *belong* to where you will *be longed*. I believe God used it for John, Paul's assistant, too. I haven't forgotten about him.

IT CAN BE A WIN-WIN SITUATION

Thanks to Paul disapproving John, he was spared from going to prison. Paul actually protected him from getting beaten with rods and thrown into the confines of a prison cell. Considering that he left Paul and Barnabas during a previous trip, Paul's assessment of his strength to handle adversity might have been right. As a minister, I know firsthand what it feels like to think *you have a ministry*. And when you are not allowed to carry out *your ministry*, or better still, the ministry God has entrusted to you, you might feel that you are being hindered.

That might not necessarily be the case. Maybe you are being protected. Perhaps God is using your overseer to shield you from making a fool of yourself. If your boss is anything like Paul, he or she is actually stopping you from falling flat on your face. The person is helping you by rejecting you.

Perhaps you might think that you are ready to run your own ministry. But, you are not ready until God says you are. Judging from Paul and John's case, I don't think it was so much that John wasn't ready for ministry. I think it was because he was not even called for the kind of ministry that Paul and Silas were called for. John didn't strike me as the prison ministry type. Therefore, by not accepting John, Paul assisted him in ending up at the ministry he was to fulfill. Paul unwittingly helped him *find his niche*. But prior to that, Paul pushed him to his cousin, Barnabas.

Barnabas' name means *son of encouragement*. After you

have been refused, it makes sense for you to be encouraged before you dare embark on any form of ministry. If you recall, I mentioned that when you get rejected, you should seek out someone to help you navigate through the disappointment. If there is no one that you can lean on, always know that God is always available for you. Incidentally, John had Barnabas.

I can't imagine the way John must have felt after his mentor dismissed him. Little did he know that he was being protected from getting flogged and locked up. His demotion was replaced by Silas' promotion. Silas was the prison ministry type. But, first, John needed consolation, which I believe he obtained from his cousin. Barnabas must have uplifted him and helped him discover where he actually fit in ministry.

If you can relate with John's plight, perhaps you realize that you were declined not only because you were not ready for the kind of ministry your mentor carried out, but also because God had something else for you to do. In some cases, you may be suited for another leadership. Being restricted by your overseer, supervisor, mentor, or pastor might be an indication that your tenure with your leader is over.

I don't believe that you have to have a conflict with your boss before you flow into your calling, but sometimes we don't listen to God when he tells us to move. We only end up moving after a conflict arises. John had assisted Paul and Barnabas but ended up under his cousin's wing. Being rejected by an authority figure leads you to another ministry. It's imperative to understand that God is getting you around those that would better nurture what He placed in you.

That, however, does not always mean that the leader who turned you down is jealous or intimidated by your gifts. It's likely you were declined in the best interest of the ministry God entrusted your overseer, and in the best interest of the ministry to which God entrusted you. The leader might not know that was why he or she rejected you, though. As in John's case, the person probably thought they fired you because of incompetence or dereliction of duty.

I do know, however, that some leaders are intimidated by their subordinates. They feel threatened by the unique gifts of their assistants. As a result, some fabricate dubious means to oust them from their establishments. I'll talk more about this shortly. Nevertheless, it's to your advantage that you conduct yourself responsibly toward leaders who seem to hinder you either by necessity or by jealousy, because regardless of why they refused you, God is protecting and directing you into His purpose for your life.

John started out with Paul and Barnabas but, after his leadership split, he was left with Barnabas. John must have learned a lot from Paul. He probably learned enough for Barnabas to take over John's ministerial education. Barnabas, as his name implies, probably encouraged and consoled his cousin. He must have also helped him discover and embark on the ministry God had for him.

You know, in the course of ministry, God places us under the auspices of certain leadership. They are to teach us the basics of our respective professions. They are to show us the ropes. Then, after we have been taught the basics by them, God gets us under the leadership of others who will take us to a new level or other dimensions of ministry. Even if we are to launch into a ministry, business or project on our own, there are still things we need to learn to ensure the success of the ministry to which God has entrusted us. The advanced education we need for the new levels in ministry is not always taught by the leadership we started with. That is why we have to transition to other leadership.

Herein lies the problem: sometimes, we don't want to move to other leadership. Sometimes we don't know that we are to transition to another ministry. In such cases, we have delineated a comfort zone. But, God causes us to come to our "come forth" zones. And sometimes He does that through conflict and adversity manifested in the form of rejection.

Friend, if you're in ministry experiencing what I've just discussed, it's likely that God is redefining your role in ministry. Despite the conflict, it is not about your CEO, manager, bishop or leader, it's about fulfilling God's purpose for your life. Don't you forget that the stone which the builders rejected became the chief cornerstone.

While I believe Barnabas played a significant role in John's life, scholars suggest that Peter played the most significant role in his life. It was Peter who they suggest had the most influence in helping John fulfill his ministry. So, what kind of ministry did John end up doing? Well, let's just say that he contributed to the Bible. He's characterized as one of the authors of the four gospels. Every time you read the book of Mark, remember that the individual to whom that book was attributed was the gentleman that Paul rejected.

Rejection ensured that Paul had the right partner in Silas for prison ministry. It also offered John the opportunity to be ministered to and encouraged by Barnabas and influenced by Peter to have his name etched in the living Bible as The Gospel According to Mark.

Oh, by the way, John was better known as "Mark." Scholars say that Peter mentored Mark and was the source of the information for his gospel, as Mark served as his interpreter.[1] The book of Mark is noted for some of the most invaluable and profound insights on faith, prayer, and forgiveness, all of which are necessary for God to respond to our requests (Mark 11:23-25). These virtues are also necessary for us to overcome and benefit from rejection.

Paul did the right thing by cutting off Mark. Paul protected his ministry and redirected Mark to his own. It was a win-win situation. You might not realize nor accept it, but in some cases, when you get rejected, it's in your best interest and that of the person who excluded you. Sometimes, people will not know how valuable you are until they let go of you. You, on the other hand, might be stifled from reaching your potential if you remained in relationship with the person who forsook you.

At times we derive our identity from those we are affiliated with. The problem with this is that we are prone to limiting ourselves to the standards of those with whom we're involved, thereby limiting our creativity and personality. And if those individuals are bad news, they could negatively affect our credibility as well.

We are set free from such relationships when we are kicked out from them. We're liberated to discover and see ourselves for who we are apart from the limited notions of those we were in-

volved with. We are opportuned to exercise and express our
true gifts and reveal our true worth. Once this is accomplished,
don't be surprised when the same people who gave you the cold
shoulder run to you with open arms. With them, and to them,
you were useless. But, apart from them, you became useful. I believe that was the case when Paul wrote in his letter to his pro-
tégé, Timothy:

*...Get Mark and bring him with you, for he is useful to me
for ministry (2 Timothy 4:11 NKJV).*

That suggests to me that sometime after Paul parted with
Mark, he concluded that Mark was useful to him. Paul wrote
that letter while he was in prison. He would have been unable
to request Mark's presence had Mark been in prison, too. But
thanks to Paul dismissing Mark, he was able to protect him
from the ordeals that he went through. It turned out to be a
win-win situation.

Talking about win-win situations, I believe the fourth in-
stallment of the reality TV show, *The Apprentice*, drives my
point. The "controversial" finale saw Dr. Randal Pinkett emerge
as the winner of the competition. When Donald Trump asked
the entrepreneur if he would share his victory with Rebecca
Jarvis, the other finalist, he refused. Dr. Pinkett declined the
offer. In essence, he did not accept Miss Jarvis as a co-winner of
the competition.

Granted that *The Apprentice* is a TV show, assuming that
the outcome of the finale was legit, the rejection that Miss Jarvis
experienced turned out to benefit her. That was evident when
she, Dr. Randal Pinkett, and Donald Trump were interviewed
on *Larry King Live*. While Dr. Pinkett remained and maintained
his victory as the apprentice, Rebecca Jarvis was showered with
other viable options. In fact, despite still having the opportunity to be part of the Trump organization, she opted to consider
the other opportunities that were on her table. At the time of the
interview, she was musing over positions *at Yahoo* and Microsoft.

Technically, had Dr. Pinkett shared his victory with her, she
would not have had the liberty to consider other lucrative
prospects because she would have been contracted to Mr.

Trump. But because she was *turned down* as one of "The Apprentices", she was *turned on* to other prospects.

I hope you are seeing how rejection can help you find your niche and fulfill your destiny. The individuals I talked about came out on top despite being pushed down below. While some dismissed them, others embraced them. While some fired them, others hired them, and those who were not hired pioneered their own gigs. Michael Bloomberg exemplifies this.

He worked for Salomon brothers as a Wall Street trader. During his fifteen years working for the company, he started out as a clerk and rose up through the ranks and became a partner in the investment firm. One day in 1981, he and his colleagues were summoned to a meeting. They were informed that their company was merging with another firm and, as a result, Mr. Bloomberg and his colleagues found themselves without a job.

Mr. Bloomberg did not lose his cool over his sudden unemployment. Perhaps his response was aided by the fact that, together with his termination, he was given ten million dollars, which was his cut from the sale of the company. He turned those millions into billions.

After he was fired, Michael Bloomberg went from being a partner at a firm to being an owner of his own establishment. He went from just being *Michael Bloomberg* to being Bloomberg News, Bloomberg Radio, Bloomberg TV and Bloomberg LP, the top financial information network in the world. His establishment supplies nonstop financial data to 126 countries and generates over three billion dollars in revenues each year. Also, since 2001, Mr. Bloomberg doubled as the mayor of New York City, and he resumed his second term in office after winning his reelection by a landslide.[3]

Dear reader, being fired might never enable you to become a billionaire but you can still do something extraordinaire. You might never pioneer an establishment, but you can still establish yourself. You might never run a city, but you can still run your life successfully.

That is how God employs rejection. He uses it to inspire and liberate you to start your own ministry. He uses it to help you find your niche. He uses it to help you redeem yourself from your past failures. He uses it to promote you and make a name for yourself. At the end of the day, once you realize that being rejected benefits you and the person who turned you down, you'll realize that being rejected was a win-win situation.

On a side note, when I said that God uses rejection to help you start your own ministry, I was in no way endorsing rebellion. I know that many of us find it hard to be submissive. I'm fully aware that instead of serving under someone else's directives, most of us would rather do "our own thing." I believe that there are a lot of ministries, businesses, and projects out there established by individuals who have no ethics and who are rebellious and selfish. Truth be told, it will just be a matter of time before their establishments crumble.

I am not saying that God utilizes rejection to help individuals who are unfaithful, lazy, and lack integrity to do their own thing. I believe such individuals should humble themselves and submit to their leadership and not use this chapter as a crutch to justify their insubordination. God does not honor rebellion—neither do I.

My discussion is only applicable to individuals who are faithful, hardworking, and conduct themselves with integrity, while submitting to their leadership. However, despite the good work ethic by some of these individuals, they still get mistreated by their leaders. What I'm saying is that sometimes God uses such experiences to inspire, liberate, and prepare such individuals for His plan for their lives. He utilizes it to promote, protect, and provide them for the vision He placed in their hearts. He takes advantage of the rejection they experienced to redeem and redirect the dismissed faithful few to find their niches and start and expand their own ministries.

Chapter 14
Experiencing It from a Leader

Now, I'll address the issue of leaders being intimidated by their subordinates. This happens a lot in organizations across the globe. Some up-and-coming ministers, executives, and other apprentices bear the brunt of their leader's jealousy. In some cases, some of them quit their ministry or industry because of the adversities and injustices they experience from their mentors. Oftentimes, these individuals are rejected by their leaders because their bosses feel threatened that their subordinates will outperform them and take over their establishments.

In addressing this issue, let us take a look at David, the guy who put his name on the map by slaying Goliath. As a result of this exploit, he quickly won the admiration of the king of Israel, Saul. Prior to beheading Goliath, David was Saul's armor bearer (1 Samuel 16:21). After David slew the giant, Saul made him the leader over a thousand of his soldiers (1 Samuel 18:5 & 13). Everything started going downhill when Saul and David were coming back home after David killed Goliath.

When the men were returning home after David had killed the Philistine, the women came out from all the towns of Israel to meet King Saul with singing and dancing, with joyful songs and with tambourines and lutes. As they danced, they sang: "Saul has slain his thousands, and David his tens of thou-

sands." Saul was very angry; this refrain galled him. "They have credited David with tens of thousands," he thought, "but me with only thousands. What more can he get but the kingdom?" And from that time on Saul kept a jealous eye on David. (1 Samuel 18:6-9)

Saul's animosity against David was triggered by the women who gave more praise to David than to him. Saul felt insecure after hearing the way the women adored David more than they adored him. But you know what? Saul's problem with David was triggered by what the women said. It was ignited by what others said. It was instigated by hearsay. How can a king dislike the newfound asset to his kingdom based on what other people said? You know, that is the same thing that happens in ministry, relationships, family, and industry. Somebody begins to dislike someone they liked previously just because a third party said something that is often not true—or half true.

Someone once said:

A half truth is a whole lie.

We can corroborate that maxim when we reexamine the women's claim. They said that Saul killed thousands, which was probably true considering scripture references that reveal the wars Saul fought. They also said that David killed tens of thousands. That was absolutely not true. Prior to the women's comments, David had only killed a lion, a bear, and Goliath, one man and two animals. That is not even close to five, much less ten thousand. Yet, a leader was miffed with his subordinate because of something he heard—which was not true. Even so, the seeds of spite had been sown in Saul's heart against David.

And it happened on the next day that the distressing spirit from God came upon Saul.... So David played music with his hand, as at other times; but there was a spear in Saul's hand. And Saul cast the spear, for he said, I will pin David to the wall! But David escaped his presence twice. (1 Samuel 18:10-11 NKJV)

Saul was out to get David. Ever since he heard the remarks from the women, Saul's perception of David changed. As a result, he opened himself to a distressing spirit. Not long after that, he attempted to kill David with a spear. Did you notice the sequence of events? First, he was jealous. Second, he was out to destroy David. Third, he inadvertently opened the door of his heart for a distressing spirit to come and influence him to do the fourth—kill David.

That is the same sequence of events that can take place in us when we are out to malign people whom we dislike. We open ourselves up for evil spirits to influence us to murder people. We might not murder them physically, but we can murder them by slandering them. We can attack them by using our words like lethal weapons, hauling them like spears to pin the reputation of those we detest to the wall of destruction.

Saul tried to stab David but missed his target. If you are like David and you are under the leadership of someone like Saul, I have good news for you: your leader's attempt to take you out will not prevail. The person's spear of rejection will miss you. The individual can't pin you. You will not be immobilized. You will not be held down. Like David, you will escape.

Let's look closely at how David handled his situation with Saul. This is important because his response to Saul's animosity toward him helped him through the ordeal. Furthermore, if you're going through similar experiences like David had with Saul, the same principles he used to survive Saul are available for you to use to overcome your adversary. The last scripture mentioned that David escaped twice. Why David waited for Saul to throw a spear at him the second time eludes me, but Saul missed his target again.

In response to Saul's attack, David did not take the spear and retaliate. Twice, David did not attack Saul. He did not try to *stab him back*. He escaped from the presence of Saul and simply turned the other cheek. David's noble and mature response to Saul's attacks did not stop Saul's attempts on David's life—at least, initially. However, David's response to Saul's attacks ensured that David was in right standing with God.

And David behaved wisely in all his ways, and the LORD was with him. Therefore when Saul saw that he behaved very wisely, he was afraid of him. (1 Samuel 18:14-15 NKJV)

David responded to Saul with wisdom. In doing so, he ensured that God was with him. Even Saul was befuddled by David's action. David behaved wisely, and God was with him. Similarly, you are to behave *wisely*, not *wildly*, in response to a leader's animosity against you. Proverbs 16:7 basically says that when a man or (woman's) ways please the Lord, God will make even the individual's enemy to be at peace with him or her. It is important that you act with wisdom in responding to the person trying to destroy you.

David's response to Saul reminds me of a piece of wisdom that I learned from Dr. John Maxwell:

No matter what our circumstances, our greatest limitations isn't the leader above us...it's the spirit within us.[1]

David had to escape from the presence of Saul lest the king annihilate him. Facing the same circumstances as David, if your life is being threatened by your boss, you will have to part with him or her, even if it means leaving the ministry, business or establishment where you served under the leader. Mind you, the reason you should leave is because your overseer is after your life. When anyone is trying to harm you physically or psychologically, it is in your best interest to leave the presence of that individual.

Now, David escaped, but he did not speak against Saul nor instigate others to slander him. Though Saul's hatred for David was public, the public's awareness of Saul's attempt at David's life was not obtained from David. David did not go around telling everybody what Saul was trying to do to him. Similarly, in dealing with a leader's rejection, you should not be broadcasting the issue to your hairstylist, barber, babysitter, or your dog. If someone is after your life, of course, you should relay this information to the authorities to protect yourself, however, you want to ensure that the proper authorities are involved, not every Tom, Dick, and Hanifa.

When David had fled and made his escape, he went to Samuel at Ramah and told him all that Saul had done to him.... (1 Samuel 19:18)

In David's case, he stated his case to Samuel, the prophet, a bonafide authority figure ordained by the Most High, a man of God. David was following the proper protocol. He reported

Saul to Samuel. David's action was indicative of him submitting the situation to God. God is a God of order. He wants things done decently and in order (1 Corinthians 14:40). Even the justice system requires order in court before any case can be heard. Regardless of how hideous a crime is or how battered the plaintiff is, the system still requires that things are done in order, and anyone out of order would be held in contempt of the court.

You know, it is the same thing with God. It doesn't matter who hurt you or what was done to you, He requires you, in presenting your petition to Him, to present it decently and in order. He requires you to follow His divine protocol. Your boss or leader being out of order does not give you wherewithal to be out of order, too. If your overseer is out of order, like David, you stay in order. Be wise—and God will be with you. If you lash back at your leader, God is now compelled to deal with two people who are out of order. Assuming God hired your boss, He most certainly has the right to fire him. You want to make sure that God does not fire you, too, or, allow judgment on you.

Samuel was the prophet God used to anoint and appoint Saul as king. David presented his case to Samuel. In essence it was up to God to deal with Saul not David. What David had to do was escape and go out of his way to avoid Saul as well as not smear the king's name. In dealing with a leader's rejection, you might have to go out of your way not to lash back and speak against the person. You have to step back and let God deal with his servant. Even if it looks like your boss is getting away with his or her conspiracy against you, trust that God is on the case way more than Perry Mason.

There is a possibility that God will influence the person to repent and make amends with you. If that does not happen, that leader's life is definitely on the line. By staying in order, you are ensuring that your life is not on the line, too. If both you and your leader cannot have a happy ending after such an ordeal, then you ensure that *you* have the happy ending.

Another thing that struck me was that David did not ostracize Saul's kids. Like I mentioned earlier, it is not fair for us to think that those affiliated with people who are against us, dislike us, too. Jonathan and Milcah were Saul's son and daughter respectively. Jonathan was David's best friend, and Milcah was his wife. David did not detest Jonathan or Milcah because of their father's behavior toward him. He didn't conclude that Jonathan and Milcah were against him because their father was trying to kill him. He maintained his relationship with them. In fact, at the expense of their relationship with their father, they helped David escape from their father's attempts to kill David (1 Samuel 19).

Saul did not relent with his attempts on David's life. He summoned 3,000 men, and they embarked on a manhunt for David. During his quest for David's whereabouts, Saul was moved to relieve himself, so he went into a cave to answer nature's call. Unbeknownst to him, David was in the vicinity. David and his men were hiding within the recesses of the cave. David's men concluded that God had delivered Saul into his hand and encouraged David to take him out. But, David refused. Despite the ample opportunity to avenge and defend his life, David refused to lay a finger on Saul. He only cut part of Saul's cloth as a token to let Saul know that he had the opportunity to kill him but decided otherwise (1 Samuel 24:1-4).

Why didn't David kill Saul? Why didn't he assassinate the man who was making life miserable for him? Why didn't he just get him back? Because David understood protocol. David understood that he would have been out of order to kill Saul because God had anointed Saul as king. It was not David's place to take Saul out. That was God's call. God hired him, so God should fire him.

In your encounter with a leader like Saul, you will have people who are on your side. There will be individuals close to you who will encourage you to lash back at the authority figure who is out to get you. They might even tell you that it is God's will for you to do so. Just like David had the opportunity to kill Saul while the king was relieving himself, you will have opportunities to destroy, discredit, and denounce your adversary when he or she is in their most vulnerable state. And, the people in your camp like your friends, colleagues, and family members will urge you to avenge yourself, professing that God is the one who has giving you the opportunity.

Friend, don't you make that mistake! Every opportunity that God gives you is an opportunity to prove your faithfulness—or foolishness. God will test you with people. In doing so, He will bring situations across your path for you to prove your integrity—or lack of it. It does not matter who tells you to do otherwise "in the name of God." Always make decisions that are consistent with God's Word. David did. David was no fool; he was faith-full. He understood that it was God that promoted Saul; therefore, it was up to God to demote Saul. So, he didn't kill Saul, neither did he let his men touch him.

And he said to his men, "The LORD forbid that I should do this thing to my master, the LORD'S anointed, to stretch out my hand against him, seeing he is the anointed of the LORD." So David restrained his servants with these words, and did not allow them to rise against Saul.... (1 Samuel 24:6-7 NKJV)

David was able to spare Saul's life because he recognized that Saul, despite his faults and insecurities, was "The Lord's Anointed." This suggests that attacking your overseer shows that you do not recognize the person as the Lord's anointed. Take note that your leader is the Lord's anointed, not your anointed; not your grandma's anointed, not your best friend's anointed, but the Lord's anointed. Whether your leader was genuinely ordained by God might remain to be known. Even so, you will never go wrong by letting God handle your boss.

...Saul got up from the cave and went his way. David also arose afterward, went out of the cave, and called out to Saul, saying, "My Lord the king!" And when Saul looked behind him, David stooped with his face to the earth, and bowed down. (1 Samuel 24:7-8 NKJV)

Let us look at some interesting points at that scripture. Did you notice how David approached the man who was after his life? David called him *My Lord; the king....* He even bowed down before him. It takes a lot of character to stare at your adversary and respond to the person with such meekness and humility. Despite the animosity and rejection he experienced from Saul, David still acknowledged Saul's authoritative position in word and deed, as evidenced by the way he paid homage to him.

David told Saul that he had the opportunity to kill him. In fact, his men urged him to kill Saul. But David declined. He passed over the opportunity because he recognized that Saul was *his Lord* and the *Lord's anointed.* Basically this was David's attitude toward Saul:

Let the LORD judge between you and me, and let the LORD avenge me on you. But my hand shall not be against you. (1 Samuel 24:12 NKJV)

Therefore let the LORD be judge, and judge between you and me, and see and plead my case, and deliver me out of your hand. (1 Samuel 24:15 NKJV)

And how did Saul respond to David's nobility?

...And Saul lifted up his voice and wept. Then he said to David: "You are more righteous than I; for you have rewarded me with good, whereas I have rewarded you with evil. "And you have shown me this day how you have dealt well with me; for when the LORD delivered me into your hand, you did not kill me. (1 Samuel 24:16-18 NKJV)

"And now I know indeed that you shall surely be king, and that the kingdom of Israel shall be established in your hand. (1 Samuel 24:20 NKJV)

The way David responded to Saul is the way we are to respond to any pastor, archbishop, coach, CEO or administrator who is trying to destroy us. David responded with the awareness that God would judge his adversary. Even Saul was humbled by David's attitude toward him. If you recall, Proverbs 16:7 paraphrased says that when your ways please God, He will make your enemies be at peace with you. Saul, out of his own mouth, said that David was more righteous than he was. He stated that David rewarded his evil with good.

Never pay back evil with more evil. Do things in such a way that everyone can see you are honorable. Do all that you can to live in peace with everyone. Dear friends, never take revenge. Leave that to the righteous anger of God. For the Scriptures say, "I will take revenge; I will pay them back," says the LORD. Instead, "If your enemies are hungry, feed them. If they are thirsty, give them something to drink. In doing this, you will heap burning coals of shame on their heads." Don't let evil conquer you, but conquer evil by doing good. (Romans 12:17-21 NLT)

David applied those passages, scriptures that did not exist until thousands of years after his death. Like David, you should reward your head's evil against you with good. Your goodness is an ingredient of your love. Your response to the rejection you experience from your leader should be one of love.

But I say to you love your enemies, bless those who curse you, and pray for those who spitefully use you and persecute you. (Matthew 5:44 NKJV)

I know that this might sound unreasonable and farfetched. I know that responding with love to someone who you trusted and looked up to, someone who is now trying to destroy you, sounds very difficult and unrealistic. It definitely does not make sense. But if you want to come out on top of the situation, I suggest you follow God's instruction. He is the One avenging you. He knows what He is doing. In fact, He is working out the situation for your benefit. Consider that your leader is doing you a favor by rejecting you.

He or she is pushing you away from him or herself to your destiny. Having this understanding should help you embrace your leader's animosity against you. By rejecting you, your leader is inadvertently preventing you from learning his or her dubious ways, since the individual does not want to be around you. By rejecting David, Saul hindered David from being affiliated with him and, as a result, prevented David from learning the king's questionable character. It also assisted David in arriving at his destiny.

Chapter 15
It Gets You to Your Rightful Place

Prior to Saul's hostility against David, Saul had designated David, who was a skillful harp player, to be the harpist who played music for him anytime he felt distressed. He also made David the head of a thousand of his men and allowed him the task of carrying his armor. But, God did not plan for David to be Saul's private solo orchestra. Neither did He purpose for David to be Saul's armor bearer nor captain of a thousand of Saul's men. David's destiny was to be the king, not the king's entertainer, armor bearer, or officer (1 Samuel 16:21; 18:5 & 13).

Saul basically rejected David to his purpose. With this in mind, your leader, in an effort to hinder you from taking his or her position, is actually assisting you to obtain the position he or she is trying so hard not to lose. That position is part of God's purpose for your life. God is using your boss's rejection to re-eject you to your destiny. He is utilizing it to push you to your calling.

David's respectful behavior toward Saul could not help but cause the king to finally spill the beans. Saul had to admit that David was a better man for the kingship than he was. He conceded that David was going to be the king and that he would establish the kingdom of Israel. Saul finally confessed what was eating him all along after the Israelite women sang more praises to David than to himself. David was the one that God appointed to take his spot. Saul's discontentment actually started way before David slew Goliath.

The Israelites had demanded for a king and God gave them Saul (1 Samuel 8:1-5). God used the prophet, Samuel, to anoint Saul as king. God had asked Saul to destroy Amalek, a nation that ambushed the Israelites on their way from captivity in Egypt (1 Samuel 15:1-2). God was basically avenging what the Amalekites did against his people. God instructed Saul to spare no one. He was not even supposed to spare the animals. But Saul did otherwise. He spared Amalek's king, the best of the animals, and the best spoils that they had obtained from their raid on Amalek. God was displeased with Saul's disobedience and, rejected Saul from being king.

God rejected Saul because Saul rejected God's Word. He did not obey God's commandment and, therefore, God rejected him from being the king of Israel (1 Samuel 15:23-26). Samuel was the one God used to relay the bad news to Saul. Saul did not take the news too well. In fact, he assaulted Samuel by grabbing the edge of the prophet's robe, which tore in the process. In response, Samuel told him that just as he tore his robe, so was the kingdom of Israel torn from Saul (1 Samuel 15:27-28). Did you notice something else? Saul assaulted an authority figure. Big mistake! Did you see what I've been trying to relay to you regarding how to deal with a leader?

Unlike David, Saul was out of order in the way he treated the prophet of God. Though he was upset about the information God gave Samuel to tell him, his reaction to God's rejection was disrespectful. His response to his demotion reinforced God's judgment on Saul. The kingdom was torn from him. For sure, Israel was taken from Saul and was given to another man better than Saul. That man turned out to be David.

Perhaps you noticed the sharp contrast between the way David responded to Saul's rejection and the way Saul responded to Samuel's rejection. I believe David and Saul's respective responses determined their fates. Saul lost the kingdom, while David gained it.

Despite the heartwarming exchange between David and Saul, even though David spared Saul's life, you'd think Saul would have called a truce with David (1 Samuel 24:8-22). You'd think the problem between Saul and David had been resolved. But, no, it had not. It was not long after David and Saul separated and went their separate ways that Saul got his 3,000 men again to go look for David (1 Samuel 26:1-2).

Saul was given intelligence about the area where David was hiding. So he proceeded with his troops to look for David. On the course of their quest, Saul and his troops set up camp in an area so that they could rest. Meanwhile, David was already aware that Saul was after him again. He also found out where Saul and his men were encamped. At night, David then took one of his men, Abishai, to scope out exactly where Saul was resting.

When David and Abishai got to the place where Saul was resting, they found Saul and his men sleeping.

So David and Abishai came to the people by night; and there Saul lay sleeping within the camp....Then Abishai said to David, "God has delivered your enemy into your hand this day. Now therefore, please let me strike him at once with the spear, right to the earth; and I will not have to strike him a second time!" But David said to Abishai, "Do not destroy him; for who can stretch out his hand against the LORD's anointed, and be guiltless?"..."As the LORD lives, the LORD shall strike him, or his day shall come to die, or he shall go out to battle and perish. "The LORD forbid that I should stretch out my hand against the LORD's anointed...."(1 Samuel 26:7-11 NKJV)

On seeing that Saul and his men were sleeping, Abishai concluded that God had provided an opportunity for David to kill Saul. In fact, Abishai volunteered to execute Saul. He just needed David to give him the green light. But David refused. Again, note how David responded to his man's encouragement to assassinate Saul. David was cognizant that Saul was appointed by God and that he had no right whatsoever to kill Saul. The following scripture gives credence to David's response to Abishai's instigation:

Who are you to judge another's servant? To his own master he stands or falls. Indeed, he will be made to stand, for God is able to make him stand. (Romans 14:4)

Saul was God's anointed. He was God's servant. And to God, he was held accountable. David understood this, that was why David dissuaded Abishai from killing Saul. I hope you understand this, too. Your leader is accountable to God, not to you. It is God that deals with him or her. You have no right whatsoever to judge your boss regardless of his or her flaws. It is to his or her master, God, that your leader accounts and either stands or falls. According to David, "Who can stretch out his hands against the LORD'S anointed and be guiltless?"

If you are someone who has undergone the pain of being mistreated by your leader, you do not want to compound your situation by falling under God's judgment. Let God reserve His judgment to his servant over you, not to you. You will be free from God's judgment by following God's order. Like David said, the leader coming against you will be judged by God. If the person does not relent from harming you, the individual is subject to death. Death could be in the form of the person's demise, divorce, the death of his or her ministry, industry, business, establishment or possibly ending up behind bars.

Furthermore, it is in your best interest that you go out of your way not to slander your leader and ensure that others close to you do not discredit the individual, either. Abishai wanted to harm Saul, but David prevented him. Abishai was actually David's nephew. He was the son of David's sister, Zeruiah (1 Chronicles 2:13-16). Abishai was a member of David's family.

Family members, close friends, and acquaintances that are aware of your leader's ways will incite you to attack your overseer. They will speak against your boss. You do what you can to dissuade them from doing this. Though you cannot control their actions, you want to ensure that you do whatever is in your power to stop them from harming your leader. By doing so, not only are you walking in God's will, you are also protecting your family, friends, and well-wishers from God's judgment. If they refuse and proceed to slander your leader anyway, that's okay; that's between them and God. You just stay in God's will and let God deal with his servant.

It is interesting that Saul tried to pin David with a spear twice, and David was opportuned to kill Saul twice. Saul missed his target twice, and David passed over the opportunity twice. Saul eventually got his reward for trying to harm David. Might I remind you that David is now "The Lord's anointed?" Unlike David, Saul had the nerve to attack the man God anointed as king. Saul experienced the repercussion of basically disobeying God. His disobedience manifested in the form of rejecting God's Word, rejecting Samuel, God's prophet, and rejecting David, God's anointed.

Who can stretch out his hand against the Lord's anointed and be guiltless? Saul attacked God's anointed, David. Therefore, he was found guilty. There was a war between the Israelites and the Philistines. Saul's three sons were killed during the war. In addition, Saul was severely wounded by the arrows that projected from the bows of the Philistine archers. Saul did not want to be found injured and tortured, so he asked the guy who carried his armor to kill him with his sword. His armor bearer refused to kill him so Saul took a sword and fell on it. Another man found Saul still not dead from his botched suicide. Saul then asked the guy to end his misery. The young man obliged Saul's request and finished him off (1 Samuel 31; 2 Samuel 1:6-10).

Later on, the young man escaped from Saul's camp and met David and his men. He told David that Saul and his sons had died in the war. David then asked him how he knew about the death of Saul and Jonathan, Saul's son and David's best friend. He explained to David that he found Saul leaning on his spear, and his enemy's horsemen and chariots were coming after him. So, Saul asked the young man, who happened to be "Amalekite," to perform a mercy killing on him. After the young man killed Saul, he took Saul's crown and bracelet and brought them to David (2 Samuel 1:1-10).

Is it not noteworthy that Saul could not kill David with his spear, yet he killed himself with his own spear? If you deal with your leader with wisdom, if you go out of your way not to speak against the person ensuring that God protects you while He deals with your boss, your leader's attempts at your life will come back to haunt the person. Your adversary will fall into the pit he or she dug for you. It seems like the spear that Saul hurled at David, like a boomerang, made a 180 degree turn from David and came back to pierce him.

Saul's death shows the possible consequence of attacking someone God has anointed. God's Word is anointed. Jesus is the Word and also the Anointed One, hence, He is the Christ. So when Saul rejected God's Word, disrespected Samuel, and attacked David, he came against the Lord's anointed. Finally, he reaped the consequences of his own actions. He lost his job; he lost his sons, and he lost his life.

Despite the death of his enemy just like David said it would happen, David was upset that the young man was not scared to kill Saul. David was miffed that the Amalekite had the nerve to kill the Lord's anointed. As a result, David gave orders for the man to be executed, and the young man was killed (1 Samuel 31:1-6, 2 Samuel 1:1-16).

Even though Saul was going to die anyway without the young man touching Saul, David was upset with the guy because he killed Saul. I didn't really get it at first, but understanding the sacredness of not messing with someone that God has ordained gave me some clarity. Even when your leader is reaping the seeds of discord that he or she sowed against you, don't interfere with your leader's judgment. Don't help God out. Let God take care of him or her. In Saul's case, had the young man not killed him, the Philistines would have annihilated him. They would have probably tortured him first, but they would have snuffed out Saul.

I believe Saul's armor bearer reverenced Saul's position as king; that was why he refused to kill Saul when Saul asked him to. But, the Amalekite in his ignorance, and thinking that David would be pleased with him for killing Saul and bringing Saul's crown and bracelet to David, was given a rude awakening.

Do not be like the Amalekite and kill your leader even when the person is in his or her most vulnerable state. If the person who has been after you is dying slowly, let the person die slowly. Don't catalyze the person's death. Do not sign your own death warrant. The judgment is for your boss, not for you.

Keep it that way. You've held on this far. You've been patient. You've weathered the storm. Don't mess things up now that you are close to being finally free from your adversary.

If you have been coming against your leader, I encourage you to ask God to forgive you. You probably lashed back out of anger, and you might not have been properly informed on how to handle the adversity. Perhaps things have gotten harder for you since your ordeal with your overseer. Perhaps you are experiencing the results of attacking the person who is out to get you. Armed with the information pertaining to how to respond to your leader, begin to apply it.

If you have slandered your boss and instigated others to malign the person, too, again, I urge you to ask God to forgive you. You might also need to go to the person to apologize and ask for forgiveness. Yes, I know it is tough and unfair. But, you know what? That might be the answer to turning your situation around. Your apology is just a reflection of your stance to follow God's divine protocol. It is more about you expressing your heart's sincerity in letting God take over the situation. It is also a way for you to wash your hands of any dirt you might have thrown at your leader.

By apologizing, you are making a positive change in response to your leader's rejection, and you are not taking God's forgiveness in vain. You are expressing your repentance from dead works—dead works of trying to avenge yourself. You are responding in love to your adversary. You are also allowing God to reverse any judgment that might have befallen you due to your attempts at getting even with your leader.

Saul lost his throne to David because of his disobedience. And, once again, David demonstrated his competence at being king, not only by how he respectfully handled Saul, but by the fact that he ordered the execution of the Amalekite—something that Saul did not do.

Ironically, Saul lost credibility with God because He did not kill the Amalekites like God had asked him to. Saul was supposed to kill everyone and every animal in Amalek, but he spared Amalek's king. In contrast, the young man from Amalek did not bat an eye in killing Saul, the Israelite king. The very "thing" that God instructed Saul to kill, but he did not kill, ended up killing him. He was instructed to take out all the Amalekites but didn't. An Amalekite ended up killing him.

The same applies to us. If we don't get rid of things that God wants us to get rid of, those things will get rid of us. In the context of this book, if we don't handle rejection properly, rejection will handle us improperly. If we don't get rid of rejection by responding to it with faith, hope, and love, it will get rid of us with hate, hopelessness, and loss. It will render us bitter, depressed, and unfruitful.

Chapter 16
Experiencing It from Followers

Thankfully, not all leaders are insecure. There are some genuine individuals who conduct their affairs with honesty and humility. You would think that leaders who conduct themselves as such would be widely accepted. Unfortunately, that is not the case. There are leaders who carry themselves with integrity and lead in the best interest of those who follow them, yet they still get ridiculed and underappreciated. I would be doing a disservice to such leaders by not deliberating on the fact that they get rejected too, even when they are doing everything within their power to help those who have been placed under their care.

Moses is a prime example of a leader who did his best to help the children of Israel, yet he was rejected by most of them. God appointed him to lead his children out of bondage in Egypt. Moses' assignment was to liberate them from the hands of Pharaoh and get them to the Promised Land. Perhaps you are familiar with Moses demanding from Pharaoh the release of his people from Egypt. And each time Pharaoh rebuffed Moses' demand, he and his people were subjected to plagues, ten in all.

Under extreme duress, Pharaoh eventually released the Israelites and Moses led them out of Egypt. On the way to the land God promised them, the Israelites faced what appeared to be a setback as they were caught betwixt the Red Sea and

Pharaoh's army, which the Egyptian leader sent to recapture the Israelites after he rescinded his decision to let them go. God instructed Moses to stretch a rod in his hand over the sea, and the water parted, resulting in a pathway through which the Israelites crossed the water. When the Egyptian army got on the path in their pursuit of the Israelites, God brought the water back, and the entire army drowned (Exodus 14:5-7, 15-28). Hence, God delivered Israel from Egypt through the man He appointed as leader over them—Moses.

For some of us, little else is known about Moses and his people after the miracle at the Red Sea. To a degree, part of Moses' mission had been accomplished. He got his people out of Egypt. The second phase of his mission was to get them into the Promised Land.

EXPERIENCING IT FROM YOUR ASSISTANTS

The LORD said to Moses, "Send some men to explore the land of Canaan, which I am giving to the Israelites. From each ancestral tribe send one of its leaders." (Numbers 13:1-2)

Canaan was the land God promised His people. He instructed Moses to send out twelve leaders representing the twelve tribes of Israel to canvass the land and bring back a report on the place that He was giving them. Moses appointed the twelve men and sent them on their mission. After they fulfilled their mission, they came back to Moses and the people to give their report. The men confirmed that the land was rich and "flowing with milk and honey" just like God told Moses. Unfortunately, ten of the men told Moses and the Israelite people that they would not be able to possess the land because there were giants in the land.

But the men who had gone up with him said, "We can't attack those people; they are stronger than we are." And they spread among the Israelites a bad report about the land they had explored. They said, "The land we explored devours those living in it. All the people we saw there are of great size. We saw the Nephilim there (the descendants of Anak come from the Nephilim). We seemed like grasshoppers in our own eyes, and we looked the same to them." (Numbers 13:31-33)

Despite the negative analysis given by ten of the men, two

men saw the light. They were Joshua and Caleb. Caleb encouraged the people and told them that they would be able to take over the land.

Then Caleb silenced the people before Moses and said, "We should go up and take possession of the land, for we can certainly do it." (Numbers 13:30)

Caleb's optimism, however, came a little too late. The negative report given by his ten colleagues had already raised concerns with the Israelite people. They were scared for their lives and they *complained against* Moses and his brother, Aaron, who assisted him.

So all the congregation lifted up their voices and cried, and the people wept that night. And all the children of Israel complained against Moses and Aaron, and the whole congregation said to them, "If only we had died in the land of Egypt! Or if only we had died in this wilderness! Why has the LORD brought us to this land to fall by the sword, that our wives and children should become victims? Would it not be better for us to return to Egypt?" So they said to one another, "Let us select a leader and return to Egypt." (Numbers 14:1-4 NKJV)

It appeared that the children of Israel developed a sudden attack of amnesia. How quickly they seemed to have forgotten that they defied the laws of science and passed through the Red Sea. Did they not recall that they were crying out so much that God heard their groaning? And, did they forget that with miraculous signs and wonders through Moses, God led them out of Egypt, their land of bondage, to get them to the land of bounty, the Promised Land?

Yet, the people who were crying due to their suffering in Egypt were crying out to go back to Egypt. They even had the gall to propose to appoint a new leader. As far as they were concerned, Moses' leadership skills were suspect. Moses must not have known what he was doing.

If you are a *good* leader, perhaps a pastor, foreman, manager, supervisor, coach, superintendent, administrator, director, or CEO, does this sound familiar to you? Despite your efforts to ensure the welfare of your congregants, subordinates, team, colleagues or employees, when things seem to go wrong, they are out for your throat. All of a sudden your successful track record in leading them does not count. They question your leadership and begin to look for someone else to take your place. In some cases, the reason they "disapprove" of your directives is because they have unconsciously appointed another leader in your stead. That new leader or leaders are the individuals who, like the ten spies, incited your followers against you.

IT KEEPS YOU IN GOD'S WILL

But Joshua...and Caleb who were among those who had spied out the land, tore their clothes; and they spoke to all the congregation of the children of Israel, saying: "The land we passed through to spy out is an exceedingly good land. If the LORD delights in us, then He will bring us into this land and give it to us....Only do not rebel against the LORD, nor fear the people of the land...the LORD is with us. Do not fear them." (Numbers 14:6-9 NKJV)

Joshua and Caleb tried to persuade their people to be courageous and trust God to help them possess the land.

But the whole assembly talked about stoning them.... (Numbers 14:10)

Instead of heeding their leaders, the people opted to stone them. Instead of attacking the challenge they faced in the Promised Land, they chose to attack Moses and the men who stood by him. Little did they know that they were not only resisting their leaders, they were also resisting God.

Then the LORD said to Moses: "How long will these people reject Me? And how long will they not believe Me, with all the signs which I have performed among them?" (Numbers 14:11 NKJV)

If you are exercising the gift of leadership that God gave you to help the people whom you oversee, but the people you are trying to help are coming against you, I've got good news for you: God takes it personally. When you are being rejected, God feels He is being rejected, too. He feels rejected because the people are rejecting the gift He placed in you to lead them to His purpose for them. God's purpose for the Israelites was to ultimately possess Canaan. Yet, the people were ready to stone Moses and the men who stood by him.

I have more good news for you. By coming against their leaders, the children of Israel kept them in God's will and on God's side. Therefore, when your people come against you, they are helping you stay in God's will. This means that they are helping you stay within God's jurisdiction and protection. Like Moses, don't let the threats of the people you oversee abort the mission that God assigned you to lead. Don't let their fear, unbelief, and cowardice derail you. Let their rejection keep you on the right track.

Count yourself blessed every time someone cuts you down or throws you out, every time someone smears or blackens your name to discredit me. What it means is that the truth is too close for comfort and that that person is uncomfortable. You can be glad when that happens—skip like a lamb, if you like!—for even though they don't like it, I do . . . and all heaven applauds. And know that you are in good company; my preachers and witnesses have always been treated like this. (Luke 6:22-23 MSG)

God was so upset with His children that He almost brought judgment on them. Fortunately, the Israelite leader, Moses, interceded on their behalf and dissuaded God from allowing them to be destroyed. Even so, God declared that those that complained against Him who were over twenty years old would not enter the Promised Land. Rather they would die in the wilderness.

. . . "I have heard the complaints which the children of Israel make against Me. Say to them, 'As I live,' says the LORD, 'just as you have spoken in My hearing, so I will do to you: The carcasses of you who have complained against Me shall fall in this wilderness, all of you who were numbered, according to your entire number, from twenty years old and above. Except for Caleb the son of Jephunneh and Joshua the son of Nun, you shall by no means enter the land which I swore I would make you dwell in....' Now the men whom Moses sent to spy out the land, who returned and made all the congregation complain against him by bringing a bad report of the land, those very men who brought the evil report about the land, died by the plague before the LORD. But Joshua, the son of Nun, and

Caleb, the son of Jephunneh, remained alive, of the men who went to spy out the land."(Numbers 14:26-38 NKJV)

Everyone who rejected Moses' leadership did not make it into the Promised Land. The ten spies who instigated the Israelites to reject their leaders were afflicted with plagues and died. On the other hand, Joshua and Caleb made it into the Promised Land. Two of the twelve spies accomplished God's purpose for their lives. Because Caleb and Joshua were rejected, they were *separated* from their ten colleagues and the Israelite congregation who came against them. Consequently, Caleb and Joshua were in right standing with God. They were protected from the ramifications that befell their colleagues. This enabled them to enter and possess the Promised Land, unlike their colleagues who died and never made it in.

Those rejecting your leadership are inadvertently separating themselves from you and liberating you to champion the cause that God assigned you to carry out. They are screening themselves out from tampering with your work and pushing you toward others who will help you accomplish the vision God gave you. In fact, those rejecting you are manifesting the fact that they do not belong in your squad. Their antagonism toward you is a cue that they were never really committed to your leadership. So, by rejecting you, they are cutting themselves off from you, thereby, liberating you from their pessimism and sparing you God's judgment on them.

They left us, but they were never really with us. If they had been, they would have stuck it out with us, loyal to the end. In leaving, they showed their true colors, showed they never did belong. (1 John 2:19 MSG)

After the fate that befell the ten spies, you would think the Israelites and other leaders under Moses would have learned from the incident. But, no, they did not. That is evident by the fact that some other leaders came against him regarding his leadership.

Getting on his high horse one day, Korah...Dathan and Abiram...and On...rebelled against Moses. He had with him 250 leaders of the congregation of Israel, prominent men with positions in the Council. They came as a group and confronted

Moses and Aaron, saying, "You've overstepped yourself. This entire community is holy and GOD is in their midst. So why do you act like you're running the whole show?" (Numbers 16:1-3 MSG)

Korah, Dathan, Abiram, and On came against Moses. Not only did they attack him, they also incited 250 other "prominent" leaders to rebel against him, too. These were all individuals who Moses appointed as leaders of the Israelite congregation.

Isn't it something? You appoint people to a position, and all of a sudden they want to tell you how to run your business, ministry, or department. Unfortunately, some people just can't handle promotion. You give them an inch, and they ask for a yard. They become prideful, and the result is rebellion. Can you relate to this scenario? Have you ever experienced a situation in which the people you fed came up and bit the fingers you used to feed them? You were their *mentor*, but they became your *tormentors*.

Like Moses was accused, your disgruntled subordinates claim that you are: arrogant, you think you are better than they are; you act like you are above them. The truth is that, from an authoritative standpoint, you are their head...their covering. But they treat you like you are their lid. If this is the case, no wonder they get exposed to their detriment, since they did not let you protect them by covering them.

If you are experiencing what Moses went through, aside from exercising your authority as a leader who has the right to dismiss a disgruntled subordinate, I encourage you to respond like Moses did. He humbled himself and left the situation in God's hands.

On hearing this, Moses threw himself facedown on the ground. Then he addressed Korah and his gang: "In the morning GOD will make clear who is on His side, who is holy. GOD will take His stand with the one He chooses." (Numbers 16:4-5 MSG)

Moses summoned his detractors to come before God and let the Lord settle the issue of who was really in right standing with God. Moses' request, however, for the presence of Dathan and Abiram was given a cold shoulder by both individuals.

Moses then ordered Dathan and Abiram, sons of Eliab, to appear, but they said, "We're not coming. Isn't it enough that you yanked us out of a land flowing with milk and honey to kill us in the wilderness? And now you keep trying to boss us around! Face it, you haven't produced: You haven't brought us into a land flowing with milk and honey, you haven't given us the promised inheritance of fields and vineyards. You'd have to poke our eyes out to keep us from seeing what's going on. Forget it, we're not coming." (Numbers 16:12-14 MSG)

Dathan and Abiram refused to respond to Moses' call. They complained that Moses was bossing them around. Furthermore, they griped that they had not received any inheritance nor entered the Promised Land. In fact, they felt that they were better off in Egypt. To them, Egypt was a land flowing with milk and honey.

Korah, Dathan, and Abiram represent individuals who resist change in an establishment. Oftentimes, when things are not going according to plan during a transition that an organization is going through, some, if not most, members of the organization complain against their leader. Due to promises yet to be fulfilled by their leader, they feel that their leader is incompetent, and they conclude that they were better off doing things the way they used to do them.

That was the kind of malady Moses was faced with. Perhaps you can relate to this scenario. They were frustrated that they had not possessed the Promised Land. I find it ironic that the rebels forgot that they were the ones responsible for the slow progress into the Promised Land, since they and the other Israelite congregants came against their leaders when God told them to enter the land. Now, they have the audacity to complain and challenge Moses' leadership.

Sometimes, God slows down your progress just enough to expose the moles in your organization. One way to figure out those who are not committed to the vision God gave you is by seeing the way they act when things seem to go wrong. Are you questioning your purpose? Are you wondering why those you considered trusted workers, associates, and friends are coming against you? As long as your heart is right before God and you are doing what you believe He has instructed you to do, it is likely God is using their rejection to expose their disloyalty.

God is interested in helping you fulfill your destiny. He is not going to let anyone in your organization abort your mission. The closer you get to fulfilling your purpose, the more important it is for you to ensure that those you are leading to accomplish the vision are in harmony with you. When that is not the case, in order to protect God's plan from being hindered, God will expose those individuals who are not in agreement with you. One way you discover them is by their lack of support for your cause and your leadership.

Moses put everything in God's hands. God gave Him the assignment though his detractors thought otherwise. Moses summoned them to come before God in the tabernacle of meeting, with censers in their hands. Moses determined that God would settle, once and for all, those who were His, and those who were not.

When they came before God, Korah had gathered the entire congregation *against* Moses at the door of the tabernacle of meeting. God told Moses and Aaron to separate themselves from the congregation. He was going to let them experience his wrath. But, again, Moses pleaded that God would not subject the Israelite congregation to His wrath because of what the leaders, Korah, Dathan, and Abiram did. So, God told Moses to tell the congregation to back away from the tents of the three culprits (Numbers 16:16-25).

And he spoke to the congregation, saying, "Depart now from the tents of these wicked men! Touch nothing of theirs, lest you be consumed in all their sins." So they got away from around the tents of Korah, Dathan, and Abiram; and Dathan and Abiram came out and stood at the door of their tents, with their wives, their sons, and their little children. Now it came to pass...that the ground split apart under them, and the earth opened its mouth and swallowed them up, with their households and all the men with Korah, with all their goods. So they and all those with them went down alive into the pit; the earth closed over them. And a fire came out from the LORD and consumed the two hundred and fifty men who were offering incense. (Numbers 16:25-27, 31-33, 35 NKJV)

All the men that came against Moses perished. Moses did not touch them; he did not fight them. He simply left the situation in God's hands, and God took care of business. Similarly, I suggest you divert those attacking your leadership into God's hands. God will take care of them. Korah and his accomplices stood their ground against Moses. Interestingly, "the ground" collapsed under them and they and their households fell in, to their demise. In the same way, the premise which your detractors are using to resist your leadership could be the very thing that destroys them.

The fact that they got *buried* alive under the earth depicts the weakness of the claims which served as the *grounds* on which they stood against Moses. Furthermore, since they refused to possess the land by following Moses' directives, God let a land "possess" them. It's unfortunate that their families were also affected by God's judgment on them.

Despite God's obvious disapproval of the mutiny against Moses, the congregation still complained against Moses and his brother, blaming them for the death of Korah and his conspirators.

The next day the whole Israelite community grumbled against Moses and Aaron. "You have killed the LORD's people," they said. (Numbers 15:41)

Some people just don't learn. Some have set their heart as stone and are bent on frustrating your efforts. They will blame you for any and everything. Have this in mind when you lead people. Don't be surprised by those who act as such. Don't let their defiance distract you. Let it keep you on course. Keep your eye on God and his vision and let Him deal with them.

And the LORD spoke to Moses, saying, "Get away from among this congregation, that I might consume them in a moment." And they fell on their faces. So Moses said to Aaron, "Take a censer and put fire in it from the altar, put incense on it, and take it quickly to the congregation and make atonement for them; for wrath has gone out from the LORD. The plague has begun." Then Aaron took it as Moses commanded, and ran into the midst of the assembly; and already the plague had begun among the people. So he put in the incense and made atonement for the people. And he stood between the dead and the living; so the plague was stopped. Now those who died in the plague were fourteen thousand seven hundred, besides those who died in the Korah incident. (Numbers 16:45-49 NKJV)

Because God was upset with the people a plague was released to afflict the congregation. Even so, Moses demonstrated the heart of an exemplary leader by asking his brother, Aaron, the high priest, to make atonement for the people in order to stop the onslaught against his people. Aaron quickly adhered to Moses' directives and the plague was stopped. However, prior to the plague being stopped 14,700 people lost their lives in such a short time. Wow!

Despite all that Moses and Aaron went through, despite their efforts at ensuring that they fulfilled God's mandate in possessing the Promised Land, they did not make it into the Land. The rebellion of the children of Israel took its toll on Moses and caused Him to be irreverent to God.

In the first month, the entire company of the People of Israel arrived in the Wilderness of Zin. The people stayed in Kadesh. Miriam died there, and she was buried. There was no water there for the community, so they ganged up on Moses and Aaron. They attacked Moses: "We wish we'd died when the rest of our brothers died before GOD. Why did you haul this congregation of GOD out here into this wilderness to die, people, and cattle alike? And why did you take us out of Egypt in the first place, dragging us into this miserable country? No grain, no figs, no grapevines, no pomegranates—and now not even any water!" Moses and Aaron walked from the assembled congregation to the Tent of Meeting and threw themselves face down on the ground. And they saw the Glory of GOD. GOD spoke to Moses: "Take the staff. Assemble the community, you and your brother Aaron. Speak to that rock that's right in front of them and it will give water. You will bring water out of the rock for them; congregation and cattle will both drink." Moses took the staff away from GOD's presence,

as commanded. He and Aaron rounded up the whole congre-
gation in front of the rock. Moses spoke: "Listen, rebels! Do
we have to bring water out of this rock for you?" With that,
Moses raised his arm and slammed his staff against the rock—
once, twice. Water poured out. Congregation and cattle drank.
GOD said to Moses and Aaron, "Because you didn't trust me,
didn't treat me with holy reverence in front of the People of Is-
rael, you two aren't going to lead this company into the land
that I am giving them." (Numbers 20:1-12 MSG)

The Israelites, who were notorious for making complaints,
complained to Moses for water. Moses approached God for
help, and God told him to speak to a rock and water would
come out for the Israelites. Moses, in his frustration with his
people, did not *speak* to the rock; rather, he *struck* it *twice* with
the staff in his hand. God was displeased with Moses' attitude
toward Him in the presence of the people, so He told Moses
and Aaron that they would not lead the Israelites into the
Promised Land.

With that in mind, I would like to caution you not to let the
insubordination of your people prevent you from fulfilling
God's purpose for your life. I know that it can be frustrating
when the people whom you are making sacrifices to help are
unappreciative. Nevertheless, don't let their ingratitude hinder
you from fulfilling the vision. Their rebellion might stop them
from accomplishing their goals, but don't let them stop you
from fulfilling your destiny.

Remember that the key to taking advantage of any rejection
you face is in how you respond to it. It's in your best interest
that you respond with faith, hope, and love, believing that
things are working out for your best. Don't retaliate toward
your adversaries. Don't recompense evil for evil. Don't take
over God's job. Let God be the judge of your opponents while
you focus on the task he assigned you to undertake. If you need
to fire or dismiss someone because of dereliction of duty, go
ahead and do so. However, let God deal with those who are
making personal attacks against you.

If anyone should have made it to the Promised Land, it
should have been Moses. His exploits for his people were ab-

solutely awesome. Unfortunately, he let their negativity prevent him from making it to the place that he tirelessly tried to lead them to. Since Moses was demoted, someone else was promoted to take his place. Guess who? Joshua. Moses' rejection lead to Joshua's promotion.

After the death of Moses the servant of the LORD, it came to pass that the LORD spoke to Joshua, the son of Nun, Moses' assistant, saying: "Moses My servant is dead. Now therefore, arise, go over this Jordan, you and all these people, to the land which I am giving to them—the children of Israel. Be strong and of good courage, for to this people you shall divide as an inheritance the land which I swore to their fathers to give them. (Joshua 1:1-2 & 6 NKJV)

Joshua became the leader of the Israelites. When Joshua and Caleb tried to motivate their people to possess the Promised Land, the people came against them. In doing so, they exposed Joshua's commitment to Moses and God's cause. Is it any wonder that God chose him as Moses' successor? Being rejected assisted Joshua in fulfilling his destiny.

Chapter 17
It Leads You to the Right Team

Chauncey Billups was used as a regular bargaining chip for the NBA player trades. In fact, it was said that he was bounced around the NBA like a basketball. Chauncey Billups first made his debut in the NBA after he was drafted to the Boston Celtics as the third pick in the first round of the 1997 NBA draft. At the end of his first season in Boston, he was traded to another team. The six-foot-three-inch guard found himself traded to four different teams in three seasons. Even so, he was offloaded to a fifth team. His rollercoaster ride did not stop with his fifth stint; he spent two years there, and he opted to be traded again.[1]

Richard Hamilton was one-half of the scoring duo that gave the Washington Wizards a good run toward the NBA playoffs in the 2001-2002 season. His scoring partner and boss was no other than the legendary Michael Jordan. It came as a shock to Richard, nicknamed Rip, when Michael Jordan traded him to another team. In his article "Sour Deal Turns out to be Sweet," Joe Lago, an NBA Editor for ESPN.com, revealed that Richard Hamilton did not understand why Michael Jordan traded him, since Rip was one of the building blocks of the Washington Wizards. Hamilton felt like being traded to another team was a slap in his face. He was devastated by the trade, and it took about seven months for him to recover from the disappointment.[2]

Rasheed Wallace was labeled as the bad boy of the NBA. He led the league in technical fouls and was considered the black sheep of the Portland Trail Blazers. He had been ejected from NBA games several times for speaking against referees. At one time, he was even suspended for allegedly assaulting a referee off court. Things got so bad for him that he even experienced rejection from his home fans. The bad press he received, coupled with the dissatisfaction of his home fans and the disapproval of his conduct on and off the court by his team management, took its toll on Rasheed and he opted to leave Portland. The Trail Blazers were very obliged to offload Rasheed to another team.

Chauncey Billups, Richard Hamilton, and Rasheed Wallace were all traded to another team. These players were basically rejected by their previous teams. As things turned out, they all ended up on the same team—the Detroit Pistons. Prior to their arrival in Detroit, little did these players know that being traded to the Detroit Pistons was the best thing that ever happened for them.

Despite his short-lived tenure on his previous teams, Chauncey Billups encouraged himself. He never gave up on his dream of playing his best and winning an NBA championship. When he landed in Detroit, the real Billups emerged even more. It seemed like landing in Detroit *built up* Billups. He played his best ever since landing in the NBA.

Richard Hamilton overcame his disappointment of being traded to the Pistons. He had to tell himself to get over the situation. He embraced Detroit and considered being in his new team a great situation. He encouraged himself to move on, and move on he did. He felt like he fit in when he landed in Detroit. Rip earned his name with the Detroit Pistons. He lead his new team in points scored and improved his assist average. All and all, he improved his game.

Rasheed made a pit stop in Atlanta before arriving in Detroit. During talks that Rasheed would be traded, some sports analysts debated on the chances of him being picked up by other teams considering his well-publicized conduct. There were talks that no one wanted him. Portland did not want him, and other teams were not too keen to invite him to their bandwagon—except, of course, the Detroit Pistons. When he landed in Detroit, sports analysts unanimously agreed that he would make the Pistons a contender for the highly coveted Larry O'Brien trophy—the grand prize of winning the NBA championship.

Bill Walton, an inductee to the NBA hall of fame and ESPN analyst, was surprised at the enormous contribution Rasheed afforded the Pistons.[3] Rasheed improved his teammates by helping their defense and presenting himself as a reliable option on the offense as well. In addition, Wallace fit well with the game plan of the Pistons. Rasheed, a skillful basketball player who was often criticized in Portland for being unselfish, was finally allowed to be himself in Detroit. He did not have to carry the team on his shoulders. His team could carry him on theirs, especially when he had a bad day with his game and the referees.

IT OFFERS YOU THE OPPORTUNITY TO BECOME A CHAMPION

In essence, Billups, Hamilton, and Wallace ended up on the right team. It was with the Pistons that their years of playing in the NBA paid off. Finally, Richard Hamilton ended up in the playoffs, something he was not able to accomplish with his previous team despite being the top scorer. Finally, Chauncey Billups played the way he believed he could always play, something he was not able to fully accomplish on his previous teams. Perhaps his ability to reach his basketball peak was impaired by all the trades he was involved in. Finally, Rasheed Wallace found a home in Detroit.

These three players who were dismissed from previous teams were featured as starters for the Detroit Pistons and, together, they won back-to-back, the 2003-2004 and 2004-2005 Eastern conference NBA championships. They also won the 2003-2004 NBA championship.

They were rejected into a good situation. They were all rejected to the right team—and the right coach. Incidentally, their hall of fame coach, Larry Brown, had his own bouts with rejection. He resigned from a previous team in which his attempts to win the NBA championship never materialized. Despite having Allen Iverson, one of the best players—a one-time NBA MVP and All-Star MVP—it was said that his relationship with Iverson was not the best. It was also said that some players did not want to play for him. They did not like his style of coaching, a style of coaching that led the Pistons to win the championship.

Coach Larry Brown had a mantra that served as the theme for the way he coached his team. His theme was for them to "play the right way." To accomplish this objective, he emphasized team play and de-emphasized individual play. His coaching antics might have been refused in previous teams and rebuffed by some players, but they paid off in Detroit.

With the Pistons, he was finally able to coach the right players, who formed the right team, to play the right way. Rasheed Wallace did not have to work as hard and put up big numbers like he was expected to in Portland. He did not have to be selfish like they wanted him to be on his previous team. Rasheed played like he always wanted to play—unselfishly, which fit well with his new coach's philosophy. In Detroit, Rasheed played more efficiently and put up relevant, not extravagant, numbers. That took the pressure off him and probably contributed to him having less trouble with game officials and less technical fouls.

Chauncey Billups excelled with the Detroit Pistons. In addition to earning a championship ring, he won the NBA Final's Most Valuable Player trophy. Other than their team president, Joe Dumars, the guy who gave him and his other teammates the chance to *redeem* themselves, Chauncey Billups became the most low profile player who had never been to an All-Star NBA game who went on to win the NBA final's Most Valuable Player trophy. Overall, Chauncey Billups, Richard Hamilton, Rasheed Wallace and their coach Larry Brown all benefited from ending up on the right team. They all ended up becoming champions with the Detroit Pistons, something they were not able to accomplish with their previous teams, despite their hard work, sacrifices, and the criticisms they withstood. Being cut by their previous teams was the best thing that ever happened for them.

Dear reader, perhaps like those NBA stars, you were dismissed by some people. Those people might have been friends, acquaintances, family, or people of influence. I know it hurts when people turn you down. I know the pain of feeling worthless and the fear that you might never amount to anything. But, rest assured that when you are armed with the understanding that you can benefit from being refused, you might even surprise yourself with how successful you can become. With this in mind, you can respond to your rejection with hope that things are actually working out for your best.

Hall of fame coach, John Wooden, articulated it best when he said:

Things turn out best for the people who make the best of the way things turn out.[4]

Those NBA players made the best use of the way things turned out for them. This is the same encouragement I'm offering to you. Make the best out of your situation. Respond "the right way" to your rejection. In doing so, you will realize that rejection offers you the opportunity to come into your own.

There is a potential in you that is lying dormant because of the people with whom you hang around. Your affiliation with them might have been by design or by circumstances beyond your control. Either way, they were unable to cultivate your strengths. As a result, they only saw your weaknesses or what they misconstrued as weaknesses. You did not meet their expectations so they rejected you.

Even so, they were doing you a favor. They might not want you, but some other people do. There are people who need you. They need to feed off your supply, a supply which was turned off by your previous acquaintances. For the sake of those who can benefit from your supply, God will allow those who do not see nor value your potential to push you to those who will bring out the best in you. Through rejection, you will be driven to the right team.

Tom Brady is another prime example of someone who underwent rejection in his craft. During the NFL draft in 1999, he was picked in the "sixth" round as the 199th pick. It was said that he was least likely to be an NFL quarterback. During an ESPN interview, Brady revealed that he was wondering why nobody wanted him. He wondered why they did not like him. He was distraught that nobody wanted him to be their quarterback.

Little did all the teams that rejected him know that Tom Brady was going to be, according to ESPN sports analyst Sean Salisbury, "The most fundamental quarterback" in the NFL. Despite the obvious rebuff by other NFL teams, the team that finally picked him in that sixth round was the New England Patriots. Brady ended up on the right team. It was with the Patriots that he honed his skills. It was with the Patriots that he earned his reputation. It was with the Patriots that he linked up with the teammates, coach, and management that believed in him.

Tom Brady emerged as an NFL quarterback, something that was said he was least likely to achieve. In addition, he won the Super Bowl's Most Valuable Player award, twice, as well as three Super Bowl championships with the New England Patriots. He won all three championships within four years, before he turned thirty.

You might never win the NBA championship. You might never lift the Vince Lombardi Trophy—the grand prize of winning the Super Bowl. Nevertheless, you can still *champion* your life. You can overcome the negative perception that people have about you. You can be somebody. You are somebody! Like the athletes I talked about, don't give up on yourself. Don't fight or lash back at those who do not accept you. Let the hurricane of their rejection blow you onto the right team.

When people overlook us for a while, God uses their neglect to preserve us for those who will take us into their confidence. The people you expect or desire to "pick" you may never do so. They might pass you over. They might slight you. They might not see any value in you, but that is just their misguided opinion. They are just leaving you for the right team of individuals who will accept you as you are and cultivate you into who you will be.

You might be the last pick but you will be "picked." You might be picked last but you will be first. Some of the athletes I talked about appeared to have been at the bottom of the barrel of their games, but after they ended up with the right team, they ended up on top of the barrel. They emerged as the cream of the crop.

And note this: Some who seem least important now will be the greatest then, and some who are the greatest now will be least important then. (Luke 13:30 NLT)

That is also what happened for Vonetta Flowers. From the age of nine, Vonetta Flowers had dreamed of being in the summer Olympics. She was an outstanding athlete in high school, lettering in volleyball, basketball, and track, where she was the MVP for three seasons. In college, she focused mainly on track, competing in the heptathlon, long jump, triple jump, 200-meter and 400-meter sprints, as well as relays. She was named all-American seven times.

On July 2000, she went to Sacramento, California hoping to achieve what she had been training her whole life for. She was going to compete in the Olympic trials for a spot to represent the United States in Sydney, Australia. Four years prior, she had tried out to compete in the 100-meter sprint and long jump for the 1996 team, but she did not make the cut. It was a hard blow to her dreams, but she kept her head up, and put in another four years of rigorous training.

Unfortunately for her, she did not meet the expectations required to make the track team that would represent the US in Sydney. She did not finish with a good enough jump. Her valiant efforts and performance was rejected. It appeared that seventeen years of relentless training went down the drain—or did it?

Interestingly, while still in Sacramento, Vonetta Flowers's husband saw a flyer posted in a hallway that offered an opportunity for people interested in participating in the Olympics to try out for the United States' bobsled team. Her husband suggested that she try out, but Vonetta was reluctant to do so. She had never lived near snow, she knew nothing about bobsleds, and she was still devastated about not making the Sydney Olympics.

Eventually, she tried out and discovered that her training with weights as a sprinter and as a triple jumper were relevant to being a bobsled brakewoman—the person who pushes the bobsled and rides with the driver. She put in another shift of two years of training and ended up fulfilling her dream of being an Olympian, not as a track athlete at the summer Olympics, but as a bobsledder in the winter Olympics.

The rejection she experienced by not making two consecutive summer Olympics as a track athlete, *redirected* Vonetta Flowers to another Olympics and to another sport where she proved her mettle. She had wanted to make the summer Olympics, but thanks to rejection, not only did she make the winter Olympics, she also *made* history. In the 2002 Winter Olympics, she became the *first* African-American to win a gold medal in a winter Olympics, when she and her driver, Jill Bakken, took the most coveted jewelry for the event.[5]

IT LEADS YOU TO CROSS PATHS WITH THE RIGHT PEOPLE

The movie *Seabiscuit*, which was based on Laura Hillenbrand's bestselling book and nominated for seven Academy Awards, also drives the point of how rejection can be a blessing. The screenplay featured four characters: a wealthy businessman, a young jockey, a horse trainer, and the racehorse, Seabiscuit. The wealthy businessman was divorced by his wife partly because she held him responsible for the death of their son in a car accident while the child drove the vehicle unsupervised. The young jockey was sold by his family because they could not afford to take care of him as they were going through a severe economic depression. The horse trainer was like an outcast, and Seabiscuit was deemed useless as a racehorse as no one could ride him because he was out-of-control. Incidentally, the paths of these four characters crossed. Together they formed the right team and helped each other out.

The wealthy businessman caught the eye of a younger and more attractive woman who married and supported him. The young jockey was sold to a callous man who dealt with horses. The jockey underwent a lot of pain and hardship but eventually ended up having to ride Seabiscuit. The horse trainer nurtured, restored and trained Seabiscuit. He was also the person who found the young jockey to ride Seabiscuit. The businessman sponsored Seabiscuit, the jockey, and the trainer. The right team was set.

In addition, they built camaraderie, formed a bond with each other and became like a family. Together they won scores of horse races with a horse everyone had given up on, a jockey that they said was too big to ride a horse and least expected to accomplish anything as a jockey, an obscure horse trainer, and the financial and emotional support of the businessman and his wife. The getting together of these individuals was facilitated by the respective individuals who dismissed them.

I believe that the relevance and significance of the film to our everyday life was one of the things that contributed to the success of the movie, which was also based on a true story. There was a very encouraging line uttered by the horse trainer in the movie. He said:

You don't throw a whole life away because it's banged up a little.

Just because rejection bangs you up a little does not mean that you should give up on yourself. God specializes in taking individuals who have been banged up a little bit, or a whole lot, and uses them to make a *big bang* in life.

Let God fire you up to stardom. Let Him make you *His star* like *Esther*. When God allows people to dismiss you, He is using their rejection as a fishing hook, line, and sinker, and you, as the bait to catch the fish of unprecedented success. He uses their rejection as the catalyst to propel you to your destiny. It's okay when people push you away; they are pushing you to other individuals who, with you, will form the right team.

If you experienced rejection in the ministry of the gospel, your colleagues, congregation, or leader is just pushing you to a better and more compatible team of ministers, leaders, and congregants with whom you will excel and be all God wants you to be—and where He wants you to be. If you experienced rejection at work from your management and or staff, they are redirecting you to a better and more fulfilling position at another corporation with a more cooperative staff.

Maybe your rejection was experienced in a relationship with a prospect. The individual is just pushing you to the right mate— the right teammate for you. Perhaps you were divorced. If reconciliation and remarriage with your ex would not promote a healthy and peaceful relationship, depending on your situation, you've either been given another opportunity to start over and get things right with a compatible spouse, or given the opportunity to be fulfilled by yourself, with God holding your hand all the way.

Whatever your case might be, God uses rejection to get you to the right team. He will direct you to the right team, but it is up to you to cooperate and make things work with your new team or teammate. For this to work, it is important for you to understand that those who rejected you just redirected you to your newfound relationship be it ministerial, managerial, or matrimonial. With this in mind, forgive those individuals that did not accept you, *forfeit* the wrongs they inflicted on you, and move on in life with your new team.

Chapter 18
It Furthers Your Cause

B rad Cohen was in the fourth grade when he began to draw unwanted attention to himself. Clearing his throat, making barking sounds, jerking his head, and twitching his eyes were some of the things he did which were beyond his control. As a result, he faced a lot of teasing, scolding, ridicule and rejection. Medical experts said that he had a behavioral problem and that he needed to be dealt with firmly. His mother was alarmed at the uncontrollable, off-and-on, tics in his face, arms, and major muscle groups in his legs. These caused her to do research on what was going on with her son.

At one time in a store, a lady approached his mother to suggest that Brad was *possessed by the devil*. In fifth grade, Brad's noises got louder and his teacher brought him to the front of the class and asked him to apologize to the class for his noises. He did so, and on his way back to sit down, his teacher told him to come back and say that he wouldn't do it again. He complied with being humiliated even more by his teacher, but, of course, that did not stop his tics, it just exacerbated them.

Because of his ordeal, Brad had no friends and was left all by himself. Mean kids mocked his noises, few understood his disorder, and he drew little sympathy outside school. But Brad wanted to be normal. He wanted to be like everyone else.

Brad spent lunch period with the school nurse because no one wanted to eat with him. The school nurse noticed this, befriended him and ate with him. In middle school, teachers were cruel to him, even more than the students. Brad was 12 years old when it was discovered that what others perceived as him "acting up" and "seeking attention" was diagnosed to be Tourette syndrome. This condition is described as a neurological disorder of the brain that causes involuntary movements and vocalizations.

Due to that discovery, a principal asked Brad to tell students and faculty about Tourette Syndrome during an all-school assembly. Brad seized the opportunity to educate them about his condition. His presentation of the subject won him an applause, acceptance, and understanding. That was a *defining* moment in Brad's life. From that point on, Brad understood that he needed to help prevent kids from going through what he went through. The seed was sown in his heart to become the teacher that he never had.

Brad went on to Bradley University where in his first week of school he had to deal with, same ole, same ole. He was a freshman living in Giesert Hall where he met new acquaintances who invited him to have lunch with them. Because of the noises he made, an employee of a campus town restaurant kicked him out of the eatery. This ejection drew a student-organized boycott of the restaurant. Even strangers stopped by Brad's room to offer him support. The restaurant eventually apologized for what they did to Brad, and Brad convinced students to stop the boycott of the restaurant.

The incident in his first week of school helped Brad immediately explain why he had uncontrollable tics and get the issue out of the way. Brad Cohen put it this way:

"I was able to educate everybody during that first week. It was such a pivotal step that it really helped my success at Bradley because I was able to get that issue - why is Brad making the noises? - out of the way. For something I never wish would have happened, it possibly could have been one of the best things to ever happen to me."

In Bradley, Brad went on to be a fraternity president, an honors student and graduated in 1996, cum laude, as an elementary education major. Despite his accomplishments, he could not find a job as a teacher. During interview after interview, principals refused to hire him because of his condition. They didn't think he would make it as a teacher. In fact, one principal even told him that his students would laugh at him and that his fifth grade students would beat him up. Brad was so hurt by that comment that he got out of the interview as quickly as he could, got into his car and drove away, sobbing so hard that the tears blurred his vision. Despite the opposition, despite the setbacks, despite the hindrances, Brad kept looking for a teaching position.

After 24 unsuccessful interviews, one principal gave him a chance. During an interview with Oprah, Hilarie Straka, the assistant principal of Marietta's Mountain View Elementary, who was instrumental in giving Brad a shot, revealed how he got her attention. She was in a meeting where she heard about a "barking" teacher going around dropping resumes. The former speech pathologist came across his file and was impressed with his accomplishments. She felt that having his information come before her was meant to be. Her school offered programs for students with disabilities and she encouraged the school principal, Jim Ovbey, who was reluctant at first, to hire Brad.

She told him that since their school inspired students with disabilities by telling them that they can be whatever they want to be, they not only need to talk the talk, but needed to walk the walk by hiring Brad Cohen. He would be a primary example of someone, who despite his limitations, was able to accomplish his goals. With that being said, after his 25th interview, Cohen was hired as a second grade teacher for Mountain View Elementary School.

To me, the fact that he was hired by Mountain View speaks volumes. It appears that the schools that had a "valley" view perspective on Brad redirected him to a school with a "mountain" view paradigm on him. Brad ended up fulfilling his destiny at a school that shared the "sky is the limit" mindset that he had. Brad was re-ejected to the *top*, so to speak. This was evident when Hilarie Straka nominated him for teacher of the year, something she had never done before. Just a year after he was rebuffed by 24 schools, on July 1997, Brad Cohen's outstanding efforts as a second grade teacher were honored when he was named Sallie Mae First Class Teacher of the Year for the state of Georgia.

Cohen's remarkable accomplishment gave rise to a book, which he co-wrote with Lisa Wysocky, *Front of the Class*. His inspirational memoir won the *2005* Independent Publisher's Book of the Year Award and was named the best education trade book by *ForeWord* magazine. His story also inspired a Hallmark Hall of Fame movie, also titled, Front of the Class, which aired on CBS on December 7 2008.

The rejection Brad Cohen faced because of Tourette syndrome not only furthered his cause, but also explained his "cause"—the cause of his condition. As the subtitle of his book reveals, How Tourette Syndrome Made Me the Teacher I Never Had, his *cause* was to become a teacher who was sympathetic to the plight of kids who were ostracized because they were different. In addition to training teachers at two Marietta elementary schools as an area lead teacher for Cobb County schools, Tourette syndrome also added author and motivational speaker to his cause. Furthermore, the antagonism he faced led to, and facilitated, the awareness and education of people about the neurological disorder that affected Brad and an estimated 200,000 Americans.[1]

What Brad Cohen accomplished through the rejection he faced reinforces a piece of wisdom that was uttered by the apostle Paul:

Every test that you have experienced is the kind that normally comes to people. But God keeps his promise, and he will not allow you to be tested beyond your power to remain firm; at the time you are put to the test, he will give you the strength to endure it, and so provide you with a way out. (1 Corinthians 10:13 GNB)

In the *New King James Version*, the last part of that passage reads:

but with the temptation will also make the way of escape, that you might be able to bear it.

In the above scripture, temptation also refers to trials or tests. The verse reveals that God will not let us go through any trial that we cannot handle. In addition, *through* the test, God will make a way of escape. *...but with the temptation will also make the way of escape....* In other words, the very thing that was meant to imprison you is the thing that God uses to set you free. It's what He uses as your way of escape— your *liberation*. What was meant to harm you, God uses to *arm* you—your *provision*. Tourette syndrome, which appeared initially to hold back Brad Cohen, ended up setting him free. Being rejected for his *disability* facilitated *the ability* for him to find and fulfill his destiny.

Rejection did the same for Nelson Mandela. This prominent humanitarian was banished for his convictions. His cause was to abolish apartheid in South Africa. His efforts to thwart the racism against black South Africans landed him in a prison on Robben Island for 18 years. Despite the rejection, despite the incarceration and despite the depravation of his human rights, Nelson Mandela responded to his plight with faith, hope and love.

In fact he wrote:

No one is born hating another person because of the color of his skin, or his background, or his religion. People must learn to hate, and if they can learn to hate, they can be taught to love, for love comes more naturally to the human heart than its opposite.

With that kind of attitude, is it any wonder that Nelson Mandela won the admiration and respect of his jailer, James Gregory? Mr. Mandela responded with forgiveness toward the man who worked for the establishment that put him in prison. Consequently, similar to how Paul influenced his jailer, Nelson Mandela influenced James Gregory. Nelson Mandela helped stir James Gregory in the right direction and became his lifelong friend. Also, just like Joseph rose from being a prisoner to a governor, Nelson Mandela went from prison to the presidency. He went from being an inmate to being an icon.

Nelson Mandela was banished for his convictions. Notwithstanding, the rejection he experienced furthered his cause. Mr. Mandela was instrumental in the abolishment of apartheid in South Africa. It cost him 27 years of his life, but it gained him and other black South Africans their freedom from institutionalized racism. It also gained him a Nobel peace price and the honor of being the first truly democratically-elected President of South Africa.[2]

Oftentimes we get rejected for our convictions. It's preposterous, but true, that some people dismiss us for what we stand for but, interestingly, sometimes when people try to foil our cause they unwittingly further it.

Now I want you to know and continue to rest assured, brethren, that what [has happened] to me [this imprisonment] has actually only served to advance and give a renewed impetus to the [spreading of the] good news (the Gospel). (Philippians 1:12 AMP)

Three young men come to mind. Their story is narrated in Daniel 3:1-25. Unlike most of the people in the province of Babylon where they lived under captivity, they had reverence for God. Though these men were captive, they were placed over certain affairs in the province of Babylon. These men were Shadrach, Meshack and Abednego.

A decree had been issued to everyone in Babylon to worship a golden image that the king of Babylon, Nebuchadnezzar, had made. Everyone was required to bow down and worship the image once they heard the sound of various kinds of music playing in harmony.

The Hebrew boys—Shadrach, Meshack and Abednego—refused to worship the image because they only worshipped the true and living God. Had they worshipped the image, they would have gone against their convictions and they would have been guilty of breaking the third and fourth of the Ten Commandments (Exodus 20:3-6).

Their refusal to adhere to the decree was made known to Nebuchadnezzar who, in his rage, summoned the Hebrew boys to be brought before him. Nebuchadnezzar told the young men that if they did not worship the golden image, he was going to throw them into a burning fiery furnace. In expressing his contempt for their beliefs, he taunted them by questioning who the God was that would deliver them from his hands. Basically, if they refused to bow down to his image, he pronounced that they would be banished to death.

In response to his threats, the boys told him that their God would deliver them. In addition they made it crystal clear to the Babylonian King that whether he threw them into the fire or not, they would not pay homage to his idol. The king was enraged at their complete disdain toward his commands. He was so ticked off that he ordered the furnace to be heated seven times more and commanded that certain mighty men from his army bind them and toss them into the furnace.

FIRED OR FIRED UP?

Fully clad in their turbans, coats and slacks, Shadrach, Meshach and Abednego were bound up by the strong men and thrown into the burning fiery furnace. These guys were rejected because of what they stood for. They were discarded; they were thrown into the fire; they were banished.

Because the king's command was urgent and the fire was blazing hot since it was heated seven times more, the men who threw the young men into the fire were barbecued by the flames. Amazing! The men who threw the Hebrew boys into the fire were burnt, but the young men thrown into the furnace did not burn up, nor were they hurt. In fact they were moving around in the fire with a *Fourth Man*! The king in awe at this development described the fourth man as one in the form of the Son of God.

Since the men that threw the Hebrew boys into the fire got burnt but the boys didn't, Shadrach, Meshach and Abednego were better off in the fire than outside of it. Similarly, at times it is better for us to be in the fire of persecution than out of it. Going through the fire of trials can get us energized and ignited! Going through nothing can get us quenched and blighted! Going through situations can make us sharp, vigilant, and on our toes. Not having things to press through can make us warped, nonchalant, and leave us on our backs. The young men moved freely in the fire while those who threw them into the furnace died. God was with them in the fire just like he was with Joseph in prison. If you are also in the inferno of rejection, rest assured that God is with you, too.

Shadrach, Meshach, and Abednego were rejected for doing the right thing. They were re-ejected into the fire; they were re-ejected into the will of God. God Himself is a consuming fire (Hebrews 12:29). In truth, they pushed them closer to God. So close that God was manifested to them out of the fire. Those who threw them in the fire got *consumed* by it, while those in the fire were *assumed* by it.

Similarly, those outside the will of God, those that pushed you into the will of God by rejecting you, are subject to the fire of God's wrath, while you who got thrown into the furnace of rejection are subject to the fire of God's love, protection, and power. While those who reject you are prone to having the light of their life quenched, in your fire, you are prone to having your light ignited.

Having God's fire burn you or birth you is based on your relationship with God. Your proper response to rejection is dependent on your understanding that God is with you to bring you through the ordeal to bring you to a great deal—a favorable outcome and your deliverance. Sometimes God brings us *through* before he brings us *to*.

...We went through fire and through water, But You brought us out to rich fulfillment. (Psalm 66:12)

When you draw close to God, God will draw close to you (James 4:8). Sometimes adversity draws us closer to God, at least for those of us who believe in His power to deliver us from harm's way.

The young men were sentenced to death because of their convictions. They were thrown into fire. They were literally fired! Fortunately, that assisted the guys in getting closer to God. Though they tossed them into the fire—fired them, they actually fired them up. They empowered them by inadvertently placing them in the blazing furnace from which God's presence and power manifested to them.

Nebuchadnezzar was astonished by that development.

With his officials beside him, he called the Hebrew boys out from the fire and was further baffled by the fact that there was no sign that they were engulfed in the flames. Their hair was intact; their clothes were not burnt; and they did not smell of smoke. Consequently, the king acknowledged the sovereignty of God so much so that he decreed that anyone who blasphemed against God would be annihilated. The king also *promoted* Shadrach, Meshack and Abednego (Daniel 3:19-30).

Before the Hebrew boys were sentenced to death, they were over the affairs in Babylon. After they were rejected, they were promoted. Their God was reverenced after they were banished to death. They commanded more respect from the king after they were dismissed. They were elevated after they were thrown into the fire. These boys advanced, were highly esteemed, and had their faith in God reinforced after they were rejected. These took place because they trusted God to deliver them from the fire. They had faith in God, and judging by their confident defiance of the king's command, they had faith in themselves. They responded optimistically after Nebuchadnezzar condemned them to death.

In fact, the repercussion of sending those men into the fire sheds more light into why God allows us to be rejected. The Hebrew boys' setback turned out to be a setup from God. Statements made and actions carried out by Nebuchadnezzar before and after he tossed the young men into the fire caused me to have an epiphany. When the boys refused to worship his image, Nebuchadnezzar responded thus:

Then Nebuchadnezzar flew into a rage and ordered that Shadrach, Meshach, and Abednego be brought before him. When they were brought in, Nebuchadnezzar said to them, "Is it true, Shadrach, Meshach, and Abednego, that you refuse to serve my gods or to worship the gold statue I have set up? I will give you one more chance to bow down and worship the statue I have made when you hear the sound of the musical instruments. But if you refuse, you will be thrown immediately into the blazing furnace. And then what god will be able to rescue you from my power?" (Daniel 3:13-15 NLT)

Within that passage, the following statement blinks out to
me like a neon sign:

*And then what god will be able to rescue you from my
power?*

Before I elaborate on that remark, let's look at Nebuchadnezzar's statements and actions after the young men survived
and came out of the fire unscathed:

*Then Nebuchadnezzar said, "Praise to the God of
Shadrach, Meshach, and Abednego! He sent his angel to rescue his servants who trusted in him. They defied the king's
command and were willing to die rather than serve or worship any god except their own God. Therefore, I make this
decree: If any people, whatever their race or nation or language, speak a word against the God of Shadrach, Meshach,
and Abednego, they will be torn limb from limb, and their
houses will be turned into heaps of rubble. There is no other
god who can rescue like this!" Then the king promoted
Shadrach, Meshach, and Abednego to even higher positions in
the province of Babylon. (Daniel 3:28-30 NLT)*

Without undermining all we can learn from what
Shadrach, Meshach, and Abednego went through, the following gives us a glimpse of why God allows us to experience
rejection:

*...what God will be able to rescue you...Then Nebuchad-
nezzar said, "Praise to the God...Therefore, I make this decree..." Then the king promoted Shadrach, Meshach, and
Abednego to even higher positions....*

There are people questioning the existence of God. Consequently, God uses us to answer their questions: *what God?*
And, *will He be able to rescue you?* Because some people are
defiant toward God's existence and omnipotence, they subject those of us who believe in Him to the heat of their wrath.
They persecute us for our convictions. God, however, uses
their rejection of us to answer their question.

*For the eyes of the LORD run to and fro throughout the
whole earth, to show Himself strong on behalf of those whose
heart is loyal to Him.... (2 Chronicles 16:9 NKJV)*

After God reveals himself through us by helping us overcome the trials they subject us to, God causes them to do the second reason why He allowed them to reject us. He uses what we went through to cause our detractors to *make a decree*. In other words God uses our triumph over our adversity to influence those who came against us to enact laws, modify laws or do away with them altogether. Nebuchadnezzar originally decreed or enacted a law that stipulated that individuals would be roasted in fire if they did not bow to his image. The young men disobeyed his law because adhering to it would have caused them to go against their convictions of serving God only. After they came out of the fire, the same king *enacted a new law* that acknowledged God and also dissuaded people from speaking against Him.

Finally, God uses our ordeal to help us achieve a great deal. Like I alluded to previously, God utilizes it to get us promoted. The Hebrew boys were promoted by the king after they came out of the fire. In a nutshell, God allows people to come against us so that He can utilize their fire to empower and energize us to higher levels of success, pass, modify or eradicate laws or policies, and make *Himself* known. After he was released from prison, Nelson Mandela was promoted by being elected as the president of South Africa. His tenure in prison also led to the enactment of the law that abolished apartheid. Believe it or not, God's sovereign power was behind it all.

Some people sentence us to death because of our convictions. They subject us to the fire of their wrath because we are different from them in some form or fashion: our work ethic, our skin color, our morality, our family values, etc. They reject us because of how we feel and what we believe about the different issues of life when it is not consistent with their beliefs. Granted, there are myriad of beliefs paramount in the world. Thus, it is important that we still respect, love, and be at peace with each other regardless of our social, political, and religious differences.

When you respond to a job loss, criticism and antagonism, like Shadrack, Meshack, and Abednego, you will realize that the job loss was rather a job gain. The criticism and antagonism hurled against you was just a means that God utilized to elevate you beyond the position you held prior to being rejected. God uses your *commotion* as *locomotion* for your *promotion*.

Your promotion could manifest itself in the form of you being elevated above those who tried to demote you and, or, get you fired. Rather, your detractors got demoted if not fired. Your advancement could also come as a better job, in a better company, with a better salary where you feel fulfilled especially when you can now spend much needed time with your family. Your elevation could be in the form of starting your own business, a vision that might have been lying dormant in your heart because you were comfortably undermining your potential with a nine-to-five.

I don't wish this on you, but if you get laid off or if you've been let go from your job already, don't take it as a *step down* but a *step up*. See your termination as your ticket to success. Whether you got fired as a result of your company downsizing, which is an unfortunate consequence, or for incompetence or confidence mistaken as arrogance, don't foul mouth your boss, thank your heavenly Boss. Thank God for the opportunity to advance.

I can understand when you get fired because you did not do a good job. Yes, it's a wake up call. Wake up to the call! Get it right for your next job. Take the necessary steps to ensure that you do not make the same mistakes you made in your previous job. That training is necessary to prepare you for the next job, which is a step up from your old one and a requirement for you to land the job.

I served as a waiter in a restaurant for about four-and-a-half years. I was tired and frustrated when I was working there, especially, when I had a college degree in biology. I applied for other jobs but to no avail. I certainly wasn't trying to get other jobs in the restaurant business. I had taken some classes in the information technology field, and I was looking for something...anything in that field.

It was even more embarrassing that my parents sent me from Nigeria to school in the US, and all I could show for my college education after "nine years" in the States was a waiter's job, and the tips were taking serious dips. Fortunately, I landed a part-time job as a customer service associate at a reputable company. Though working for that reputable company did not mean reputable money, at least to me, although I was grateful for it.

I worked hard for the company. I did a good job for them. However, my shortcoming was that I came to work late occasionally. I was tardy. Their policy in layman's terms was three strikes and you're out! I struck out on seven. I worked there for close to four months. They were nice enough to allow me to stay after exhausting my three chances. My supervisor had given me a pep-talk about my tardiness, and I uttered not a word because he was right.

The reason why I occasionally came to work late was because I often disobeyed the *alarm clock*...hmmm. I often slept overtime—which often led to way overtime. A little sleep, a little slumber and your poverty will come like an armed man, the Bible says (Proverbs 6:10-11).

Evidently sleeping a little extra after I hit the "snooze" button and most times just stopped the alarm, wasn't a good idea. Incidentally, poverty through layoff came like an armed man and robbed me of my employment.

I came to work one morning, strolled into the warehouse-like call center, and told the lady behind the desk, in the call center that I was late—again. I then went to a computer station to sign on. A few minutes later, I was signing off after my supervisor came and gave me the "red light"...verbally. I didn't argue; it was my tardiness that got me fired. I guess I should have had some form of consolation that I still had the restaurant job. Unfortunately, I had handed my resignation letter to the restaurant about a week before I was laid off from the reputable company.

Please don't try this at home. I gave my resignation to the restaurant because I believed I was exercising my faith that God would get me another job. I was waiting for Him to get me another job while I was holding the restaurant job. However, it seemed to me that God was waiting on me to make a move by putting myself in a position that proves that I was really depending on Him. Please don't get me wrong. I didn't just sit home waiting for a job to fall in my lap those four-plus years I worked at the restaurant. I went looking for other jobs but to no avail.

Nonetheless, I wouldn't say I was completely in faith, since I did have a part time job at the reputable company. In the back of my mind, I considered that if I didn't find a job after I left the restaurant, at least I still had the Customer Service gig. And if that was all I was left with, I would strive to work full-time. But it turned out that God assisted my faith by allowing me to get fired. Obviously, I aided my job loss through my tardiness, and I had about a week left in the restaurant after I was fired from the customer service job before I was completely out of work.

Even so, I didn't fret. God was still with me. It was a very uncomfortable situation but I had to trust that God would work things out. A few days later, I called a temp agency that I reluctantly registered with, thanks to the insistence of my sister. For months, claims by friends and well-wishers that the agency had job openings did not materialize.

Six months after I registered with the agency, I called to update my new address information because I had moved. I also inquired if they had any job prospects for me. Well, what do you know? They did. The position was with a Fortune 500 company, in their information technology department, paying thirteen dollars per hour. Wow!

Less than a week after I was fired, and before I was to bid good riddance to my restaurant job, I was given another opportunity to *redeem* myself. I was grateful to God. My faith in Him was reinforced. I was rejected to be promoted. I was fired from a less reputable company to be hired by a more reputable one. Being fired forced me to try the agency again, and it paid off!

Similarly, being rejected causes you to re-evaluate your situation and make the necessary adjustments to improve your predicament. At least, that is the way you're supposed to respond to any setback you face. Even if you did not contribute to your demotion like I did, it's still in your best interest not to cry over spilled milk. Clean the spill and get another glass!

When you respond properly to rejection experienced through a layoff, a refusal of your proposal, losing a contract, or an attack on your personal beliefs, you'll end up better than you ever envisioned. Your rejection was just your ejection to a higher plateau.

Chapter 19
It Makes You a Test Case

On December 1, 1955, Rosa Parks boarded a bus and sat on a seat close to the last section of the bus designated for whites. When the bus got to the next stop, several white people boarded the bus and filled up all the seats reserved for whites. As a result, there was a Caucasian man left standing in the bus. The bus driver then asked Rosa Parks and three other African-Americans to leave their seats, which were in the front of the section designated for blacks, so that the white man could have a seat.

Three blacks moved out of their seats, but Rosa Parks merely moved to the window. The bus driver, who had also put her off his bus twelve years earlier, asked Rosa Parks to relinquish her seat, but she refused. The bus driver threatened to have her arrested, and she told him that he could go ahead and do that. And, do that he did. He called the police and had Parks arrested. The African-American lady was put off the bus because she refused to give up her seat. She did not like the way African-Americans had been pushed around. She could no longer tolerate the social injustice she had been dealing with all her life. She was removed from the bus. She was rejected for her convictions.

Rosa Parks was involved in the civil rights movement. She was behind the scenes supporting the men who fought for the rights of blacks. Her involvement in the civil rights movement was limited to typing, setting up meetings, and other secretarial-type jobs. But after her encounter on the bus, she was propelled to the forefront of the civil rights movement. She became the poster child for the movement. She emerged as the heroine who not only liberated blacks from the back of the bus, but from other injustices of segregation. She was able to accomplish this unprecedented feat by getting rejected.

The attorneys fighting for the cause of African-Americans were looking for a test case that they could use to file a suit with the Supreme Court to abolish segregation on buses. Rosa Parks became that test case. Her case was taken straight to the top. The Supreme Court outlawed segregation on buses. And the rejection of Rosa Parks and her convictions contributed to the Supreme Court's decision.[4]

I found it amusing to learn that, after the Supreme Court's decision, which outlawed separation on buses, Rosa Parks boarded the bus that started the whole fiasco. She ended up sitting where she desired on the same bus driven by the same driver who got her arrested. The driver was still on his driver's seat, but Rosa Parks was the person who *drove* the policies that governed the bus transit system. The bus driver did her a favor. He did blacks a favor.

In an effort by the bus driver to push her to a back seat, he pushed her to the front seat. The attempts by prejudiced whites to foil her cause only furthered her cause. The lady who they tried to make a scapegoat turned out to have escaped while making them the goat. Not only did she escape from the social injustice she encountered, she also liberated other African-Americans as well.

Her success and determination also helped redefine the roles of women. She exemplifies someone whose victory over rejection helped other people going through similar experiences overcome theirs, too. Being rejected and removed from that bus was the best thing that ever happened to Rosa Parks and one of the best things that ever happened for African-Americans.

She was just a little, frail African-American woman who

REJECTED *for a* PURPOSE

doubled as a seamstress and secretary before she got dismissed from the bus. After she was put off the bus, she became the person who fueled the civil rights movement, the person who won the Presidential Medal of Freedom, the person who had a library and a museum named after her, and the person for whom The Rosa and Raymond Parks Institute for Self-Development was established, amongst other things.

Like Rosa Parks, you are a test case. You are the person whose rejection is being used to liberate others. There are scores of people hurting and going through the same experiences as you. The way you overcome your trials will help others overcome theirs, too. Equipped with this knowledge, you can handle your adversity better. You can utilize the injustice inflicted on you to bring justice for yourself and others.

The way you overcome your adversity starts with responding properly to your rejection. Don't get violent or insolent. Rosa Parks was non-violent. She did not move from her seat; she maintained her stance. She held on to her convictions. She was well within her rights because she was seated in the section that blacks were restricted to. She was innocent, like those Hebrew boys. If you are innocent and people are coming against you, that should be a cue for you to know that something big is about to happen for you, and through you, to bless others. Allow the rejection of your convictions to earn you and others an invaluable commission, commendation, and compensation.

Like Rosa Parks, don't argue with your adversaries. Take your case straight to the top. She took her situation to the Supreme Court. Take yours to the Supreme God. And watch Him use your trials to promote you. It was this mode of action that led to Daniel's promotion.

IT ISOLATES YOU FOR PROMOTION

Daniel went through a similar experience like his friends, Shadrach, Meshack and Abednego. I believe his relationship with his friends breeded in him a healthy perspective on how to handle adversity. Whether he got them from his friends or they got it from him remains to be known. The bottom line, according to 1 Corinthians 15:33 (KJV) is that:

Evil communications corrupt good manners.

Conversely, good communications and associations enhance and promote good manners. He who walks with wise men will himself be wise, but the companions of fools will be destroyed (Proverbs 13:20). When you face rejection, do you have a pity party? Do you get your response tips from whiners or shiners? Do you hang out with the chickens or do you soar with the eagles? The eagle uses the resistance of the wind to soar to greater heights. We can learn from an eagle the invaluable wisdom in using rejection as a propeller to greater achievements.

In fact, hanging around the wrong friends, in the wrong career and the wrong relationship is reason enough for God to allow you to get re-ejected to the right relationships and associations. Rejection is also a way that God uses to screen out the parasites from your life, even if they are coworkers, family, or church members. Sometimes they are the reason why you haven't progressed. Out of sheer jealousy and envy, Daniel was about to get backstabbed.

Darius assumed kingship over Persia after the demise of Nebuchadnezzar's son, Belshazzar. When Belshazzar was king, he used gold and silver vessels taken by his father from Jerusalem to drink wine with his wives and concubines. His disdain of the sacredness of those vessels resulted in his death. While he was merry-making, a hand appeared from out of the blue and started writing on a wall in his palace (I believe that this is where we get the saying "see the handwriting on the wall"). Belshazzar was deeply troubled about this and consulted his advisors, soothsayers, and astrologers to explain the meaning of the writing on the wall.

His experts were unable to explain the writing. Nonetheless, his Queen consoled him and told him that Daniel would be able to explain the inscription on the wall. Daniel was consulted and basically explained that Belshazzar would die because of the way he bastardized God's property. Daniel's interpretation came to pass, which led to Darius assuming the throne (Daniel 5).

Darius set 120 leaders over his kingdom, and he placed three governors over them. Daniel was one of the governors. Daniel, however, distinguished himself from the other administrators.

An excellent spirit was found in him. In essence, his track record was impeccable. As a result, Darius considered making him head over all his administration. On realization of this, the other governors and leaders schemed to oust Daniel from his position.

Their initial attempts to find something against Daniel proved futile Instead, this is what they found about him:

...but they could find no charge or fault, because he was faithful; nor was there any error or fault found in him. (Daniel 6:4 NKJV)

Isn't that interesting? They could not find anything against him. Consequently, they concluded that the only way they could get him was to devise something that would affect his beliefs about God. So, the governors, satraps, counselors and advisors consulted with Darius the king and tricked him to make a decree which stipulated that anyone who prayed to their God within 30 days, instead of to him, would be thrown into a den of lions (Daniel 6:5-7).

My friend, does this development sound familiar to you? To me this sounds like a corporate conspiracy. Their action against Daniel is a reflection of what unfortunately takes place in the workplace and in our world at large: Coworkers and people getting together to oust another colleague.

King Darius, oblivious to their conspiracy against Daniel, enacted the decree and signed it. Daniel did not let the decree dissuade him from praying to God. In fact, with his windows open he prayed to God three times on the day he heard about the decree. His colleagues of course, discovered him praying and went to the king to report Daniel. They reminded him that, according to the rule, anyone who prayed to God instead of to the king within 30 days was to be thrown into the den of lions (Daniel 6:8-15).

Darius now discovered what he had done. He was displeased with himself. Had he known the motives behind his governors' and leaders' proposal, he would not have agreed to the statute. He tried hard to find a way to release Daniel from the consequence of breaking the decree that he signed with his own hands, but he could not. His officials did not make things easier by insisting that he enforce the decree that he signed. As a result, Darius commanded that Daniel be thrown into the den of lions.

Even so, King Darius said something remarkable. He told Daniel that His God would deliver him. In addition, a stone was used to cover the mouth of the lions' den and the king sealed it with his signet ring and the ring of his Lords. That was done so that the purpose concerning Daniel might not be changed (Daniel 6:17). Marvelous!

The escape route from the lions' den in which Daniel was tossed, was closed with a stone, which was sealed by the king, so that the purpose concerning Daniel would not be changed. My friend, the question is: What purpose—and whose purpose? Based on the narration presented by scripture, the purpose was to oust Daniel from his administrative position by getting him killed by the lions. This purpose, of course was instigated by the other governors and leaders.

Basically that was Daniel's adversaries' plot. That was their plan. However, God had other plans—a bigger plan. Daniel's colleagues, in their ignorance, might have thought that they got Daniel exactly where they wanted him, but actually, they helped Daniel get on the path toward where God wanted him. Therefore, the real purpose, the divine purpose, the true purpose of Daniel going to the Lions' den was God's purpose. Though he was thrown into the den by his colleagues, God was using it to promote Daniel.

Having mentioned the true purpose of Daniel being banished to the den of lions and established whose purpose it was—God's purpose, let's look a little more closely at some fine details about this account.

First off, after the lions got surprised with an uninvited but palatable guest who also doubled as their potential free dinner, an excerpt of Daniel 6:18 (NKJV) reads:

Now the king went to his palace and spent the night fasting....

Darius, the king, spent the night fasting for Daniel's deliverance. That is remarkable. The name Darius means *possessing the good*. You see, in a sense, Darius, a king, was a reflection of The King, Jesus. Like king Darius fasted for Daniel, so does The King Jesus fast for His children. Fasting involves abstaining from eating food or certain types of food and, or, drinks for a period of time. So Jesus is fasting according to this statement he made:

Assuredly, I say to you, I will no longer drink of the fruit of the vine until that day when I drink it new in the kingdom of God. (Mark 14:25 NKJV)

God is a good God. He is the epitome of good. Since Jesus is God the Son, He is the possessor of good. Goodness is an imprint of His love. With that in mind, we can see how God was working through Darius to help Daniel, whose name means, *God is my judge*.

The mouth of the den was sealed by the king with his signet ring. A signet is like a seal used to mark or endorse something. The word "signet" is actually coined from the word, "sign." A signet is like a notary on a legal document. The presence of a signet, sign or mark endorses the document on which the signet is found. The signet authenticates whatever it is found on. It is a seal that endorses the validity of a document.

In Daniel's case, Darius endorsed Daniel being sent into the lions' den. The stone which was used to close the mouth of the den was sealed with the signet rings of king Darius and his lords. Jesus is the King of Kings and Lord of Lords. He also has a signet, a seal, a sign that authenticates his children: The Holy Spirit, the third Person of the Triune God. God's Spirit in a believer is a sign that that individual is Christ's (Ephesians 1:13).

The devil recognizes this sign and is out to get any child of God. On the one hand, Satan is described as a roaring lion looking for who to devour (1 Peter 5:8). On the other hand, Jesus is also described as the Lion of the tribe of Judah (Revelations 5:5). Throwing Daniel into the lions' den was like throwing Daniel into the hands of Satan to be devoured by him. But in truth, he was thrust closer into the protection of the Lion of the tribe of Judah.

The stone blocking Daniel's escape route was sealed to ensure that the purpose concerning Daniel would not be changed.

And the stone was sealed by the king. At face value, the plan was to destroy Daniel by having the lions turn Daniel into their "Happy Meal." But the King, God, sealed the den to ensure that *His purpose* for Daniel would not be changed. This purpose had nothing to do with the lions getting their "grub on." That purpose had to do with Daniel getting promoted. God was using Daniel's commotion as locomotion for his promotion

God chose to allow Daniel to be rejected by his colleagues. Daniel was rejected into his purpose. Being pushed into the Lions' den pushed Daniel closer to His God, the Lion of the tribe of Judah.

God worked through King Darius' fast and faith in affirming to Daniel that God would deliver him. God also brought him through the lions' den, where He sent an angel to close the mouths of the lions so that they couldn't hurt Daniel. The lions had to take a back seat because the bigger Lion was calling the shots. Similarly the devil is rendered speechless and effortless when he tries to attack a person who is sealed by the Spirit of God. He cannot hurt an individual who, like Daniel, is *innocent before God*, *trusts* and *believes* in, and expects to be delivered by God's power (Luke 10:19).

The other administrators disliked Daniel. Their distaste for him was fueled when they discovered that Darius was thinking of making him their boss. That, my friend, was God's purpose for Daniel. That was set in motion when the other officials deceitfully entrapped the king to throw Daniel into the den of lions. In doing so, they actually threw him into the den of God—the will of God—the presence of God, manifested in the form of the angel who sealed the lions' mouth.

Being thrown in the den actually served as a catalyst to advance Daniel to the position that Darius considered for him. God used Daniel being rejected by his peers to get him to the position He ordained for him. God used Daniel's opposition to position him.

Darius could not sleep after he banished Daniel to the den of lions. He spent the night fasting. Early in the morning the next day, he ran to the entrance of the den calling out Daniel to find out if God delivered him. And Daniel in not so many words replied that God "had his back." God protected Daniel from being "devoured" by the lions. God disallowed the devil from having his way with His servant. That was realized after God sent an angel to shut the mouth of the lions (Daniel 6:19-24).

Daniel mentioned to the king that God protected him because he was innocent before God and he did not do anything wrong to the king. Not only did Daniel not displease God, neither did he disregard the king—even after the king endorsed his execution. That is so important! How you come out of rejection is dependent on how you go through it, and how you go through it is dependent on how you act in it.

As hurtful as rejection is, particularly in a situation where you are innocent, it is imperative that you maintain a good attitude toward God and toward those that tossed you into the den of rejection. While going through pain and suffering, you want God to be your judge not judge you—or, allow a negative sentence on you.

I encourage you to be like Daniel—someone whose judge is God. Mark these words:

For You have maintained my right and my cause; You sat on the throne judging in righteousness. (Psalm 9:4 NKJV)

So will God do for you if you're His beloved, innocent before Him and before your accusers.

On hearing that Daniel was not harmed by the lions, Darius was elated and commanded that Daniel be brought out of the den. On closer examination of Daniel, he discovered that he was not harmed or injured in any way. Just like there was no mark or sign of smoke on Daniel's friends, Meshack, Shadrack, and Abednego after they came out of the fire, there was no mark on Daniel, either.

...and no injury whatever was found on him, because he believed in his God (Daniel 6:23 NKJV).

Daniel survived the belly of the beasts because he *believed* in his God. He had *faith in God*. Believing in the power of God and His presence with you to acquit you from any crisis you face is fundamental to your survival. In facing rejection, are you going to be a victim or victor? Are you going to whine through your dilemma or shine through it? Whatever part you play in your ordeal, you don't want to end up receiving the fate imputed to Daniel's accusers.

Then the king gave orders to arrest the men who had maliciously accused Daniel. He had them thrown into the lions' den, along with their wives and children. The lions leaped on them and tore them apart before they even hit the floor of the den. (Daniel 6:24 NLT)

After Daniel's deliverance from the lions' den, the king commanded that those officials who came against Daniel be cast into the lions' den with their wives and children. Whoa! Can you imagine the lions' delight? Because the lions' obeyed God by not making a meal of Daniel—not that they had a choice—they were rewarded with a buffet of Daniel's accusers and their families. The beasts did not even let them hit the bottom of the den before they tore them up and had them for brunch. How sad.

Another thing that Darius did after he ordered Daniel out of the lions' den reinforces a significant point I made earlier about why God allows us to be rejected:

Then the king Darius sent this message to the people of every race and nation and language throughout the world: "Peace and prosperity to you! "I decree that everyone throughout my kingdom should tremble with fear before the God of Daniel. For he is the living God, and he will endure forever. His kingdom will never be destroyed, and his rule will never end. He rescues and saves his people; he performs miraculous signs and wonders in the heavens and on earth. He has rescued Daniel from the power of the lions." (Daniel 6:25-27 NLT)

Just like the men who tossed Daniel's friends into the fiery furnace got burned instead of Daniel's friends, so did Daniel's adversaries get eaten instead of Daniel. Similarly, people or companies that treat you despicably are subject to having a much more bitter taste of their own medicine. Their destruction might not be by fire or by a feeding frenzy carried out by the king of the jungle, it might manifest as an unforeseen collapse of the company that fired you, while you assume a promotion and better pay at a bigger company which, incidentally, had also been contracted to audit and clean up the mess of your previous employer.

The consequence of slander and conspiracies carried out by your colleagues and, or, boss at work against you could also result in your accusers finding themselves behind bars, bankrupt, and having a nervous breakdown. And, unfortunately, if your accusers have family, they could lose them through divorce and distrust. You on the other hand, because of your understanding that God was with you to bring you through the situation, would be better off than you were before you got rejected.

Since Daniel's accusers were digested and defecated by the lions, I guess that left the administrative positions in Persia wide open. Hmmm, I wonder who Darius hired to fill those positions? Well, I'll let you draw your own conclusions with this:

So this Daniel prospered in the reign of Darius and in the reign of Cyrus the Persian. (Daniel 6:28 NKJV)

Not only did Daniel succeed and fulfill His God-given destiny during Darius' regime, he also prospered and fulfilled his destiny during the reign of Darius' successor, King Cyrus. Based on this revelation, it seems like Daniel served for "two terms" in his office. But before he got "re-elected" by God, he had to go through the lions' den.

If you feel like Daniel in your den, it could be that you're being set up for a second term or a double portion. Be encouraged by this:

Because you got a double dose of trouble and more than your share of contempt, Your inheritance in the land will be doubled and your joy will go on forever. (Isaiah 61:7 MSG)

Just like God did with Daniel, Shadrach, Meshach, Abednego, Joseph, Paul, and Silas, sometimes God has to confine you so that when He drops His blessing on you, He won't miss. At times God straps you with the bull's eye of rejection so that your adversaries can have target practice on you. While your enemies propel *arrows at you,* God turns their arrows into *rockets for you.* God utilizes their attempts to annihilate you to elevate you. I guess this explains part of what David meant in

Psalm 23:5 when he said that *God sets* a table for us in the presence of our enemies. I always wondered why God had to prepare a table for us *in the presence* of our antagonists.

While pondering about this, it occurred to me that part of the reason could be because our enemies were the ones that brought the table, and the ones who inadvertently set it up for us. Their plan was to have us for dinner but God foiled their plan, and they ended up serving us dinner. Daniel's colleagues wanted to prevent Daniel from heading them up by getting him killed. They ended up getting themselves killed instead while they helped Daniel get the position and find their replacements. Nebuchadnezzar tried to kill Daniel's friends because they did not bow down to his image. He ended up killing some of his elite mighty men and bowing down to their own God and promoting them in the process. Joseph's brothers sold Joseph into slavery to prevent him from fulfilling his purpose. They ended up helping him achieve it. The magistrates in Philippi threw Paul and Silas in prison to stop them from spreading the gospel. They unwittingly assisted them in proselytizing the inmates and their jailer. Hmmm...I wonder if this is one of the main reasons why we have a record number of jail time conversions today.

With those in mind, be encouraged to know that God can utilize the rejection you're experiencing to help you fulfill His mandate for your life. Just remember that your response to your plight is key to the outcome of your situation. Just like the aforementioned Bible characters, it's in your best interest to respond to the opposition you're facing with faith, hope, and love.

PART 6: IT'S A ROAD TO REDEMPTION

Chapter 20

It Gets You Back on the Right Track

B arely dressed and perhaps too ashamed to look up, the woman was slumped over on the dusty ground, sobbing and probably bruised by the way she was manhandled by her accusers. With her tears beginning to make tiny puddles on the cement, she hid her face under the shade of her tattered hair, avoiding the gaze from the man who was to pass judgment on her, and from the men who captured and dragged her out of the house where she was caught in the act of infidelity.

"*Any second now those stones will scar my flesh and pierce my soul until I fade to eternity*" she must have thought while she awaited her fate.

She held her breath as the seconds trickled by. Nothing happened. She cherished what she must have considered her last few gasps for air. Still, nothing happened. No stones were hurled at her. In fact it seemed everything grew quiet as she heard shuffling feet gradually fade out of her hearing. She was likely startled at the voice that spoke to her with a tone in sharp contrast to her detractors.

When she heard the man's voice, she must have felt the weight of reproach and remorse lifted off her shoulders as she looked into his eyes gleaming with love. Jesus, still stooping down, inquired of her wellbeing. He asked her if her accusers had stoned her, to which she answered that none of them had. He told her that he did not condemn her, either. He then told her to go her way—and sin no more.

IT LEADS YOU TO GOD

You might be all too familiar with the story of the lady who was caught in the act of adultery. Some men nabbed her, dragged her, and threw her before Jesus, and asked Him what was to be done to her. They reminded the Lord of their law which mandated them to stone her based on her misdeed. Jesus stooped down to the ground like he never heard what they said and began to write on the earth. He then told her accusers that those of them who had not sinned before should cast the first stone. On hearing that statement, the men dropped their stones and walked off—one by one—beginning with the eldest (John 8:1-11).

The woman was rejected because of the sin she committed. As if dragging her out of the bed or wherever she was being immoral with her accomplice wasn't enough humiliation, they tossed her before Jesus in an attempt to justify their case before they stoned her. Fortunately, they did the woman a favor; the best thing that ever happened for her, for me, and for you, too.

In an attempt to take her life, they gave her life. Not only did they drag her to the right person, they rejected her to the best person who was best equipped to help *liberate* her from her predicament. Perhaps in her attempt to find love, she sought it in an illicit affair with the wrong man. By apprehending her and thrusting her before Christ, her accusers, unbeknownst to them, helped her find the fulfillment she desired. They yanked her from the arms of the wrong man into the embrace of the right man. Being rejected by those men translated her from an act of infidelity to a life of liberty.

Though Jesus did not condone her for her transgression, He did not condemn her, either. He convicted her accusers instead. He rightly judged the situation.

You might wonder how what happened to that woman is beneficial to us. Well, she also exemplifies someone whose experience with rejection helps us overcome our experiences with rejection, too. If you've ever responded to anyone's accusation against you by saying something like, "If you have not sinned cast the first stone," note that that expression originated from that woman's experience. It was her experience that afforded you the opportunity to use that statement. It was her rejection that gave you ammunition to combat those that came against you. Although we should not use that statement as a crutch to justify our sins, it's a word of caution, conviction, and correction for those who are out to get us.

The woman was thrown to the right person. That is what rejection can do for you and me. When people ostracize us for mistakes we've made, they sometimes throw us into the embrace of those that would take us in our mess and help us become our best. The woman ending up at the feet of Jesus was a humbling gesture. I believe that anytime we make a mistake, our first destination should be on our knees at the feet of God to ask for forgiveness and restoration.

Interestingly, the men who dragged the woman to the Lord were the Scribes and Pharisees. They were *leaders*. The builders brought her to be executed but unwittingly helped her to be acquitted. The men condemned the woman to be destroyed, but their rejection got her restored. And this is the kicker: They brought her to the temple. It was while Christ was teaching in the synagogue that they shoved her before Him (John 8: 2-3).

The main point I'm bringing out from that account is that if we are heading in the wrong direction, God can use rejection to get us back on the right track. He uses it to redirect us to His house of worship so that we can receive forgiveness, restoration and proper direction to get back on the right track.

So, those who are coming against you are only pushing to God. Although they are trying to frustrate you, their antagonism is leading you to God. If you did not realize this, I encourage you to let the thrust of your antagonists push you into God's house of worship where He will not condemn, but set you free.

IT POINTS YOU BACK IN THE RIGHT DIRECTION

The book of Jonah enlightens us about the prophet Jonah whom God assigned to deliver a life-changing message to the people of Nineveh. But Jonah did exactly the opposite. Instead of going to Nineveh as God instructed him, he went the opposite direction by boarding a ship going to Tarshish "away from the presence of the Lord."

God sent a storm that rocked the boat and caused those in the ship to panic and pray to *their gods* for help. Meanwhile, Jonah was fast asleep in the lowest part of the ship. The captain of the ship found Jonah sleeping, woke him up and asked him to pray to his God to deliver them from the raging storm. The other travelers in the ship also huddled together and concluded that the reason they were going through the raging of the storm was because of Jonah. Jonah in turn admitted that he was the cause of all the brouhaha. Later on, reluctantly, at Jonah's request, the travelers in the ship tossed Jonah out of the boat into the sea in which a great fish, prepared by God, swallowed him and lodged him for three days and three nights (Jonah 1).

Jonah's story adequately illustrates how God uses rejection to help us fulfill our destiny. God had instructed him to go to Nineveh to deliver a message, but Jonah did the opposite and went to Tarshish away from God's presence. Like Jonah, some of us head in the wrong direction. God told him to go one way, and he went another way. Furthermore, the Bible said that he paid a fare to board the ship that took him to Tarshish (Jonah 1:3).

Like Jonah, as a result of going in the wrong direction or doing something that is contrary to God's will, we *pay* a price. It costs us. Going away from God's will can cost us our dignity, our emotions, and our dreams, just to mention a few. Interestingly, Jonah boarded a ship that was to take him to Tarshish. Indulge me as we explore the significance of the ship that Jonah boarded.

You see, friend, in our everyday language we say things like "we are in the same boat." This means that we are in the same situation or predicament. This means that we are dealing with similar circumstances. With this in mind, since a ship is a boat, to better understand Jonah's drama's relevance to our lives, let's envision Jonah getting in the ship as him getting into a situation, a predicament or a circumstance because he left God.

Furthermore, there are different kinds of ships. There are friend-ships, sponsor-ships, companion-ships, intern-ships and relation-ships. However, the most important ship of all is the Lord-ship—the Lordship of Jesus Christ, having Jesus Lord over our lives. When we go out of His will like Jonah did, we basically jump ship. Like Jonah, we get out of God's presence, God's will, and place ourselves in another's presence, someone else's will, some other ship. This usually leads to "hard-ships." God is not pleased when we do that. Sometimes if we don't repent, it will take an act of God to bring us back into His presence.

So, Jonah goes in the opposite direction from where God told him to go, he paid to get on a ship, and he also ended up on a ship with unbelievers since they prayed to *their* gods for help from the storm (Jonah 1:5). When God sent a storm to rock the boat, the ship was about to be broken and, yet, Jonah was sleeping in the lowest point of the ship (Jonah 1:5). Along the same lines, when we get ourselves in situations because we left God's will, we can also end up in the *lowest point* of the ships or boats we boarded. We can end up depressed. We can hit rock bottom.

The ship was about to be broken up due to the tempest on the sea. Yet, Jonah was in the lowest part of the ship "fast asleep." This is how it is with us sometimes. When we get out of God's will by getting ourselves in relationships or things that we have no business with, situations arise. Storms emerge. We feel rocked in the boat we placed ourselves in. And yet like Jonah we wallow in it. We stay in the destructive ship.

Even in a relationship that is obviously not working, a relationship that is about to be broken, a relationship tossed to and fro with the tempest of disobedience, some of us still stay in it. As heart-wrenching and devastating as the relation-*ship* is, some of us still flounder in it. Like the lowest part of the ship Jonah slept in, some of us hit rock bottom—the lowest part of that ship.

Sometimes we anesthetize our shame by acting like everything is all right. Despite the obvious decadence in the relationship, we sleep in our mess. We've carved out a comfort zone in the lowest part of the ship. Despite the impending danger in the ship, despite the fact that our boat is about to be broken, some of us still try to sleep our problems away. We try to act like nothing is wrong, everything is all right, it's just a nightmare, just a bad dream, it will all go away. We might even quote, "Weeping might endure for the night but joy cometh in the morning" (Psalm 30:5).

The only way joy will come in the morning is when we weep at night to God for forgiveness and repent for getting out of His will. Unfortunately, sometimes, we've sunk so low in the ship and gotten desensitized to our alienation from God's presence. In that regard, we are like a person who endures his or her stench while moving his or her bowels but gradually adapts to the smell of their defecation.

God, however, in demonstration of his love for us comes to rescue us from our pitfalls. Though we might not know or have the courage to get out of situations, boats or ships we get ourselves into, God will assist us in getting us out. How He goes about it at times, like he did for Jonah, is through rejection.

The ship's crew was frantic about what was happening and their captain had to find Jonah and wake him up from his sleep. Sometimes, when we get ourselves in situations that we were not supposed to be in in the first place and end up with people we were not supposed to be with, too, God can use the very people that we were not supposed to be hanging out with to wake us up from our slumbers. The captain woke Jonah up, and Jonah told him that he was the cause of their chaos (Jonah 1:6). The ship crew asked him what they needed to do to resolve the raging storm and Jonah told them that they needed to throw him out of the ship.

They said to him, "What are we going to do with you—to get rid of this storm?" By this time the sea was wild, totally out of control. Jonah said, "Throw me overboard, into the sea. Then the storm will stop. It's all my fault. I'm the cause of the storm. Get rid of me and you'll get rid of the storm." (Jonah 1:11-12 MSG)

Isn't this something? Jonah knew that he was the problem.

Jonah knew that he was the one that brought the storm, yet he was not going to leave the boat. He was not going to jump off himself. The only way he was going to get off the boat is if they threw him out.

Wikipedia reveals that the word "rejection" was first used in the year 1415, and it meant "to throw" or "to throw back."[1] Therefore, when Jonah told his ship mates to throw him out he was basically telling them to reject him. He was telling them to disallow him from being in the boat. He was telling them not to accept him on the boat.

Some of us are like Jonah. We know or sense that we are going in the wrong direction. We know that we are in the wrong boat, with the wrong person(s), in the wrong job, or just in a place that we're not supposed to be. You don't like it. You are frustrated by it. You are unfulfilled in it, but like Jonah you still stay in it. In fact, you carve out a comfort zone and sleep in it. Given this scenario, one is left to wonder why people choose to remain in such broken ships. But if you look at Jonah's options, perhaps you can empathize with his situation.

Jonah, from his perspective, only had two options: 1) to remain on the boat or 2) to jump into the sea. Now, I don't know about you, but as bad as the ship is, it seems better than the sea. Some of us have gotten ourselves in situations that are depressing and emotionally and psychologically unfulfilling. Yet, we stay in such predicaments.

You might say to yourself, "I don't like this place," "I hate this situation," "I hate this job," "I can't stand this relationship any longer," "I'm not getting my needs met," "I'm not getting fulfilled," "I'm not happy," yet, you still stay in the depressing situation. Perhaps it's because you feel that staying in a sinking ship is better than drowning in a sea of uncertainty.

You might feel that staying at the bottom of a draining relationship is better than not having a relationship at all; at least that's what it looks like. The ocean of uncertainty might be an outlook of not finding anyone else that will take you after what you have been through. It might look like there is nothing out there better for you. But that is not the case. God has bigger and better things for you to do, places for you to go, jobs for you to have, and someone to share your life with.

However, if your mental state is such that you are not going to leave a situation despite the fact that it is making you miserable, unfulfilling you, depressing you and swallowing you up like quicksand, then the only way for you to be "saved" from your slow death is to be *thrown* out—hence, God's purpose for rejection. Sometimes the only way God can get you out of a rut is to get you rejected from it.

Sometimes, you are not the person to be thrown out. Sometimes you are the person that needs to throw someone out. Why don't you put yourself in the position of the ship's crew for a moment? You are the one that invited someone into your ship—be it your business, your ministry, or your heart. And as soon as the person came in, all hell broke loose. All of a sudden your ship is about to be broken.

You don't have to be Einstein to figure out the cause of the brouhaha. You know that your guest is the main culprit behind the potential implosion you're about to face, even if the person is acting nonchalant, passive and is nowhere in sight like Jonah at the bottom of the ship.

It's in your best interest to dismiss that person. It doesn't matter who that person is. In Jonah's case, he was a prophet. It's especially hard to toss someone who is supposed to be revered. It's hard to let go of someone you look up to. It's difficult to part with a man or woman of God, a family member, a mentor, someone who helped you out significantly some time in your life or someone that is important and dear to you. Don't let your sentiment lead to your detriment.

If you don't get rid of any Jonah in your life, especially when you are fully aware that the individual is causing problems for you, your ship will sink. Your boat will go under. You will no longer have the option of choosing between a sinking ship and a sea of uncertainty. Rather, your sinking ship will sink in the sea with certainty.

Even after Jonah made it clear to the ship crew that he was the cause of their problem, they still tried hard to salvage the ship.

Jonah said, "Throw me overboard, into the sea. Then the storm will stop. It's all my fault. I'm the cause of the storm. Get rid of me and you'll get rid of the storm." But no. The men tried rowing back to shore. They made no headway. The storm only got worse and worse, wild and raging. (Jonah 1:12-13 MSG)

That's kind of how we are sometimes. After God or the dire circumstances that you're facing has made it clear sometimes through the culprit, that he or she needs to go, some of us try harder to keep the person in our lives. You go for counseling. You hit the gym. You try the Atkins diet, the "you" diet, "Alli's" diet, and it's a surprise that you haven't *died yet.* Notwithstanding, despite your sincere efforts to keep the boyfriend or girlfriend, husband or wife, roommate or family member, employee, business partner, deacon, usher, church member or worker that is *clearly* sinking your ship, in your boat, the situation gets worse. Your boat sinks even faster.

Eventually the ship crew threw Jonah out of the boat and there was calm. Likewise, the sooner you dismiss whomever God wants you to part with, the sooner you'll get your restoration. If you don't, your ship will sink. You will go under, and if you're not careful, depending on your situation, you can end up six feet under.

Jonah got rejected off the boat because God had something better for him to do, somewhere better for him to go, and some people better for him to save from God's wrath. Likewise, God has something better for you to do, some place better for you to go, and someone better for you to be in relationship with. God allows you to be cast off from a wrong relationship to the right relationship: His Lordship.

Can you imagine the slap in God's face to see his beloved prophet in the lowest part of the ship? Jonah paid to board on the wrong ship, and he rode with the wrong folks. He paid to be in a mess. Similarly, it costs us dearly when we get away from God's presence. We often pay unnecessary prices when we get ourselves in a mess. It saddens our Father to see some of us pay to shoot up, get drunk, or get sexually, psychologically and emotionally exploited and abused. That being the case, we end up bound in situations we get ourselves in. In our melancholy, it seems there is no way out of our despair; but there is.

In such cases, something drastic and radical has to take place. God has to do something to deliver us from our predicament. Rejection is one of those drastic measures that God uses to liberate us. When we get rejected, we usually don't see how that is a good thing. When we are oblivious of the fact that God uses rejection to get us where he wants us to be, we often end up dejected. That is why it's imperative for us to understand why God allows us to be rejected. When He facilitates rejection, He's only getting us to where we need to be and whom we need to be with.

Jonah, a prophet, a man of God, God's mouthpiece, erred when he tried to run away from doing God's will. He took what he thought was the easy way out of his responsibility. He boarded the wrong ship with the wrong folks going the wrong way. But Jonah got thrown out of the boat.

When he got tossed out of the boat, he ended up in the belly of a big fish prepared by God. Hmmm, God prepared a place for him in the belly of the fish. While in the fish Jonah asked God to forgive him, and God did. From the belly of the fish, he cried out to God and God heard his cry (Jonah 1:17; 2).

Dear friend if you feel that you're like Jonah in the lowest point of your life, in the belly of the fish of despair and you know that you got there by making poor decisions, don't just cry—cry out to God! He will hear, heal, forgive and restore you. After Jonah reconciled with God, God spoke to the fish, and the fish vomited him (Jonah 2:10). Interesting.

When we ingest food that does not sit well in our stomachs, our bodies respond by rejecting the ingested food. In other words, we vomit out what we ate. So, by vomiting Jonah, the fish rejected him out of its belly. Jonah was back in the Lord's ship. God again commanded Jonah to go to Nineveh once he was out of the belly of the fish, and this time around He followed instructions (Jonah 3). It appears that Jonah was rejected from Tarshish back to Nineveh.

In essence, God uses rejection to maneuver us from going in

the wrong direction to the right direction. He uses it to get us from a bad relationship to a good one. He employs it to get us from an unfulfilling career to a fulfilling one. He utilizes it to lead us back to His presence, back to His will—His purpose for our lives.

LOST AND FOUND

You might also be familiar with the story of the kid who left home prideful and with plenty, but later came back home humble and empty. He was the younger of two sons. He demanded that his dad give him the portion of his father's inheritance that belonged to him. His father adhered to his request, and not long after he got his cut, he left home and went to a *distant* country.

The young man squandered his possessions in his newfound land and was soon hit by a severe famine that plagued the country he relocated to. Desperate, the lad hooked up with a citizen of the country. His sponsor then assigned him the task of feeding his pigs. The young man was so hungry that he even desired to eat from the pig's slop; but, no one gave him anything.

The Bible says the young man came to himself, and when he contemplated on how his father's servants were faring better than him, he decided to go back home and ask his father to forgive him and hire him as one of his servants. On his way back home, while he was afar off, his father saw him. Oozing with compassion for his son, he ran to him, kissed him and received him back home. He then threw a party for him (Luke 15:11-32).

For whatever reason, the kid took his portion of his father's wealth and left home. He left a loving father and the security and provisions of his father's house. He ended up in the insecurity and lack of provision in another man's house. The young man basically went astray. He headed in the wrong direction and thereby ended up in the wrong place. He blew all his dough and ended up broke. To make matters worse, a famine hit the country he went to. Consequently, he was forced to secure employment feeding pigs.

But what caused him to come back home? What was the turning point that got him back in the right direction? Rejection!

He was so hungry he would have eaten the corncobs in the pig slop, but no one would give him any. That brought him to his senses. He said, "All those farmhands working for my father sit down to three meals a day, and here I am starving to death. I'm going back to my father. I'll say to him, Father, I've sinned against God, I've sinned before you; I don't deserve to be called your son. Take me on as a hired hand." He got right up and went home to his father. (Luke 15:16-20 MSG)

The story reveals that he desired to eat of the pig's food, *but no one would give him any*. He was not even given pig food. The dude was disallowed from eating hog's slop, let alone bacon, ham or chitterlings. Can a brother eat?

After he was rejected from receiving anything, he came to himself; he came to his senses. Sometimes when we are not thinking straight or when we make uninformed decisions, being rejected for our poor decisions causes us to wake up and re-think our actions. When we get ourselves in situations that bring us low, like the situation where the prodigal son was confined to feeding pigs, we are forced to take a good look at ourselves and contemplate our plight. We are humbled and compelled to look up to God to deliver us from the pit we got ourselves into.

Think about it: the young man was required to feed the pigs but was prevented from eating pigs' food, and neither could he eat the pigs. There goes the sausage links and the pork chops. How low can one get? That triggered him to come back home. Likewise, when we go astray, when we take for granted God's love and get out of his will to do our own thing, we are subject to being disappointed. God, however, uses our disappointments to reappoint us back to our destiny.

THREE KINDS OF PEOPLE

I believe we all fall within three classifications of people. I believe that we are either mature believers, baby believers, or non-believers. The mature believers are those that have a strong relationship with God. They hear from Him, and they are familiar with what He wants them to do. The baby believers also have a relationship with God but are more susceptible than the mature believers to go astray and let their own agendas distract them from hearing and adhering to God's directives. The non-believers are those that do not have a relationship with God and usually don't care to know Him or hear from Him.

For illustrative purposes, I believe Jonah represents a strong believer, the prodigal son represents the baby believer, and the woman caught in infidelity represents a non-believer.

Jonah depicts the strong saint because He was God's Prophet; he heard from God, had a relationship with Him and knew exactly what God wanted him to do. The prodigal son depicts the immature saint because although he had a relationship with his father who was symbolic of God, the Father, he chose to do his own thing by packing all his belongings and moving to a "distant" country away from his pops. He chose to live his live apart from his father like so many of us who've received God as our loving Father but sometimes take His love and grace for granted by living our lives apart from Him. The woman caught in adultery represents the non-believer because we have no indication that she knew God. All that was revealed about her prior to her encounter with Christ was that she transgressed.

Despite the classifications, they all had one thing in common; like us all, they made poor decisions. They also had something else in common; they were stirred or sent back to God through rejection. Friend, that puts us all on the same playing field. It doesn't matter where you're from, what you've done, what you believe or don't believe; living apart from God will land us in the same boat. Our decisions can drop us in the same ship. If the ship is not the Lord's, God can use rejection to get us *all* on, or back to His ship. In this context, I'm not better off than you are. Regardless of the different side of tracks we come from, God uses rejection to get us to Him—or back to Him.

The woman caught in the act of adultery was rejected into the arms of The Savior. The prodigal son was rejected back into the arms of his father. Jonah the "prophet" was rejected back to do God's will. Seems to me that compared to the other two, Jonah had it worst. I'd rather be dragged to church or be hungry for some pig slop and intestines, than risk that "Jaws" have my intestines for dinner. It was only by the grace and mercy of God that Jonah was not masticated by the fish. That must have freaked him out. That sure got his attention. He cried out to God from the fish, and God delivered him. God spoke to the fish, and it vomited Jonah out of its belly. How bad did Jonah taste that the fish refused him? That in itself is a humbling experience, and it got Jonah back on track.

Chapter 21
We Need to Do It, Too

For the most part I've been discussing how we should respond to rejection and how God uses the experience to help us discover and fulfill His plan for our lives. Notwithstanding, there are things in life that we face that warrant us to reject, too. In order to be all God wants us to be, it's beneficial for us to exercise the courage to say "no" to others. If not, we are likely to get the short end of the stick. We will lose out if we do not refuse, resist or rebuff individuals and situations detrimental to our overall well-being.

I believe that there are at least three main things that we need to reject:

1. *Reject Being Like Other People.*

Don't try to be like other people. Don't try to do things like them. Be yourself. One of the reasons why some people are unsuccessful at who they are and what they do is because they try to be like others. We can only be successful at being who we are. We're all unique individuals. Trying to be like someone else is like a duck trying to be a squirrel. This is impossible! Is it any wonder we often disappoint ourselves?

Some of us have not even scratched the surface on how special we are. That's because we've spent most of our lives chasing the wind by trying to be and do things like other people. Don't get me wrong; we should learn from others. Their successes should inspire us to make something of ourselves, and their mistakes should dissuade us from making nothing of ourselves. However, how we go about applying what we learn from other individuals does not have to be exactly like the way they applied their learning experiences.

I'm not saying that we should reinvent the wheel; if need be, we should *renovate* it. Some people don't feel good about themselves because they've been comparing themselves to others. That is why some people feel that they are not beautiful. It's been said that beauty lies in the eye of the beholder. We need to be the beholder of ourselves.

In order to be beautiful, you need to *be-you-to-full*. Be yourself to the fullest. Be the unique person God created you to be. You're beautiful! Behold your beauty! Behold yourself! God's masterpiece. You are God's masterpiece because you're a piece of the Master. Genesis 1:26 revealed that God created you like Himself. You are a piece of God—the *Master's piece*.

David was ready to fight Goliath. Saul gave David his armor to take on the giant. When David put on Saul's armor, he felt weighed down. He could hardly move. That is what happens when we try to be like others. Our inability to be like them weighs us down. We feel immobilized because we can't think, act, or do things like they do. That is the case because God did not create us like them. He created us to be unique.

Then Saul outfitted David as a soldier in armor. He put his bronze helmet on his head and belted his sword on him over the armor. David tried to walk but he could hardly budge. David told Saul, "I can't even move with all this stuff on me. I'm not used to this." And he took it all off." (1 Samuel 17:38-39 MSG)

We experience failure when we put on armor, gadgets, personalities or styles that are "suited" for others but not for us. If David had worn that armor to fight Goliath, he would have lost the battle before it started. Goliath would have fed him to the dogs. He would have been minced meat. But thank God David rejected being like Saul. He refused to proceed with a tactic that even Saul could not use. We should not reinvent the wheel; we should renovate it.

In any and every battle we need to be courageous; we need faith; we need hope; we need persistence and determination. However, how we apply those virtues does not have to be exactly like others. David needed an armor to fight Goliath. But based on his uniqueness, he did not need an armor of steel; he needed an armor of skill. Five smooth stones and a sling shot did not necessarily do the job. It was his shield of faith in God, the helmet of salvation that God "got his back," and the sword of God's Word in his mouth that God would help him prevail, that did the job. It was these armor that provided the support for David to catapult the stone that brought down Goliath (1 Samuel 17:40-50; Ephesians 6:10-14).

David rejected Saul's armor because he had no experience with it. David had experience with his own armor—the same one he used to protect his father's sheep from a lion and a bear, both of which he took out with faith in God's protection. He applied his experience with the animals against Goliath and prevailed.

We are not experienced in being other people. Some of us are even inexperienced in being ourselves because we've exhausted lots of time and energy and suffered defeat by trying to be like others. We should be ourselves. We should take time to begin to discover and cultivate the gifts, talents, abilities and personalities that God has placed in us. We should begin to express our hearts. If we don't, well, like I've been discussing throughout this book, rejection is hired to cause us to dig deep into ourselves and withdraw the things that have been lying dormant in us.

Friend, reject trying to be like others. In your own unique way, you're beautiful. If you haven't discovered that, just be-you-to-full.

2. Reject anything or anyone that will cause you to get out of God's will.

Don't let any circumstance or situation cause you to get out of God's will. Don't let anyone induce or seduce you to stop going to the "well." Rather, refuse to be sidetracked from fulfilling God's mandate for your life. Turn down anyone that will lure you away from God. Cast off anything that will tempt you to turn your back on God. Resist the devil and he will flee from you (James 4:6-7). Say no to the enemy and say yes to God.

Joseph was in a precarious situation. His boss's wife was attracted to him. How couldn't she be? Joseph was hot! His employer had charged him with the responsibility to manage all his affairs. Joseph oversaw his house, his food and all his other possessions, except his wife. But Potiphar's wife wanted to be part of the "affairs" under Joseph's supervision.

Joseph was not having it. He rejected her advances toward him. He did not want to go out of God's will, so, he turned her down. Despite the pressure she mounted on him, he refused to have an affair with her. Consequently, she rejected him, too. She falsely told Potiphar that Joseph tried to violate her. Her husband fired him and put him in prison (Genesis 39:6-23). That is unfair, isn't it?

Joseph was incarcerated for doing the right thing. He was rejected for *exceeding* his boss' wife's expectations. Yet, he was tossed behind bars. It seemed that Joseph was setback from fulfilling his purpose. But as you now know, he was setup for it. In fact, rejecting Potiphar's wife triggered the next phase of Joseph's progress toward his destiny. He was demoted to prison where he linked up with the King's servant who connected him to his promotion (Genesis 40 & 41). With this in mind, like Joseph, reject anything or anyone that will cause you to get out of God's will.

3. Reject anything or anyone that will ruin your destiny.

While doing research on the one thing people need to know to have sustained individual success, leadership and management consultant Marcus Buckingham made a discovery that led him to classify people into two groups: Eighty Percenters and Twenty Percenters. The twenty percenters were of course, the ones that achieved sustained individual success. This is what Marcus Buckingham said about them:

"From my research, the difference between the twenty percenters and the rest of us can be found less in what they choose to do and more in what they choose not to do." [1]

As a result of that conclusion, Marcus Buckingham said that the one thing that we all need to know to sustain success is to discover what we don't like doing and stop doing it.[2] In other words, twenty percenters *reject* doing things that stand in the way of their success. It has been said that success is finding out your purpose and doing it. Well, to accomplish and sustain this, as revealed by Mr. Buckingham, we need to reject things that impede our destiny, which in turn is tied to our success in life.

Don't get involved with anything that will ruin your destiny. Regardless of how appealing or lucrative a thing might look, stay far away, refuse or reject it if you know that it's going to negatively affect your future. It doesn't matter how attractive an individual is; it doesn't matter the number of endorsements a person receives; it doesn't matter if a man or woman's credentials is impeccable; if you know that that person is going to ruin you, reject him or her!

When I talked about Boaz and Ruth in chapter seven, I alluded to the close relative who refused to marry Ruth. Consequently that enabled Ruth to marry Boaz. Nevertheless, let me address his refusal of Ruth from another perspective.

Ruth, of course, was an outstanding young lady. She had the exclusive privilege of being called virtuous in the Bible (Ruth 3:11). Yet, the close relative refused her. He did not accept Ruth because, according to him, marrying her would ruin his inheritance (Ruth 4:5-6). It's possible that he rejected the offer to marry Ruth simply because she was a Moabite, a non-Israelite and foreigner from a pagan nation. Despite this possibility, if the reason he gave for refusing her was legit, the close relative made the right decision by rejecting her.

Despite Ruth's rising popularity, morality and integrity, the man rejected her. Why? Because it would have ruined his inheritance. Similarly, you should reject anyone that you know will ruin your inheritance. Your inheritance is connected to your destiny. If you're going to inherit something, that means you are going to receive something in the future. That is something in your destiny. If someone is going to cause you to miss out on what you're supposed to get from God, it's in your best interest that you lose the person; if not, you'll risk losing your inheritance and fulfilling your destiny.

Furthermore, like the close relative did for Ruth, you'll be doing the person a favor. By refusing the individual you're saving and preserving the person for his or her destiny, you're redirecting and helping the person to end up with someone else better suited for him or her. The person might not understand why you turned them down; the individual might blacklist you; but, in time, the person will be grateful that you said "no" to him. If not, at least you said "yes" to your destiny. You chose to end up where God wanted you, and with whom He destined for you.

Again, the fourth season of *The Apprentice* drives my point. Like I said before, I understand that this was a television program and things might have been tweaked to suit the objectives of the program. Nevertheless, for illustrative purposes, let's assume that what went on, at least, on the finale was for real.

Dr. Randal Pinkett emerged as The Apprentice. He earned the winner's title. However, Donald Trump asked him if he would share his title with Rebecca Jarvis, the other finalist. But Dr. Randal Pinkett rejected the notion. As a result Dr. Pinkett drew a lot of criticism. In fact his response to Donald "Trump's card" led some viewers to pull the "race" card and every other card.

Even so, Pinkett's response is a classic example of what I'm saying. His refusal of Miss Jarvis was not because he did not want her to work for the Trump organization. He dismissed the notion of having a tie with her. He felt he earned it. He felt that he "inherited" the title of The Apprentice. Based on his impressive resume, exceptional work on and off the program, he felt he was destined for the victory. Tying with Miss Jarvis would have ruined his destiny of being the "sole" winner of that competition.

What did I say about encountering anything that would ruin your destiny—you reject it. Miss Jarvis, of course, was outstanding; a fact that Dr. Pinkett also acknowledged. Nonetheless, despite her impressive attributes, he turned down the idea of sharing the title with her. Whether we liked or disliked what he did is beside the point. He did what he felt was best for him. We might think that his response tarnished his nice guy persona. But what we think does not matter to him; what Dr. Randall thinks about himself and his convictions, does.

It was his decision, not ours. It was his destiny, not ours. It was his call, not ours. He made what he felt was the right decision for *himself*. The ball was on his court, and he chose to slam dunk it, instead of giving an assist to Miss Jarvis to put the ball in the basket—so to speak. Despite his solo effort, they *both* won. Randall won the accolade of being The Apprentice, and Rebecca Jarvis' disappointment won her an appointment with at least, *Yahoo* and *Microsoft*. It was a win-win situation.

Not only did Dr. Randal Pinkett exemplify what I'm saying about rejecting anyone that would ruin your destiny, he also exemplified someone who did not try to be like others. He heard Mr. Trump but did not adhere to his proposal despite the fact that Mr. Trump was a potential mentor, boss, and the one responsible for hiring him. He made the tough decision of rebuffing his competitor despite going against the wishes of the court of popular opinion. He did not respond to Donald Trump's request based on what might please us, not even what might have pleased Mr. Trump. He made his response based on *his own* convictions. He did not make the decision based on what we think, how we felt, or what we thought was right. He made his decision which did not undermine Miss Jarvis from being part of Mr. Trump's bandwagon. His decision only meant that he won the competition over her.

Along the same lines, you should make decisions based on *your* heart's conviction and not on other people's. We can only hope that you make the right decision, because it has been said that life is choice-driven and we live or die by the choices we make. I'd rather make a mistake by following my own convictions than make a mistake by following someone else's convictions.

DON'T DO IT TO GOD

It's in your best interest not to be exactly like other people. Refuse anything or anyone that would lure you out of God's will and prevent you from fulfilling your destiny. If you don't adhere to these guidelines, you're setting yourself up for major disappointments. And since God desires for you to walk in accordance with the way He created you, walk in His will and walk to your destiny, not rebuffing circumstances and people that dissuade you from fulfilling God's purpose for your life is like rejecting God; the One Person you should *not* reject.

There was a prophet whom God assigned to deliver a message to a particular region. God told him that after he delivers the message, he should not turn into anyone's house to eat or drink, and he should not leave the town where he prophesied God's oracle the same way he came into it. The prophet received the instruction and went on to fulfill his mandate.

After declaring God's Word over the place, the town's king who was present when he was giving his prophesy asked him to come to his house to eat and drink. The prophet refused. The prophet told the king that God instructed him not to go into anyone's house to wine and dine, nor should he leave the vicinity the way he came into it. So, the prophet departed the place using another route.

Later on, an "old prophet" caught up with the man that God sent to the town. The old prophet asked the younger prophet to come to his house to have some repast. The young prophet turned down the offer and gave the older prophet the same spiel he gave the king. But the older prophet told the young man that he was a prophet, too. He said that God sent an angel to him to tell the young prophet that it was okay for the young man to come to the old prophet's house and get his grub on. The young prophet then changed his mind and went to the older prophet's house to eat and drink.

After eating in the old prophet's house, while seated at the table with his host, God spoke through the old prophet to the young man. He told the young prophet that because he disobeyed God's command, his body would not make to his ancestor's tomb.

After the young man left the old prophet's house, he encountered a lion on the way, and the animal killed him (1 Kings 13).

Whoa! Perhaps, like me, you have a question mark in your head. For the life of me, I don't know how to explain why God spoke judgment on the young prophet through the same old prophet that deceived the young man. That is a puzzle that has still left me puzzled.

When I first read this story I was ticked off! I was partly upset because I could relate with the young man. Perhaps you do, too. It was likely that the young man complied with the old prophet's request out of respect for him, and he probably rationalized that the older man was more experienced and knew more of the things of God. He probably also thought that the old prophet was telling the truth when he said that God had sent an angel to let him know that he could fellowship with the old prophet. But it was a lie. The young man paid dearly for not rejecting what the older prophet said.

That is part of what I meant when I said that we should reject anything or anyone that would cause us to get of God's will. My heart goes out to all the people that have lost their lives, marriages, ministries, businesses, contracts, friendships, relationships, promotions and other great opportunities because contrary to their better judgment, they adhered to the wrong advice given by those they thought were more experienced in what they where trying to achieve.

Have you ever asked someone you considered a mentor, leader or expert about something, and they gave you their advice on what to do? And despite something in you that dissuaded you from heeding their suggestion, you decided to adhere to their "two cents" because you felt that the person had more experience about the situation? But what you were trying to accomplish blew up in your face and devastated you; and, to add insult upon injury, the very person who advised you to do what you did denigrated you for carrying it out. You're further heartbroken when the individual denies that he or she gave you advice about the situation or claimed that you should have known better than to apply his or her opinion.

That was what that young prophet went through. Unfortunately, he lost his life. By adhering to the old prophet's instruction, he disobeyed God's directives. Unbeknownst to him, he rejected God. In a sense, by hearkening to the older prophet, the young man was trying to be like him. He chose another man's opinion instead of what he knew as truth in himself. As a result he got out of God's will, and he ruined his destiny. Did you see the pattern?

When we try to be like others by listening and adhering to their opinions in the expense of what God has placed in our hearts, we get out of God's will and ruin our destiny. When we get out of God's will, we also get out of His jurisdiction. And when we're out of His jurisdiction, we're out of His protection, and, hence, we're exposed to the enemy—the devil. Remember? He's like a roaring lion looking for whom to devourer (1 Peter 5:8). I believe the prophet being devoured by the lion was symbolic of being destroyed by the devil. Had he refused the old prophet, the young man would've been in God's will and would've been protected by the Lion of the tribe of Judah—Jesus.

With that in mind, may I give a suggestion? Don't accept anyone's two cents if it's going to cost you a million dollars. Don't even accept my two cents when you know that adhering to it will cost you a dime.

Saul made a similar mistake like the young prophet. God had ordained him as the king of Israel. God instructed Saul to raid Amalek, destroy everything in the area and spare no one, not even the animals. But Saul did otherwise. He spared Amalek's king, kept some of the spoils from their raid and kept some of the best animals. When God called him on the carpet about his disobedience through the prophet, Samuel, Saul, at first denied that he did not do anything wrong. He claimed that he did all God told him to do (1 Samuel 15:16-21).

But Samuel was not fooled by Saul. Despite the fact that God had already told Samuel that Saul had disobeyed His order, the bleating of the flock of sheep that was brought back from Amalek, which Samuel heard was evidence that Saul was guilty. Saul then conceded that he did not do everything he was told. Do you know why? Because he was afraid of his men that raided with him. They told him to keep back some things, and he heeded their suggestion (1 Samuel 15:24).

Here again is another prominent example of someone who adhered to other people's suggestions and paid dearly for it. God dethroned Saul for his disobedience. He heeded his men at the expense of obeying God. As a result Saul was rejected from being king because he rejected God's Word (1 Samuel 15:23).

Since the idea to hold back some of the best animals came from his men, by going along with their suggestion, Saul was agreeing with them, therefore, he was being like them. He got out of God's will and therefore lost his crown; he ruined his destiny. Did you notice the pattern again? He did what others wanted him to do in lieu of what God assigned him to do. This got him out of God's will and ruined his purpose. In fact, everything went down hill for Saul after that incident. He lost his throne, lost his family and lost his life. Sad, isn't it?

The guy who replaced him, David, did the opposite. He chose to be himself. He rejected Saul's technique and fought and prevailed over Goliath with his own tactic. If you might recall when I deliberated on the friction between Saul and David, David was told by his men and cousin to kill Saul; but, he refused. He refused to be, or think like others. David knew that he would have been out of order if he killed Saul. So he rebuffed his men's suggestion to kill his boss. Consequently, David remained in God's will and fulfilled his destiny of being one of the greatest king's of Israel.

Interestingly, the young prophet and Saul represent two sides of the coin of leadership and followership. While the young prophet erred by adhering to someone above him, Saul messed up by hearkening to individuals under him. With this in mind, whether you're a husband or wife, parent or young adult child, Pastor or parishioner, employer or employee, experienced or inexperienced, professional or amateur, don't let anyone, whether your senior or junior, your leader or subordinate, your head or underling, get you out of God's will. We should hear them but not adhere to them if what they suggest to us violates God's mandate for our lives.

That is why it is imperative for us to know God for ourselves. Learning from others is good, but it's still in our best interest to seek God on our own. At least cross-check what others are telling us about God. We should be like the individuals in Acts 17:11 who were open to hear about God from Paul but searched the scriptures to make sure that all they were being taught were true. Likewise, you should check your Bible to make sure that all the messages that others are sharing with you, me inclusive, are true.

It's God's desire for you to live a godly life (2 Peter 1:5-8, Galatians 5:16-26). It's His purpose for you to be successful. It's His heart for you to be prosperous; He wants you to be healthy, wealthy and wise (3 John 1:2, Psalm 112, Deuteronomy 8:18). God longs to have a relationship with you; it's also His will to reward you (Isaiah 55:6, Hebrews 11:6). God's Word is God's will. I encourage you to search the scriptures to become more familiar with His will for your life. Reject anyone or anything that will lure you away from Him.

By rejecting individuals who would cause you to get out of God's will, I don't mean that you should plant a crowbar on the backside of their head. No. Please don't misunderstand me. You can say "no" with tact. In fact, you can refuse someone's opinion without the person knowing that you turned down his two cents. You can listen to someone's recommendation, but unless you're required to respond immediately to the person's suggestion, or guide someone who's misguided, you don't have to tell the individual to his face that you did not accept his input. You should be open to hear, but don't adhere—if it infringes on what God told you to do. Familiarizing yourself with the Bible will give you a better feel of what's God's and what's not.

THE CORNERSTONE

The stone which the builders rejected became the chief cornerstone. That verse is the underlying theme of this book. That stone which was rejected was Jesus Christ. He is the chief cornerstone. God used rejection as a means to lead His Son to the cross to redeem the world. One Man underwent rejection to inspire, rescue and liberate us all. The Lord personifies how God uses rejection to help us fulfill our destiny.

Christ was rejected in His relationships, in His ministry, by His family and for his convictions. Jesus was widely known for spreading the gospel and performing miracles but when He came to *His own country* He was rejected (Mark 6:1-4). They questioned His wisdom and abilities because the Jesus they knew was just a carpenter's son, not a healer, Evangelist and miracle worker. They were offended at Him and did not accept His ministry. Hence Christ uttered that quote that is often heard in our day:

a prophet is not without honor except in his own country, among his own relatives, and in his own house. (Mark 6:4)

Even Jesus' brothers did not believe in Him (John 7:5). John the Baptist, the Lord's own relative, who had baptized and once acknowledged Jesus as the Christ, perhaps because he was incarcerated and offended at Jesus for not visiting him, sent two of his followers to question Jesus if He was truly the Messiah or if they should look for someone else (Matthew 11:2-3).

While Jesus was praying fervently in the garden during the final hours before His crucifixion, the elite disciples He brought with Him—James, Peter and John—to intercede and support Him were fast asleep. Can you imagine the pain He must have felt when He came and saw them snoring while He was going through the anguish of what was about to happen to Him?

On top of that, Judas *betrayed* Him, Peter *denied* Him, and when He was captured to be crucified, the disciples who were with Him forsook Him (Mark 14:50). Even the so-called leaders of the law, the clergy, the elders, the scribes and Pharisees *despised* Him. When the Lord's own people were given the option to decide who should be set free and who should be crucified between Jesus and Barabbas, a notorious criminal, they chose to set the criminal free and condemn the Lord to death (Mark 15:6-15 & John 1:11).

He is despised and rejected by men, A Man of sorrows acquainted with grief. And we hid, as it were, our faces from Him; He was despised, and we did not esteem Him. (Isaiah 53:3)

And to cap it all, even Jesus "felt" rejected. He felt that His own father, God, forsook Him. That is evident by this statement which He made:

... "My God, My God, why have you forsaken me?" (Matthew 27:46)

But God did not reject His Son. If so, why did Jesus make the above statement? You might ask. I believe it's because He was "feeling" rejected. I concluded that God never rebuffed

His Son because:

For the LORD will not forsake His people, for His great name's sake.... (1 Samuel 12:22)

"And the LORD, He is the One who goes before you. He will be with you, He will not leave you nor forsake you; do not fear nor be dismayed." (Deuteronomy 31:8)

"(for the LORD your God is a merciful God), He will not forsake you nor destroy you, nor forget the covenant of your fathers which He swore to them. (Deuteronomy 4:31)

Where can I go from Your Spirit? Or where can I flee from Your presence? If I ascend into heaven, You are there; If I make my bed in hell, behold, You are there. (Psalm 139:7-8)

If God will not forsake His people or leave you even if you transgressed, then why would He neglect His only begotten Son? He won't! God was with His Son, before, during and after Jesus was on the cross.

What Jesus said about the father leaving Him was just the result of the toll of our transgressions on Him. He was speaking out of the condemnation He felt because of our sins upon Himself. If we commit sin and we are conscious of our misdeed, usually we'll feel guilty and feel like God is furious with us and Has turned His back on us—that's if we don't turn our back on Him first in an attempt to hide from Him. But that's not God's heart toward us. It's just Satan speaking in our minds telling us that God is angry with us and no longer loves or cares for us because of our misconduct.

The devil is a liar! Please don't misunderstand me. God hates sin; but He loves us. If we sin, He wants us to come to Him immediately to confess our impropriety, forsake it, and ask for forgiveness, and He will forgive us and cleanse us from all unrighteousness (1 John 1:9).

After Adam and Eve sinned in the Garden of Eden they went to hide themselves from God. Their response was triggered by the newfound knowledge or consciousness of their transgression. The feeling of guilt and condemnation they felt made them take cover. Interestingly, God did not strike them with thunder and lightening. In fact God came *looking for them* in the cool of the day, even after knowing what they had done.

Despite their disobedience, they still *heard* from God. In other words, God still *spoke to them*. Since God sought them in the *cool* of the day, that suggests that God was *cool* with them—pun intended. He was *not cool* with their disobedience, though.

Some, if not most of us, usually don't think that God would want to talk to us when we mess up. We are prone to think that He'll leave and forsake us and would not want to have anything to do with us. Friend, that is further from the truth. Although He is displeased with our wrongdoing, He desires for us to repent. He is willing to forgive and wash us from our sins if we are upfront and honest with Him regarding our indiscretions.

I don't think the feeling that we experience when we sin is the *absolute* absence of God. I think it's the *imminent* presence of the enemy who feeds on the environment of our transgression and torments our minds with guilt and condemnation, which we then express through our actions and emotions by trying to cover up our misdeeds, blaming others like Adam did Eve and Eve did the serpent, and some of us blame God.

Imagine your sins, my sins, and everybody else's sins lumped on Christ. If we feel that God is not only displeased with us when we transgress, but also feel that He writes us off, how much more do you think Christ felt having taken our iniquities upon Himself. He was feeling the torment, guilt and condemnation of our iniquities on Himself. That was why He said what He said. That statement, "My God, My God, Why have you forsaken me," is also further evidence that He indeed bore our sins upon Himself.

Furthermore, Jesus did not only experience and feel rejection, He also had to reject, too. He rejected Satan three times when the devil tempted Him to turn stone to bread, worship him, and jump off the highest point of a temple to prove that God would send angels to save Him. Jesus rebuffed the devil to ensure that He did not go out of His father's will (Luke 4:1-13). Christ also dismissed Peter when he professed that Jesus would not go to the cross. He also rebuked Peter for slashing the ear of one of Jesus' captors. Christ rejected Peter's futile attempts at helping Him because he would have ruined Christ's destiny

(Matthew 16:21-23 & John 18:10-11).

Jesus was rejected; but it was for a purpose—to redeem and save us all. His rejection was the best thing that ever happened for us, as His death paid the price for our sins and enabled us to be reconciled to God.

CONCLUSION

During organ transplant procedures, an organ is surgically placed in the body of a patient who needs the tissue in order for his or her body to function properly. Unfortunately, a major challenge with this operation is tissue rejection, which happens when the body of the patient receiving the organ rejects the organ. Tissue rejection occurs as a result of the immune system attacking the organ.

Our bodies have an immune system which is designed to protect us from infections and harmful substances like toxins and microorganisms. These harmful substances have proteins on their cells known as antigens. When they enter our bodies, our immune system is able to detect these antigens. This is because the antigens from the foreign agents are different from the ones in our bodies. Once our immune system notices this difference, they then identify the source of the foreign antigens and proceed to attack it.[1]

The bottom line is that the rejection took place because the organ and patient were incompatible. God is the Great Physician who designed our bodies to refuse anything that does not conform to them. In the same way, God has orchestrated our lives in a manner that when we try to place ourselves in the lives of people who are incompatible with us, like an organ that is a mismatch to a patient, we get rejected. The rejection is a safeguard to protect and preserve us for others who match us. The rejection is to protect us from people who are harmful, toxic and can infect our lives with their toxicity.

Interestingly, organ transplants are successful with no rejections when the recipient of the tissue is an identical twin of the organ donor. This is the case because the antigen on the tissue from the donor is identical with the antigen in the recipient's body. Therefore, the immune system recognizes the foreign tissue as part of the body of the recipient, so it does not attack the tissue.

That concept of immunological rejection reinforces how God uses rejection to help us end up with people, in places, or at positions that are compatible with God's purpose for our lives. If the person, project, or environment that you're trying to associate with is not "identical" to God's plan for your life, rejection is triggered to protect, preserve, and redirect you to the individuals and areas which are in line with God's plan for your life.

Other than tissue transplants between identical twins which ensure that rejection does not take place, one way that physicians minimize tissue rejection is through a process they call tissue typing. This process is used to identify the antigen on the tissue that they are planning to transplant into the patient. This helps them ensure that they find a tissue with antigens that are as close to those of the patient so that tissue rejection is minimized. Even so, unless the tissue or organ is a close match to the recipient's body, acute rejection is inevitable.

If a tissue that is incompatible with a patient is left in the patient, the person is going to die, and so can the organ. The organ will not fulfill its purpose and the patient will not fulfill his destiny. Likewise, when we stay in relationships or situations that we are not suited for, our dreams will die, and we will not fulfill our destiny. The same thing will happen to those with whom we're involved in the relationship.

However, thanks to rejection, we can be saved from such dire consequences. Rejection acts as a safeguard to alert us to our mismatch. It's an alarm clock that buzzes us to leave the situation. Like a debit card rejected by an ATM because it had no money, it expired, or was incompatible, God allows us to be rejected to prevent us from defrauding our lives and the lives of others.

Another way that physicians reduce tissue rejection is by their use of an immunosuppressant. These are drugs that suppress the immune system from attacking the transplanted organ. With this in mind, if rejection is the tissue that God is transplanting in you, I encourage you not to let your natural "immune system"—your natural reaction to personal rejection—cause you to respond by attacking it. Rather, respond by embracing it.

Knowing that God uses rejection for your good and to help you fulfill your destiny, you can embrace the tissue of rejection by applying the spiritual "immunosuppressant" that I presented to you in chapter two. They are faith, hope and love.

Friend, being rejected is *not* the end of your life. It's a means to an end *for* your life. That end is your destiny.

Dear reader, what more can I say? At this point I hope you've discovered that God uses rejection to help you fulfill your destiny. Despite all you have learned through this book, the most important thing that I'll like to leave you with is a relationship with God. If you've been unaccepted and cast aside by people, Jesus is the One person who has His hands wide open to receive you. If you haven't done so already, I encourage you to receive Him into your life. If you would like to do this, I invite you to pray the following prayer to accept Him or ask Him back into your life.

Lord, Jesus, thank you for allowing yourself to be rejected and dying on the cross for me. I ask You to forgive me my sins. Come into my heart and save me. I receive you now. I confess you as my Lord, and I believe in my heart that God raised you from the dead. Thank you for saving me. I am your child. In Your Name I pray, Amen (Romans 10:9-13).

If you've prayed that prayer, congratulations to you! Welcome to the family of God. I encourage you to seek a good Bible-teaching church in your area and begin to cultivate you relationship with God.

If this book was a blessing to you I would like to hear from you. Please email me at: toks@ojtoks.com.

ENDNOTES

CHAPTER 2: WHY DOES IT HAPPEN TO US?

1. Rick Warren, *Purpose Driven Life* (Michigan: Zondervan, 2002), 236.

2. Edwin Louis Cole, *Irresistible Husband* (Texas: Watercolor Books, 2001), 65.

3. Jim Bakker, *I Was Wrong* (Nashville: Nelson, 1996), 295.

CHAPTER 3: EIGHT BENEFITS OF IT

1. Sidney Poitier, *Measure of a Man* (New York: HarperSanFransisco, 2007), 56-57.

2. Mary Kay. http://www.marykay.com/company/aroundtheworld/default.aspx (accessed October 22, 2009).

3. Green Business Innovators. http://www.greenbusinessinnovators.com/2008/09 (accessed October 22, 2009); Terracycle. http://www.terracycle.net (accessed October 22, 2009).

4. Harvey MacKay, *We Got Fired!* (New York: Ballantine, 2004), 225-226.

CHAPTER 4: WRONG TIMING CAUSES IT

1. John C. Maxwell, *21 Irrefutable Laws of Leadership* (Tennessee: Thomas Nelson, 1998), 197.

CHAPTER 10: YOU MIGHT BE SETBACK BUT YOU'RE STILL SET!

1. T.D. Jakes, *Reposition Yourself* (New York: Atria Books, 2007), 116.

2. Metro Ministries. http://www.metroministries.org/About/AboutBillWilson/tabid/2395/Default.aspx (accessed October 22, 2009).

3. Integrity Music. www.integritymusic.com/artists/bio/israel-html (accessed October 22, 2009); Kristi Watts and Julie Blim. "Israel Houghton: An Intimate Portrait of Worship." 700 Club. www.cbn.com/cbnmusic/Interviews/700club_Israel-Houghton _041205.aspx (22 October 2009); Richard Young, *The Rise of Lakewood Church and Joel Osteen* (Pennsylvania: Whitaker House, 2007), 133.

CHAPTER 11: IT PUTS YOU IN THE SPOTLIGHT

1. Carissa. http://www.carissaproject.com/press.html (accessed October 22, 2009).

CHAPTER 12: IT HELPS YOU START YOUR OWN MINISTRY

1. Joel Osteen, *Your Best Life Now* (New York: Warner Faith, 2004), 171-173, 213.

2. MacKay, 49-55; John C. Maxwell, *17 Indisputable Laws of Teamwork* (Tennessee: Nelson, 2000), 189; http://en.wikipedia.org/wiki/Home_depot (accessed October 22, 2009).

3. MacKay, 55.

4. Jennifer Mann. "IHOP's big plans for Applebee's." McClatchy Newspapers. http://www.heraldextra.com/content/view/232455/3/ (accessed August 08, 2007).

5. Katie Benner, Eugenia Levenson, and Rupali Arora. "The Power 50." Fortune. http://money.cnn.com/galleries/2007/fortune/0709/gallery.women_mostpowerful.fortune/49.html (accessed November 25, 2009).

CHAPTER 13: IT HELPS YOU FIND YOUR NICHE
1. J. ED Komoszewski, M. James Sawyer, and Daniel B. Wallace, *Reinventing Jesus* (Grand Rapids: Kregel, 2006), 138.

CHAPTER 14: EXPERIENCING IT FROM LEADERS
1. John C. Maxwell, *The 360 Degree Leader* (Tennessee: Nelson, 2005), 40.

CHAPTER 17: IT LEADS YOU TO THE RIGHT TEAM
1. Associated Press. "Guard averages 21 points, 5.2 dimes in series." ESPN. http://sports.espn.go.com/nba/playoffs2004/news/story?id=182 2717 (accessed June 16, 2004).
2. Joe Lago. "Sour deal turned out to be sweet." ESPN. http://sports.espn.go.com/nba/playoffs2004/columns/story?id= 1820861 (accessed June 13, 2004).
3. Bill Walton. "The turnaround of Rasheed." ESPN. http://sports.espn.go.com/nba/columns/story?columnist=wal-ton_bill&id=1763139 (accessed March 26, 2004).
4. John C. Maxwell, *Today Matters* (New York: Warner, 2004), 50.
5. John C. Maxwell, *Talent is Never Enough* (Tennessee, Nelson, 2007), 125-128.

CHAPTER 18: IT FURTHERS YOUR CAUSE
1. Ryan Ori. "From Ostracized to front of the class." Journal Star. http://www.pjstar.com/news/x2060888911/From-os-tracized-to-front-of-class (accessed October 23, 2009); Brad Cohen. http://www.classperformance.com/press-people-maga-zine/ (accessed October 23, 2009); http://www.martinliterary-management.com/vid-oprah-brad-win.htm (accessed October 23, 2009).
2. John McCain and Mark Salter, *Character Is Destiny* (New York: Random House, 2005), 168-175.
3. MacKay, 210-211.
4. Cammie Wilson, *Rosa Parks Biography* (Scholastic Paperbacks, 2001).

CHAPTER 20: IT GETS YOU BACK ON THE RIGHT TRACK

1. http://en.wikipedia.org/wiki/Rejection (accessed December 9, 2009).

CHAPTER 21: WE NEED TO DO IT, TOO

1. Marcus Buckingham, *The One Thing You Need to Know* (New York: Free Press, 2005), 216.

2. Buckingham, 217.

CONCLUSION

1. Medline Plus. http://www.nlm.nih.gov/medlineplus/ency/article/000815.htm (accessed December 15, 2009).